The Great
Ninja Foodi
Cookbook for Beginners

A Superb Ninja Foodi Recipe Book Allows You to Cook and Enjoy A
Wide Variety of Cuisines with Multiple Functions

Francesca Fox

Table of Contents

Introduction

With the Ninja Foodi XL Pressure Cooker Steam Fryer with SmartLid, get ready to revolutionize your culinary world. This amazing kitchen appliance is not just another multicooker; it is a revolutionary invention that will change the way you think about cooking. The Ninja Foodi SmartLid is distinguished by its clever lid, which was created to effortlessly carry out a variety of cooking tasks. The Ninja Foodi SmartLid makes cooking easier and more pleasurable than typical multicookers, which involve changing out the lid for various operations. As we explore its features and the countless advantages of cooking with the SmartLid, this cookbook serves as your entry point to fully utilising the capabilities of this culinary marvel. The Ninja Foodi SmartLid will allow you to experiment with various culinary skills, whether an experienced cook or a kitchen newbie. Bid farewell to the challenges of conventional cooking and welcome this amazing appliance's convenience and adaptability. Come with us on a tour of the Ninja Foodi SmartLid's universe, where flavour, originality, and culinary brilliance await. It's time to step up you're cooking and go on a brand-new gourmet journey.

Fundamentals of Ninja Foodi XL Pressure Cooker Steam Fryer with SmartLid

What is Ninja Foodi?

The revolutionary new gadget, the Ninja Foodi XL Pressure Cooker Steam Fryer with SmartLid will transform the way you cook. A major difference from other multicookers is that the lid does everything. Numerous dishes can be prepared using the SmartLid by steaming and crisping, steaming and baking, air frying, and pressure cooking. You can prepare a complete dinner with protein, vegetables, and carbs in a single appliance. Even though there are many other multicookers available, the Ninja Foodi SmartLid is unique since you don't have to switch out the lid depending on the functionalities you require. To fully utilise the capabilities of this cooker, you will learn about these features and the advantages of cooking with SmartLid in this cookbook.

Why SmartLid?

Sounds apparent but true: Different cooking techniques are required to bring out the best in different ingredients. Although pressure cooking cooks food quickly and intensifies things like meats in a short amount of time, pressure-cooked chicken breasts lack that delicious crispy skin. While steaming gently cooks food while preserving flavour and nutrients does not give Brussels sprouts a crisp edge. The SmartLid's Tender Crisp and Steam & Crisp technology pressure cooks or steams these meals until they are perfectly tender, then add a crisp finish for consistently great results. Home cooks have traditionally prioritized convenience over flavor.

Yes, throwing food into a pressure cooker or steamer is simple, but thanks to this appliance's adaptability, you may enjoy convenience and flavour simultaneously. The cover seamlessly transitions between air frying, steaming, and pressure cooking. Imagine a salmon fillet that has been finished with the air frying function, leaving it with a lovely browned exterior and a delicate and moist interior from the general cooking with steam.

With the 14-in-1 SmartLid, you can easily switch between cooking methods by sliding a lever on the lid's distinctive design. You can proof dough, air fry, bake, roast, broil, dehydrate, sear/sauté, steam, pressure cook, sous vide, produce yogurt, and keep food warm. You can also steam and crisp and steam and bake. You can prepare meals faster and more effectively than using the Ninja Foodi SmartLid in dry mode.

Parts & Accessories

Unit Lid:
The cover on the top of the Ninja Foodi Smart XL Pressure Cooker is known as the unit lid. It aids in sealing the cooking chamber and maintaining the internal temperature and pressure during the cooking process.

Deluxe Reversible Rack:
This rack cooks several things at once. It features two sides, one for steaming and the other for roasting or broiling. It lets you make the most of the cooker's internal cooking space.

Cook & Crisp Basket:
Food is air-fried and crisped in the Cook & Crisp basket. It is very helpful for giving meals like French fries, chicken wings, and other things a crispy feel.

Detachable Diffuser:
The diffuser aids with even heat distribution throughout the cooking pot, avoiding hot patches and guaranteeing uniform cooking outcomes.

8-Quuart Removable Pot:
This is the main cooking vessel used to make meals. It is a detachable, 8-quart non-stick pot for simple cleaning.

SmartLid Slider:
The cutting-edge SmartLid technology, which the SmartLid Slider is a part of, enables you to swiftly and simply open and close the lid while cooking.

Cooker Lid:
A crucial part of pressure cooking is the cooker cover. It speeds up cooking by assisting with pressure building and cooker sealing.

Pressure Release Valve Vent and Seal:
This essential safety function releases the cooker's excess pressure. Additionally, it has a sealing system that can be used to maintain internal pressure.

Control Panel:
The control panel is the interface for setting cooking periods, temperatures, and choosing different cooking modes and functions.

Cooker Base:
The heating element is housed in the cooker base, which also serves as the frame of the Ninja Foodi Smart XL Pressure Cooker.

Lid Handel:
When monitoring or removing food, the lid handle is utilised to safely lift and lower the stove lid.

Anti-Clog Cap:
This cover ensures optimum ventilation during cooking and assists in preventing clogging in the air outlet vent.

Heating Element:
Using pressure cooking, air frying, or another cooking method, the heating element creates heat inside the cooker.

Silicone Ring:
Pressure is maintained during pressure cooking because of the silicone ring's tight seal between the unit lid and the cooker base.

Air Outlet Vent:
This vent prevents pressure building by allowing extra air and steam to escape the cooker while cooking.

Condensation Collector:
The condensation collector's purpose is to catch any extra moisture that might build up while you're cooking and keep it from dripping onto your tabletop.

Accessory Assembly Instructions

Deluxe Reversible Rack:
Higher Position: Use this higher position to broil chicken, steak, shellfish, and other foods.
Lower Position: Excellent for adding capacity while boiling vegetables and sides.
Deluxe Assembly: Up to eight chicken breasts or salmon fillets can be cooked at once with the Deluxe Assembly.
1. Put the Deluxe Reversible Rack's bottom portion in

the lower position.

2. Place the ingredients on the rack's lower portion.

3. Through the handles of the bottom layer, slide the Deluxe rack layer.

4. Add ingredients to the Deluxe layer to improve cooking capacity.

Cook & Crisp Basket:

1. Pull the two fins out of the groove on the diffuser's basket to clean it, and then firmly pull the diffuser down. (Note: The diffuser should always be attached to the basket before usage and aids in ventilation.)

2. Place the Cook & Crisp Basket on top of the diffuser and firmly press down to assemble it.

Using The SmartLid Slider:

1. The slider allows you to select between cooking modes and notifies the lid of the function you're employing, such as SteamCrisp, Air Fry/Stovetop, or Pressure.

How to Open & Close the lid:

1. To open and close the lid, you should always use the handle that is above the slider.

2. The lid can be opened or closed when the slider is set to STEAMCRISP or AIR FRY/STOVETOP.

3. While the slider is in the PRESSURE position, lid cannot be opened. To open the lid, make sure that there is no pressure inside the appliance, slide the dial to STEAMCRISP or AIR FRY/STOVETOP.

 Using the Control Panel

Cooking Functions

Pressure: Maintains food softness while cooking it swiftly. In order to hasten cooking, pressure is used.

Steam & Crisp: Ideal for producing fresh artisan breads, juicy and crisp veggies and proteins, and one-touch entire meals.

Steam & Bake: Faster and with less fat for baking fluffier cakes and quick breads.

Air Fry: little to no oil is required to give food its crisp and crunch.

Broil: To caramelise and brown the tops of your food, apply intense heat from above.

Bake/Roast: Serves as an oven for baked goods, tender meats, and other things.

Dehydrate: Meats, fruits, and veggies are dehydrated to make

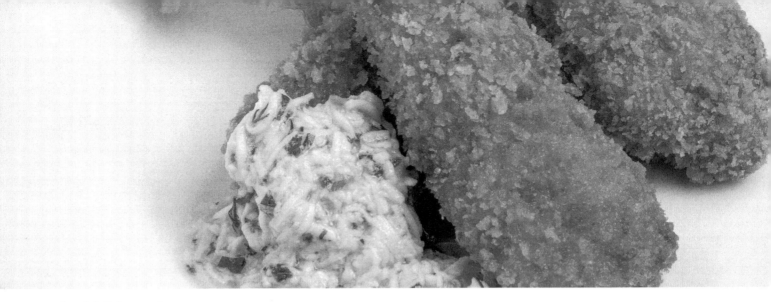

healthful snacks.

Proof: Creates a space where dough can rest and rise.

Sear/Sauté: Serves as a hub for several purposes, including browning meats, sautéing vegetables and simmering sauces.

Steam: Cooks delicate dishes gently at a high temperature.

Sous Vide: Food is slowly cooked in a water bath that has been precisely controlled.

Slow Cook: Cooks food for a long time at a reduced temperature.

Yogurt: Ferments milk after pasteurization to make creamy homemade yogurt.

Keep Warm: Automatically changes to keep warm when a certain function (Steam, Slow Cook, Pressure) is finished. By hitting the keep warm button once the feature has begun, you can turn it off.

Operating Buttons

SmartLid Slider: Slider movement lets you choose from each mode's available features. You can decide with the lit features.

Dial: Use the dial to cycle between the different functions after choosing a mode with the slider until the one you want is highlighted.

Left Arrows: Use the up/down arrows to the left of the display to adjust the cooking temperature.

Right Arrows: Use the up/down arrows to the right of the display to adjust the cooking time.

START/STOP BUTTON: To start cooking, press. While cooking, pressing it will halt the current function.

POWER: The Power button pauses all cooking modes and turns off the appliance. It switches the gadget on and off.

Benefits of Using It

With an extensive list of accessories, the Ninja Foodi Smart XL Pressure Cooker revolutionizes cooking in the contemporary kitchen. Each add-on has been painstakingly created to sync with the appliance, enhancing its functionality and transforming it into a multipurpose cooking partner. Here, we examine some of the advantages of utilizing this equipment and its specially designed accessories:

Intuitive Cooking:
Your entryway to a variety of cooking options is the SmartLid Slider. You can quickly choose

between pressure cooking, steam and crisp, air frying, and other cooking methods with only one slide. The cooking procedure is made simple by its user-friendly control system, making it easy to experiment with different culinary trends.

Precision Cooking:
Your culinary companion, the Smart Thermometer, ensures that your meals are perfectly prepared. It ensures consistency by keeping track of the food's interior temperature. This tool removes the guesswork from cooking, whether for a tender roast or a medium-rare steak.

Expanding Cooking Capacity:
This adaptable rack greatly increases your cooking space. Larger goods like whole chickens or roasts fit in the lower position. You may cook many layers of food simultaneously by sliding the Deluxe layer through the handles of the bottom layer. For throwing dinner parties or making multi-course dinners, it's a game-changer.

Healthier Cooking:
Using the Cook & Crisp Basket is simple while air frying. It uses little to no oil to give your food that crispy feel. Say goodbye to fried foods that are greasy and high in calories, and say hello to healthy, guilt-free treats.

Versatility:
The Ninja Foodi Smart XL offers an astonishing range of cooking options, including Sous Vide, Dehydrating, and Pressure Cooking. This device can handle everything from fast weeknight meals to elaborate weekend feasts with its accessories. Its unparalleled versatility makes it a priceless culinary asset.

Tailored Precision:
The control panel is carefully constructed to offer precise customization for each cooking operation. The controls are simple to use and ensure that every item is prepared to your preferences, whether you're modifying temperature, time, or doneness level.

Energy Efficient:
Energy efficiency has been optimised for this item. Compared to conventional cooking methods, it uses less energy to prepare meals quickly and evenly, lowering your carbon footprint while sparing you time and money.

Before First Use

Initial Setup and Preparation:
1. All tape, stickers, and packaging should be removed from the unit and thrown away.
2. Read operational guidelines, cautions, and crucial safety precautions as soon as possible to avoid harm to yourself or your property.

Cleaning Accessories:
1. Warm, soapy water should be used to wash the following accessories: the silicone ring, the removable cooking pot, the Cook & Crisp Basket, the premium reversible rack, and the condensation collector.
2. Before using, give these accessories a good rinse and ensure they are dry.

Installing Silicone Ring:
1. The silicone ring can be put in any direction because it is reversible.
2. On the underside of the lid, attach the silicone ring to the outer edge of the silicone ring rack.
3. Make sure the silicone ring is positioned beneath the silicone ring rack flat and is fully inserted.
4. Removing & Installing Condensation Collector

Installing the Condensation Collector:
1. Search for the condensation collecting slot on the cooker base.
2. Once it clicks into place, slide the condensation collector into its slot.

Removing the Condensation Collector:
1. Carefully remove the condensation collector from the cooker base's slot after use.
2. To make sure the condensation collector is clean and ready for the next use, hand wash it.
3. Removing Installing the Anti-Clog Cap

Removing the Anti-Clog Cap:
1. Disconnect the anti-clog cap for cleaning after each use.
2. Hold the anti-clog cap with your thumb and index finger bent.
3. To unscrew & remove the anti-clog cap from the lid, turn your wrist in a clockwise direction.
4. Use a brush to thoroughly clean the anti-clog cap.

Reinstalling the Anti-Clog Cap:

1. Place the anti-clog cap back in its proper location on the lid to reinstall it.
2. To fix it in place, firmly press down.

Water Test

First-time users are advised to do a water test to get comfortable with pressure cooking.

1. Add three cups of room-temperature water to the cooking pot before setting it in the cooker base.
2. Close the lid and move the slider to the PRESSURE position.
3. A pressure release valve should be in the SEAL position.
4. Select QUICK RELEASE using the dial. High (Hi) pressure will be the unit's default setting. Use the right down arrow to change the time to 2 minutes. To start, press START/STOP.
5. The display will show "PrE" and progress bars when the unit starts building pressure. The timer will begin to count down once the pressure reaches its maximum level.
6. The appliance will beep and display "End" when the cook time reaches zero before swiftly releasing the pressurised steam on its own. The moment the pressure release valve is going to open, a warning chime will play. The valve will allow steam to escape. Move the slider to the right to unlock the lid once the display says "OPN Lid," then open the lid when it has been unlocked.

Using The Pressure Function

Press the power button after inserting the power cord into a wall outlet to turn on the device.

Pressure

1. Fill with ingredients and 1 cup of liquid, but don't go over the PRESSURE MAX line.
2. Turn the pressure valve to SEAL, then close the lid.
3. Select the pressure level (Hi or LO) and pressure type (NATURAL, QUICK, or DELAYED).
4. Adjust the cooking time for up to 4 hours.
5. To start, press START/STOP.
6. When completely pressurised, the timer begins to count down.
7. When finished, the pressure is released in the chosen manner (natural, rapid, or delayed).
8. The timer begins to run as the unit beeps and shifts to Keep Warm.
9. It is depressurized and ready to open when "OPN Lid" appears.

Using The Steam Crisp Functions

Press the power button after inserting the power cord into a wall outlet to turn on the device.

Steam & Crisp

1. Using the up and down arrows on the right, adjust the cook duration in minutes up to an hour.
2. To START/STOP cooking, press START/STOP.
3. The progress bars and "PrE" indicator will show that the unit is generating steam. The amount of ingredients determines how long it will take.
4. The display will show the set temperature and the timer will begin to count down once the machine reaches the preset steam level.
5. The appliance will sound a buzzer and display "End" for five minutes when the cook time reaches zero.

Steam & Bake

1. Put the multipurpose pan on the pot's lower rack.
2. Using the dial, choose STEAM & BAKE after setting the slider to STEAMCRISP. Using the arrows, change the temperature (225°F to 400°F) and cooking time (up to 1 hour 15 minutes).
3. To begin cooking, press START/STOP.
4. During the 20 minutes of preheating, "PrE" will be shown. It displays the set temperature after preheating, and the timer starts to count down.
5. "End" is displayed for five minutes after the timer hits zero. If further time is required, press the right arrow (preheating is skipped).

Using the Air Fry/Stovetop Functions

Air Fry

1. In the pot, set the Cook & Crisp Basket or the premium reversible rack. Make sure the diffuser is fastened to the basket.
2. Fill the Cook & Crisp Basket or the premium reversible rack with your ingredients. Put the lid on.
3. Slider should be set to AIR FRY/STOVETOP. The default setting is AIR FRY. Using the left arrows, adjust the temperature (300°F to 400°F) in 5-degree increments.
4. Using the right arrows, change the cook time (up to 1 hour) in minute increments.

5. To START/STOP cooking, press START/STOP.
6. The device will beep and "End" will flash a total of three times on the display when the cook time ends.

Broil
1. Follow the directions in your recipe or place the premium reversible rack in the pot in the highest broil setting.
2. On the rack, arrange your ingredients, then secure the cover.
3. Use the dial to select BROIL while the control is set to AIR FRY/STOVETOP.
4. By using the right arrows, you may change the cook time (up to 30 minutes).
5. To begin cooking, press START/STOP.
6. The device will beep and flash "End" three times on the display when the timer approaches zero.

Bake/Roast
1. Close the lid after adding the ingredients and accessories to the pot.
2. Slide the dial to BAKE/ROAST and select AIR FRY/STOVETOP on the control. The default temperature is displayed; use the left arrows to change it in 5-degree steps (250°F to 400°F).
3. Using the right arrows, adjust the cook duration in 1-minute increments (up to 1 hour) and five-mins increments (1 hour to 4 hours).
4. To begin cooking, press START/STOP.
5. The device will beep and flash "End" three times on the display when the timer approaches zero.

Dehydrate
1. The lowest position of the deluxe reversible rack should be used. On the rack, layer the ingredients.
2. Add another layer of ingredients after placing the premium layer on top of the reversible rack. Put the lid on.
3. Slide the dial to DEHYDRATE, then select AIR FRY/STOVETOP on the control. With the left

arrows, change the temperature (80°F to 195°F).

4. Using the right arrows, adjust the cook time (1 hour to 12 hours) in 15-minute intervals.

5. To begin cooking, press START/STOP.

6. The device will beep and the word "End" will flash a total of three times on the display when the timer approaches zero.

Proof

1. Close the cover after placing the dough in the pot or Air Fry Basket.

2. Slide the dial to PROOF and choose that option from AIR FRY/STOVETOP. The default temperature will be displayed; use the left arrows to change it from 75°F to 95°F.

3. Using the right arrows, adjust the proof time (20 minutes to 2 hours) in minute increments.

4. To start the procedure, press START/STOP.

5. The device will beep and flash "End" three times on the display when the timer approaches zero.

Sear/Sauté

1. Fill the pot with the ingredients.

2. Open the lid or slide the control to AIR FRY/STOVETOP, then use the dial to select SEAR/ SAUTÉ. The standard temperature will show up. Choose from "Lo1," "2," "3," "4", or "Hi5" with the left arrows.

4. To begin cooking, press START/STOP.

4. To turn SEAR/SAUTÉ off, press START/STOP. To switch to a different cooking function, press START/STOP to end the cooking function then use the slider and dial to select your desired function.

Steam

1. Add 1 cup of liquid to the pot (or as directed by the recipe). Put the Cook & Crisp Basket or reversible rack containing the ingredients in the pot.

2. Slide the dial to STEAM, then select AIR FRY/STOVETOP from the menu.

3. With the right arrows, change the cook duration in 1-minute increments (up to 30-minutes).
4. To begin cooking, press START/STOP.
5. When the liquid reaches a boil, the device will preheat and show "PrE." The timer will begin to count down once it reaches temperature. The device will beep and flash "End" three times on the display when the timer approaches zero.

Sous Vide
1. Fill the cooking pot with 12 cups of room-temperature water.
2. When you set the cooking temperature (120°F to 190°F) and cook time (up to 24 hours), close the lid and choose SOUS VIDE in the AIR FRY/STOVETOP mode.
3. To reheat, press START/STOP.
4. When the message "ADD FOOD" appears, drop sealed bags into the water.
5. Put the lid on.
6. "End" will flash three times on the display and sound when the timer expires.

Slow Cook
1. While adding ingredients, watch out for the MAX line so as not to overfill the pot.
2. Turn the dial to SLOW COOK, slide the control to AIR FRY/STOVETOP, and use the left arrows to select "Hi," "Lo," or "bUFFEt" for the temperature.
3. Using the right arrows, change the cook time in 15-mins increments (up to 12 hours).
4. To begin cooking, press START/STOP.
5. The device will beep, go into Keep Warm mode, and begin counting once the timer reaches zero.

Yogurt
1. Fill the pot with milk.
2. Put the lid on.
3. With the control set to AIR FRY/STOVETOP, select YOGURT with the dial, and with the left arrows, choose "FEr" for temperature.
4. With the right arrows, adjust the incubation time (6 to 12 hours) in 30-mins increments.

5. To begin pasteurization, press START/STOP. Throughout this process, the device will show progress bars and "boiL."
6. When pasteurization is complete, the device will beep and show "COOL." Let the milk cool down.
7. The device will show "ADD," "STIR," and the incubation time once it has cooled. After skimming the top, adding yoghurt cultures, stirring, and then closing the lid.
8. To start the incubation, press START/STOP.
9. "FEr" and a countdown will be displayed on the display. The device will beep, and the word "End" will flash three times once incubation is finished.
10. The yoghurt should be chilled for a maximum of twelve hours before serving.

Must-Have Accessories

Extra Cooking Pot: It can be convenient to have a second cooking pot to prepare different foods without cleaning the first one between cooking cycles.

Silicone Sealing Rings: Silicone sealing rings are susceptible to deterioration and odour absorption over time. If you have a spare, you may always use a new seal for pressure cooking.

Air Fryer Accessories Kit: A multipurpose rack, a grill pan, and an air fryer basket are usual additions to this set. These tools are ideal for grilling, baking, and air frying.

Steamer Basket: A steamer basket comes in handy when steaming vegetables, seafood, and dumplings. It may be prepared using the pressure cooker feature and is a healthy cooking choice.

Non-Stick Inner Pot: A non-stick inner pot can simplify cooking and cleanup for dishes that tend to cling.

Silicone Trivet: Using a trivet will allow you to cook food in layers and keep delicate items out of contact with the pot's bottom.

Stackable inserts: By enabling you to cook many items at once, stackable inserts or stacking pans can expand your cooking capacity.

Silicone Lid Cover: To make it simple to keep leftovers in the refrigerator, use a silicone lid cover to cover your inner pot.

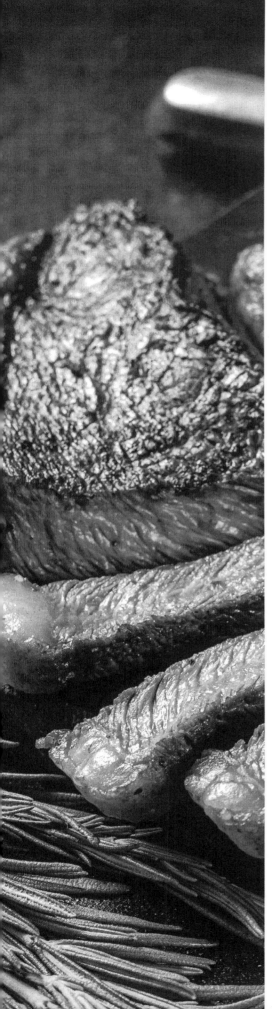

Dishwasher & Handwashing

1. Before cleaning, unplug the appliance.
2. Clean the control panel and base of the stove with a moist cloth.
3. Dishwasher-safe components include the cooking pot, silicone ring, deluxe reversible rack, Cook & Crisp Basket, and detachable diffuser.
4. With water and dish soap, clean the pressure release valve and anti-clog cap.
5. Before cleaning, soak the pot, rack, and basket in water to remove any remaining food residue. Avoid using scouring pads; use a liquid dish soap or non-abrasive cleaner with a nylon pad or brush, as needed.
6. After cleaning, let all parts air dry.

Steam Cleaning

1. Add three cups of water to the pot.
2. Set the dial to "AIR FRY/STOVETOP."
3. Choose STEAM and 30 minutes as the duration. Click START/STOP.
4. Use a moist sponge or towel to clean the interior of the lid after the timer expires and the device has cooled.
5. While cleaning the inside of the lid, take care not to touch the fan.

Frequently Asked Questions

Why is my unit taking so long to come to pressure? How long does it take to come to pressure?
- Depending on the chosen temperature, the cooking pot's current temperature, and the temperature or quantity of the contents, cooking times may vary.
- Verify that the silicone ring is flush with the lid and fully seated. If placed properly, you should be able to rotate the ring by giving it a small tug.
- When pressure cooking, make sure the lid is completely closed and the pressure release valve is in the SEAL position.
- If there is not sufficient liquid, the unit won't pressurise.

Why can't I open the lid after pressurizing?
- As a security measure, the lid won't open until the appliance has entirely lost pressure. To quickly release the pressurised steam, turn the pressure release valve to the VENT position. Steam will suddenly erupt from

the pressure release valve. The appliance will be prepared to open once all of the steam has been discharged.

"PRESSURE FAIL" error message appears on display screen when using the Pressure function.

● Before starting the pressure cook cycle again, add more liquid to the cooking pot.
● Ensure that the seal position is selected on the pressure release valve.
● Verify that the silicone ring is properly fitted.

The unit is hissing and not reaching pressure.

● Check to see that the pressure release valve is in the SEAL position. After doing this, if you still hear a loud hissing sound, the silicone ring may not be firmly seated. To halt cooking, press START/STOP, then VENT if necessary, then open the lid. Make sure the silicone ring is properly placed and flatly underneath the ring rack by applying pressure on it. Once everything is put in place, you ought to be able to rotate the ring by giving it a gentle tug.

4-Week Meal Plan

Week 1

Day 1:
Breakfast: Artichoke Pizza
Lunch: Vegetable Bowls
Snack: Deviled Eggs
Dinner: Grilled Salmon with Capers
Dessert: Honey Chocolate Cookies

Day 2:
Breakfast: Turkey Sausage Roll-Ups
Lunch: Creamy Fiesta Corn
Snack: Cheese Quesadillas
Dinner: Beef Lettuce Wraps
Dessert: Vanilla Pecan Pie

Day 3:
Breakfast: Parmesan Bread
Lunch: Cheese Beans Burritos
Snack: Chili Tomato Nachos
Dinner: Bacon Pork Chops
Dessert: Zesty Raspberry Muffins

Day 4:
Breakfast: Chocolate Rolls
Lunch: Simple Garlic Chickpeas
Snack: Olive-Stuffed Jalapeños
Dinner: Mustard Coconut Prawns
Dessert: Pumpkin Pudding

Day 5:
Breakfast: Hush Puffs
Lunch: Crispy Courgette Fries
Snack: Cheese Quesadillas
Dinner: Italian Turkey with Vegetables
Dessert: Easy Butter Cake

Day 6:
Breakfast: Peach Vanilla Fritters
Lunch: Simple Garlic Chickpeas
Snack: Hot Wings
Dinner: Crispy Fried Chicken
Dessert: Walnut Bread

Day 7:
Breakfast: Air Fried Grapefruit
Lunch: Tomato & Ricotta Risotto
Snack: Cauliflower Pizza Crusts
Dinner: Enchilada Chicken Soup
Dessert: Air-Fried Peach Slices

Week 2

Day 1:
Breakfast: Pita Bread
Lunch: Lemon Quinoa
Snack: Hot Wings
Dinner: Cod with Grapes
Dessert: Chocolate Mug Cake

Day 2:
Breakfast: Pepperoni Cheese Pizza
Lunch: Cheesy Black Beans and Green Chilies
Snack: Honey Barbecue Beef Meatballs
Dinner: South African Lamb Curry
Dessert: Butter Peach Crumble

Day 3:
Breakfast: Walnut Apple Muffins
Lunch: Creamy Cheese Mushroom Risotto
Snack: Deviled Eggs
Dinner: Chicken Mushroom Kabobs
Dessert: Red Wine–Poached Pears

Day 4:
Breakfast: Mango Steel-Cut Oats
Lunch: Bacon-Corn Casserole
Snack: Parmesan Pizza Bread
Dinner: Korean Beef Rolls
Dessert: Bread Pudding

Day 5:
Breakfast: Yogurt Parfait with Berry Crunch
Lunch: Crispy Courgette Fries
Snack: Mustard Wings
Dinner: Cheese Ribeye Steak
Dessert: Cream Chocolate Cheesecake

Day 6:
Breakfast: Boiled Eggs with Prosciutto Slices
Lunch: English Cucumber & Quinoa Tabbouleh
Snack: Honey Barbecue Beef Meatballs
Dinner: Cream Chicken & Ziti Casserole
Dessert: Fudge Cookie Dough Tart

Day 7:
Breakfast: Pumpkin Pie Oatmeal with Cranberries & Pecans
Lunch: Cheese Roasted Broccoli
Snack: Buffalo Chicken Wings
Dinner: Classic Beef Stock
Dessert: Rose Water Poached Peaches

Week 3	Week 4

Day 1:
Breakfast: Pepper Bread
Lunch: Mashed Potatoes with Kale
Snack: Chili Tomato Nachos
Dinner: Crispy Fried Chicken
Dessert: Banana Cake

Day 2:
Breakfast: Blueberry Morning Muffins
Lunch: Parmesan Cauliflower
Snack: Baked Baby Potatoes
Dinner: Soy Dipped Beef Tenderloin
Dessert: Apple Brown Betty

Day 3:
Breakfast: Yogurt Parfait with Berry Crunch
Lunch: Vegetable Bowls
Snack: Cereal Party Mix
Dinner: Root Beer-Braised Pulled Chicken
Dessert: Red Wine–Poached Figs with Toasted Almond & Ricotta

Day 4:
Breakfast: Creamy Berry Chia Porridge
Lunch: Cauliflower Mash
Snack: Teriyaki Beef Meatballs
Dinner: Lemon Prawns with Asparagus
Dessert: Honey Apple and Brown Rice Pudding

Day 5:
Breakfast: Cheese Sausage and Egg Strata
Lunch: Sweet-Sour Red Cabbage
Snack: Aubergine Caponata
Dinner: Mushroom Beef Patties
Dessert: Maple Dates Dip

Day 6:
Breakfast: Egg Fried Rice
Lunch: Tomato & Ricotta Risotto
Snack: Cheddar Cream Bacon Beer Dip
Dinner: Raisin Chicken with Capers
Dessert: Poached Pears with Yogurt & Pistachio

Day 7:
Breakfast: Creamy Polenta
Lunch: Honey Peas & Carrots
Snack: Curried Chicken Meatball Lettuce Wraps
Dinner: Lamb with Chickpea & Pitas
Dessert: Delicious Maple Crème Brule

Day 1:
Breakfast: Steel-Cut Oats with Dried Apples
Lunch: Cheese Snap Pea Pasta
Snack: Cheese Quesadillas
Dinner: Rice Pilaf with Corn and Prawns
Dessert: Lemon Cake

Day 2:
Breakfast: Strawberry Oatmea
Lunch: Creamy Fiesta Corn
Snack: Olive-Stuffed Jalapeños
Dinner: Beef mince & Pasta Casserole
Dessert: Peach-Berry Cobbler

Day 3:
Breakfast: Monkey Bread Pieces
Lunch: Cheesy Cauliflower Casserole
Snack: Cheese Artichoke Dip
Dinner: Juicy Chicken & Broccoli
Dessert: Pear-Applesauce

Day 4:
Breakfast: Cheese Polenta with Eggs
Lunch: Cheese Snap Pea Pasta
Snack: Breaded Chicken Meatballs
Dinner: Simple Salmon Fillets
Dessert: White Chocolate Cocoa with Raspberry

Day 5:
Breakfast: Taco Huevos Rancheros
Lunch: Delicious Summer Ratatouille
Snack: Classic Muddy Buddies
Dinner: Korean Beef Rolls
Dessert: Cheesecake with Peaches

Day 6:
Breakfast: Beer-nana Loaf
Lunch: Pressure-Cooked Russet Potatoes
Snack: Orange, Apple and Pear Compote
Dinner: Spicy Chicken Breast Halves
Dessert: Oats Lemon Bars

Day 7:
Breakfast: Spinach Eggs Florentine
Lunch: Bacon Brussels Sprouts Hash
Snack: Chili Pork Picadillo Lettuce Wraps
Dinner: Bacon Pork Chops
Dessert: Honey Blueberry Compote

Chapter 1 Breakfast Recipes

Pepper Bread

Prep Time: 10 minutes | Cook Time: 7 minutes | Serves: 8

18 cm round bread boule
Olive oil
120g mayonnaise
2 tablespoons butter, melted
115g grated mozzarella
25g grated Parmesan cheese
½ teaspoon dried oregano

70g black olives, sliced
70g green olives, sliced
75g coarsely chopped roasted red peppers
2 tablespoons minced red onion
Black pepper, to taste

1. Place the Cook & Crisp Basket in your Pressure Cooker Steam Fryer. 2. Cut the bread boule in half horizontally. If your bread boule has a rounded top, trim the top of the boule so that the top half will lie flat with the cut side facing up. Brush both sides of the boule halves with olive oil. 3. Place one half of the boule into the Ninja Foodi Pressure Steam Fryer basket with the centre cut side facing down. 4. Put on the Smart Lid on top of the Ninja Foodi Steam Fryer. Move the Lid Slider to the "Air Fry/Stovetop". Select the "Air Fry" mode for cooking. 5. Air-fry at 185°C for around 2 minutes to toast the bread. Repeat with the other half of the bread boule. 6. Mix the mayonnaise, butter, mozzarella cheese, Parmesan cheese and dried oregano in a suitable bowl. Fold in the black and green olives, roasted red peppers and red onion and season with black pepper. Spread the cheese mixture over the untoasted side of the bread, covering the entire surface. 7. Put on the Smart Lid on top of the Ninja Foodi Steam Fryer. 8. Move the Lid Slider to the "Air Fry/Stovetop". Select the "Air Fry" mode for cooking. 9. Air Fry bread at 175°C for 5 minutes until the cheese is melted and browned. Repeat with the other half. Cut into slices and serve warm.

Per serving: Calories: 389; Fat: 11g; Sodium: 501mg; Carbs: 28.9g; Fibre: 4.6g; Sugar 8g; Protein 6g

Artichoke Pizza

Prep Time: 10 minutes | Cook Time: 18 minutes | Serves: 2

2 tablespoons olive oil
90g fresh spinach
2 cloves garlic, minced
1 (200g) pizza dough ball
55g grated mozzarella cheese
25g grated cheese

45g artichoke hearts, chopped
2 tablespoons grated Parmesan cheese
¼ teaspoon dried oregano
Salt and black pepper, to taste

1. Heat the oil in a suitable sauté pan on the stovetop. Add the spinach and half the garlic to the pan and sauté for a few minutes, until the spinach has wilted then transfer to a bowl. 2. Place the Cook & Crisp Basket in your Pressure Cooker Steam Fryer. 3. Line the Ninja Foodi Pressure Steam Fryer basket with aluminum. Brush the foil with oil. Shape the prepared dough into a circle and place it on top of the foil. 4. Brush the prepared dough with olive oil and transfer it into the Ninja Foodi Pressure Steam Fryer basket with the foil on the bottom. 5. Put on the Smart Lid on top of the Ninja Foodi Steam Fryer. 6. Move the Lid Slider to the "Air Fry/Stovetop". Cook the prepared pizza dough on "Air Fry" mode at 200°C for around 6 minutes. 7. Turn the prepared dough over, remove the aluminum foil and brush again with olive oil. Air-fry for 4 minutes. 8. Add the mozzarella and Fontina cheeses over the prepared dough. Top with the spinach and artichoke hearts. Sprinkle the Parmesan cheese and dried oregano on top and drizzle with olive oil. 9. Put on the Smart Lid on top of the Ninja Foodi Steam Fryer. Move the Lid Slider to the "Air Fry/Stovetop". Cook on "Air Fry" mode at 175°C for around 8 minutes, until the cheese has melted and is browned. 10. Serve.

Per serving: Calories: 372; Fat: 20g; Sodium: 891mg; Carbs: 29g; Fibre: 3g; Sugar 8g; Protein 17g

Peach Vanilla Fritters

Prep Time: 10 minutes | Cook Time: 6 minutes | Serves: 8

185g bread flour
1 teaspoon active dry yeast
50g sugar
¼ teaspoon salt
120ml warm milk
½ teaspoon vanilla extract

2 egg yolks
2 tablespoons melted butter
310g small diced peaches
1 tablespoon butter
1 teaspoon cinnamon
1 to 2 tablespoons sugar

Glaze

95g icing sugar   4 teaspoons milk

1. Mix the flour, yeast, sugar and salt in a suitable bowl. Add the milk, vanilla, egg yolks and melted butter and mix until the prepared dough starts to come together. Transfer the prepared dough to a floured surface and knead it by hand for around 2 minutes. Shape the prepared dough into a ball, place it in a suitable oiled bowl, cover with a clean kitchen towel and let the prepared dough rise in a warm place for around 1 to 1½ hours, or until the prepared dough has doubled in size. 2. While the prepared dough is rising, melt one tablespoon of butter in a suitable saucepan on the stovetop. Add the diced peaches, cinnamon and sugar to taste. Cook the peaches for about 5 minutes, or until they soften. Set the peaches aside to cool. 3. Place the Cook & Crisp Basket in your Pressure Cooker Steam Fryer. 4. When the prepared dough has risen, transfer it to a floured surface and shape it into a 15 cm circle. Spread the peaches over half of the circle and fold the other half of the prepared dough over the top. With a knife or a board scraper, score the prepared dough by making slits in the prepared dough in a diamond shape. Push the knife straight down into the prepared dough and peaches, rather than slicing through. You should cut through the top layer of dough, but not the bottom. Roll the prepared dough up into a log from one short end to the other. It should be 20 cm long. Some of the peaches will be sticking out of the prepared dough – don't worry, these are supposed to be a little random. Cut the log into 8 equal slices. Place the prepared dough disks on a floured cookie sheet, cover with a clean kitchen towel and let rise in a warm place for around 30 minutes. 5. Put on the Smart Lid on top of the Ninja Foodi Steam Fryer. 6. Move the Lid Slider to the "Air Fry/Stovetop". Select the "Air Fry" mode for cooking. 7. Air-fry 2 or 3 fritters at a time at 185°C, for around 3 minutes. Flip them over and continue to air-fry for another 2 to 3 minutes, until they are golden brown. 8. Mix the icing sugar and milk in a suitable bowl. Mix vigorously until smooth. Allow the fritters to cool for at least 10 minutes and then brush the glaze over both the bottom and top of each one. 9. Serve warm or at room temperature.

Per serving: Calories: 334; Fat: 7.9g; Sodium: 704mg; Carbs: 6g; Fibre: 3.6g; Sugar 6g; Protein 18g

Pepperoni Cheese Pizza

Prep Time: 10 minutes | Cook Time: 18 minutes | Serves: 2

1 (200g) pizza dough ball
Olive oil
120g pizza sauce
85g grated mozzarella cheese
70g thick sliced pepperoni

50g sliced pickled hot banana peppers
¼ teaspoon dried oregano
2 teaspoons honey

1. Place the Cook & Crisp Basket in your Pressure Cooker Steam Fryer. 2. Cut out a piece of foil the same size as the bottom of the Ninja Foodi Pressure Steam Fryer basket. Brush the foil circle with olive oil. Shape the prepared dough into a circle and place it on top of the foil. Dock the prepared dough by piercing it several times with a fork. Brush the prepared dough with olive oil and transfer it into the "cook & crisp basket" with the foil on the bottom. 3. Put on the Smart Lid on top of the Ninja Foodi Steam Fryer. Move the Lid Slider to the "Air Fry/Stovetop". Select the "Air Fry" mode for cooking. 4. Air-fry the plain pizza dough at 200°C for around 6 minutes. Turn the prepared dough over, remove the aluminum foil and brush again with olive oil. Air-fry for an additional 4 minutes. 5. Spread the pizza sauce on top of the prepared dough and sprinkle the mozzarella cheese over the sauce. Top with the pepperoni, pepper slices and dried oregano. 6. Put on the Smart Lid on top of the Ninja Foodi Steam Fryer. Move the Lid Slider to the "Air Fry/Stovetop". Select the "Air Fry" mode for cooking. Adjust the cooking temperature to 175°C. 7. Cook for around 8 minutes, until the cheese has melted and browned. Transfer the prepared pizza to a cutting board and drizzle with the honey. Slice and serve.

Per serving: Calories: 354; Fat: 10.9g; Sodium: 454mg; Carbs: 10g; Fibre: 3.1g; Sugar 5.2g; Protein 10g

Pita Bread

Prep Time: 10 minutes | Cook Time: 48 minutes | Serves: 8

2 teaspoons active dry yeast
1 tablespoon sugar
360 ml warm water
405g plain flour

2 teaspoons salt
1 tablespoon olive oil
Salt, to taste

1. Dissolve the yeast, sugar and water in the bowl of a stand mixer. Let the mixture sit for around 5 minutes to make sure the yeast is active. Mix the flour and salt in a suitable bowl, and add it to the water, along with the olive oil. Mix with the prepared dough hook until mixed. 2. Knead the prepared dough until it is smooth. Transfer the prepared dough to an oiled bowl, cover and let it rise in a warm place until doubled in bulk. 3. Place the Cook & Crisp Basket in your Pressure Cooker Steam Fryer. 4. Divide the prepared dough into 8 portions and roll each portion into a circle about 10 cm in diameter. Don't roll the balls too thin, or you won't get the pocket inside the pita. 5. Brush both sides of the prepared dough with olive oil, and sprinkle with salt if desired. 6. Put on the Smart Lid on top of the Ninja Foodi Steam Fryer. 7. Move the Lid Slider to the "Air Fry/Stovetop". Cook one at a time on "Air Fry" Mode at 200°C for 6 minutes, 8. flipping it over when there are two minutes left in the cooking time.
Per serving: Calories: 284; Fat: 9g; Sodium: 441mg; Carbs: 7g; Fibre: 4.6g; Sugar 5g; Protein 19g

Turkey Sausage Roll-Ups

Prep Time: 10 minutes | Cook Time: 24 minutes | Serves: 3

6 links turkey sausage
6 slices of white bread, crusts removed
2 eggs
120ml milk

½ teaspoon cinnamon
½ teaspoon vanilla extract
1 tablespoon butter, melted
Icing sugar (optional)
Maple syrup

1. Place the Cook & Crisp Basket in your Pressure Cooker Steam Fryer. 2. Place the sausage links in the Ninja Steam Fryer. 3. Put on the Smart Lid on top of the Ninja Foodi Steam Fryer. 4. Move the Lid Slider to the "Air Fry/Stovetop". Select the "Air Fry" mode for cooking. 5. Air-fry the sausage links at 195°C for 8 to 10 minutes, turning them a couple of times during the cooking process. 6. Roll each sausage link in a piece of bread, pressing the finished seam tightly to seal shut. 7. Mix the eggs, milk, cinnamon, and vanilla in a shallow dish. Dip the sausage rolls in the egg mixture and let them soak in the egg for around 30 seconds. Grease the bottom of the "cook & crisp basket" with oil and transfer the sausage rolls to the basket, seam side down. 8. Put on the Smart Lid on top of the Ninja Foodi Steam Fryer. 9. Move the Lid Slider to the "Air Fry/Stovetop". Select the "Air Fry" mode for cooking. 10. Air-fry the rolls at 185°C for around 9 minutes. Brush melted butter over the bread, flip the rolls over. Cook on the "Air Fry" mode for an additional 5 minutes. 11. Remove the French toast roll-ups from the basket and dust with icing sugar, if using. Serve with maple syrup and enjoy.
Per serving: Calories: 284; Fat: 9g; Sodium: 441mg; Carbs: 7g; Fibre: 4.6g; Sugar 5g; Protein 19g

Hush Puffs

Prep Time: 10 minutes | Cook Time: 8 minutes | Serves: 20

240ml buttermilk
55g butter, melted
2 eggs
185g plain flour
240g polenta

65g sugar
1 teaspoon baking soda
1 teaspoon salt
4 spring onions, minced
Vegetable oil

1. Place the Cook & Crisp Basket in your Pressure Cooker Steam Fryer. 2. Mix the buttermilk, butter and eggs in a suitable mixing bowl. In a second bowl mix the flour, polenta, sugar, baking soda and salt. Add the dry recipe ingredients to the wet recipe ingredients, stirring just to mix. Stir in the minced spring onions and refrigerate the prepared batter for around 30 minutes. 3. Shape the prepared batter into 5 cm balls. Brush or grease the balls with oil. 4. Put on the Smart Lid on top of the Ninja Foodi Steam Fryer. 5. Move the Lid Slider to the "Air Fry/Stovetop". Select the "Air Fry" mode for cooking. 6. Air-

fry the hush puffs in two batches at 180°C for around 8 minutes, turning them over after 6 minutes of the cooking process. 7. Serve warm with butter.
Per serving: Calories: 349; Fat: 2.9g; Sodium: 511mg; Carbs: 12g; Fibre: 3g; Sugar 8g; Protein 17g

Chocolate Rolls

Prep Time: 10 minutes | Cook Time: 8 minutes | Serves: 6

1 (200g) tube of puff pastry
110g semi-sweet or bittersweet chocolate chunks
1 egg white, beaten

25g sliced almonds
Icing sugar, for dusting
Butter or oil

1. Unwrap the thawed puff pastry and separate it into triangles with the points facing away from you. Place a row of chocolate chunks along the bottom edge of the prepared pastry. 2. Roll the prepared pastry up around the chocolate and then place another row of chunks on the prepared pastry. Roll again and finish with one or two chocolate chunks. Be sure to leave the end free of chocolate so that it can adhere to the rest of the roll. 3. Brush the tops of the pastry with the beaten egg white and sprinkle the almonds on top, pressing them into the pastry so they adhere. 4. Place the Cook & Crisp Basket in your Pressure Cooker Steam Fryer. 5. Brush the bottom of the Ninja Foodi Pressure Steam Fryer basket with butter or oil and transfer the crescent rolls to the basket. 6. Put on the Smart Lid on top of the Ninja Foodi Steam Fryer. 7. Move the Lid Slider to the "Air Fry/Stovetop". Select the "Air Fry" mode for cooking. 8. Air-fry rolls at 175°C for 8 minutes. 9. Remove and let the pastries cool before dusting with icing sugar and serving.
Per serving: Calories: 372; Fat: 20g; Sodium: 891mg; Carbs: 29g; Fibre: 3g; Sugar 8g; Protein 17g

Monkey Bread Pieces

Prep time: 15 minutes | Cook time: 25 minutes | Serves: 4

310g plain flour
4 teaspoons baking powder
½ teaspoon salt
230g unsalted butter, chilled and divided
240ml plus 2 teaspoons whole milk, divided

200g granulated sugar
3 tablespoons ground cinnamon
105g packed light brown sugar
360ml water
65g icing sugar
½ teaspoon vanilla extract

1. In a medium bowl, whisk together flour, baking powder, and salt. 2. Cut 115 g butter into small cubes and place into dry ingredients. 3. Mix in the butter until dry ingredients are crumbly and about the size of peas. 4. Slowly pour in 240ml milk, mixing until a dough forms. Use clean hands to knead the dough about 10 minutes until smooth. 5. Pour dough onto a lightly floured surface and pat into a 25cm round. 6. Cut dough up into 2.5cm pieces and set aside. 7. Combine granulated sugar and cinnamon in a zip-top bag by shaking the bag. 8. Place cut pieces of dough into bag of cinnamon sugar. 9. Gently knead bag until each piece of dough is coated in cinnamon sugar. 10. Remove dough pieces and arrange evenly in the Cook & Crisp Basket pressed in the diffuser. 11. Add the sugar and butter to the cooking pot; press FUNCTION and turn the dial to select SEAR/SAUTÉ. 12. Press TEMP and turn the dial to select MD, and press START/STOP to begin cooking. 13. Cook the mixture for about 2 minutes until the butter is melted and brown sugar is dissolved. 14. Pour butter mixture over the top of Monkey Bread pieces. 15. Clean the cooking pot and add 360ml of water to it. 16. Place the basket in the cooking pot and cover the food with paper towel and foil. Crimp the edges. 17. Install the pressure lid and turn the pressure release valve to the SEAL position. 18. Select PRESSURE COOK, set the cooking temperature to LO and adjust the cooking time to 21 minutes. 19. When cooked, let the unit naturally release pressure. 20. Remove foil and paper towel from the top of pan and let cool on a rack 5 minutes. 21. To make the vanilla icing, whisk together icing sugar, remaining 2 teaspoons milk, and vanilla in a small bowl. 22. Drizzle the vanilla icing over the dish with while it is still warm. Enjoy immediately and you can store any unused portion in an air-tight container at room temperature up to 3 days.
Per Serving: Calories 800; Fat 34.22g; Sodium 355mg; Carbs 113.85g; Fibre 5.3g; Sugar 45.46g; Protein 12.31g

Baked Eggs

Prep Time: 10 minutes | Cook Time: 12 minutes | Serves: 1

1 teaspoon olive oil	tomatoes
2 tablespoons finely chopped onion	Salt and black pepper
1 teaspoon chopped fresh oregano	2 slices of bacon, chopped
Pinch crushed red pepper flakes	2 large eggs
1 (350g) can crushed or diced	25g grated Cheddar cheese
	Fresh parsley, chopped

1. Start by making the tomato sauce. Preheat a suitable saucepan over medium heat on the stovetop. Add the olive oil and sauté the onion, oregano and pepper flakes for around 5 minutes. Add the tomatoes and bring to a simmer. Season with salt and black pepper. Cook for on a simmer for around 10 minutes. 2. Place the Cook & Crisp Basket in your Pressure Cooker Steam Fryer. 3. Meanwhile, place the prepared bacon in the "cook & crisp basket". 4. Put on the Smart Lid on top of the Ninja Foodi Steam Fryer. 5. Move the Lid Slider to the "Air Fry/Stovetop". Select the "Air Fry" mode for cooking. 6. Cook on the "Air Fry" mode at 200°C for 5 minutes, shaking the basket every once in a while. 7. When the bacon is almost crispy, remove it to a paper-towel lined plate and rinse out the Ninja Foodi Steam Fryer, draining away the bacon grease. 8. Transfer the tomato sauce to a shallow 18 cm pie dish. Crack the eggs on top of the sauce and scatter the cooked bacon back on top. Season with salt and black pepper and transfer the pie dish into the Ninja Foodi Pressure Steam Fryer basket. 9. Air-fry eggs at 200°C for 5 minutes until the eggs are almost cooked to your liking. Sprinkle cheese on top. Cook on the "Air Fry" mode for 2 minutes. 10. Sprinkle with a little chopped parsley and let the eggs cool for a few minutes.

Per serving: Calories: 289; Fat: 14g; Sodium: 791mg; Carbs: 8.9g; Fibre: 4.6g; Sugar 8g; Protein 16g

Bacon Knots

Prep Time: 10 minutes | Cook Time: 8 minutes | Serves: 6

455g maple smoked centre-cut bacon	55g brown sugar
80g maple syrup	Cracked black peppercorns

1. Place the Cook & Crisp Basket in your Pressure Cooker Steam Fryer. 2. Tie each bacon strip in a loose knot and place them on a suitable the Cook & Crisp Basket. 3. Mix the maple syrup and sugar in a suitable bowl. Brush each knot generously with this mixture and sprinkle with coarsely cracked black pepper. 4. Put on the Smart Lid on top of the Ninja Foodi Steam Fryer. 5. Move the Lid Slider to the "Air Fry/Stovetop". Select the "Air Fry" mode for cooking. 6. Air-fry the bacon knots in batches. Place one layer of knots in the Ninja Foodi Pressure Steam Fryer basket. Cook on the "Air Fry" mode at 200°C for around 5 minutes. Turn the bacon knots over. Cook on the "Air Fry" mode for 2 to 3 minutes. 7. Serve warm.

Per serving: Calories: 282; Fat: 19g; Sodium: 354mg; Carbs: 15g; Fibre: 5.1g; Sugar 8.2g; Protein 12g

Air Fried Grapefruit

Prep Time: 10 minutes | Cook Time: 4 minutes | Serves: 2

1 grapefruit	2 to 4 teaspoons brown sugar

1. Cut the grapefruit in half. 2. Slice the bottom of the grapefruit to help it sit flat on the counter if necessary. Using a sharp paring knife, cut around the grapefruit between the flesh of the fruit and the peel. 3. Then, cut each segment away from the membrane so that it is sitting freely in the fruit. 4. Place the Cook & Crisp Basket in your Pressure Cooker Steam Fryer. 5. Sprinkle 2 teaspoons of brown sugar on each half of the prepared grapefruit. 6. Transfer the grapefruit half to the "cook & crisp basket". 7. Put on the Smart Lid on top of the Ninja Foodi Steam Fryer. 8. Move the Lid Slider to the "Air Fry/Stovetop". Select the "Air Fry" mode for cooking. 9. Air-fry at 200°C for 4 minutes. 10. Remove and let it cool for just a minute before enjoying.

Per serving: Calories: 82; Fat: 10.9g; Sodium: 354mg; Carbs: 20.5g; Fibre: 4.1g; Sugar 8.2g; Protein 6g

Broccoli Quiche

Prep Time: 10 minutes | Cook Time: 4 minutes | Serves: 4

90g broccoli florets	180g heavy cream
125g chopped roasted red peppers	½ teaspoon salt
140g grated mozzarella cheese	Black pepper
6 eggs	

1. Place the Cook & Crisp Basket in your Pressure Cooker Steam Fryer. 2. Grease the Cook & Crisp Basket. Place the broccoli florets and roasted red peppers in the Cook & Crisp Basket and top with the grated Fontina cheese. 3. Mix the eggs and heavy cream in a suitable bowl. Season the beaten eggs with salt and black pepper. Pour the egg mixture over the cheese and vegetables and cover the basket with aluminum foil. Transfer the basket to the Ninja Foodi Pressure Steam Fryer. 4. Put on the Smart Lid on top of the Ninja Foodi Steam Fryer. 5. Move the Lid Slider to the "Air Fry/Stovetop". Select the "Air Fry" mode for cooking. 6. Air-fry at 180°C for around 60 minutes. Remove the aluminum foil for the last two minutes of cooking time. 7. Unmold the quiche onto a platter and cut it into slices to serve with a side salad or perhaps some air-fried potatoes.

Per serving: Calories: 221; Fat: 7.9g; Sodium: 704mg; Carbs: 6g; Fibre: 3.6g; Sugar 6g; Protein 18g

Walnut Apple Muffins

Prep Time: 10 minutes | Cook Time: 11 minutes | Serves: 8

125g flour	1 egg
65g sugar	4 tablespoons pancake syrup
1 teaspoon baking powder	4 tablespoons melted butter
¼ teaspoon baking soda	185g unsweetened applesauce
¼ teaspoon salt	½ teaspoon vanilla extract
1 teaspoon cinnamon	30g chopped walnuts
¼ teaspoon ginger	30g diced apple
¼ teaspoon nutmeg	

1. In a suitable bowl, stir flour, sugar, baking powder, baking soda, salt, cinnamon, ginger, and nutmeg. 2. In a suitable bowl, beat egg until frothy. Add syrup, butter, applesauce, and vanilla and mix well. 3. Place the Cook & Crisp Basket in your Pressure Cooker Steam Fryer. 4. Pour the prepared egg mixture into dry recipe ingredients and stir just until moistened. 5. Gently stir in nuts and diced apple. 6. Divide batter among the 8 muffin cups. 7. Place 4 muffin cups in "cook & crisp basket". 8. Put on the Smart Lid on top of the Ninja Foodi Steam Fryer. 9. Move the Lid Slider to the "Air Fry/Stovetop". Select the "Air Fry" mode for cooking. 10. Air fry at 165°C for around 9 to 11 minutes. 11. Repeat with remaining 4 muffins or until toothpick inserted in centre comes out clean.

Per serving: Calories: 289; Fat: 14g; Sodium: 791mg; Carbs: 8.9g; Fibre: 4.6g; Sugar 8g; Protein 16g

Blueberry Morning Muffins

Prep Time: 10 minutes | Cook Time: 14 minutes | Serves: 8

155g flour	1 egg
100g sugar	120ml milk
2 teaspoons baking powder	100g blueberries, fresh or frozen
¼ teaspoon salt	and thawed
80ml rapeseed oil	

1. In a suitable bowl, stir flour, sugar, baking powder, and salt. 2. In a separate bowl, mix cooking oil with egg, and milk and mix well. 3. Add egg mixture to dry recipe ingredients and stir just until moistened. 4. Gently stir in blueberries. 5. Spoon batter evenly into muffin cups. 6. Place the Cook & Crisp Basket in your Pressure Cooker Steam Fryer. 7. Place 4 muffin cups in "cook & crisp basket". 8. Put on the Smart Lid on top of the Ninja Foodi Steam Fryer. 9. Move the Lid Slider to the "Air Fry/Stovetop". Select the "Air Fry" mode for cooking. 10. Air fry at 165°C for around 12 to 14 minutes or until tops spring back when touched lightly. 11. Repeat previous step to cook remaining muffins.

Per serving: Calories: 219; Fat: 10g; Sodium: 891mg; Carbs: 22.9g; Fibre: 4g; Sugar 4g; Protein 13g

Mango Steel-Cut Oats

Prep Time: 25 minutes | Cook Time: 15 minutes | Serves: 4

1 (340 ml) can coconut milk	1 large mango, pitted, peeled, and diced
100 g steel-cut oats	
Salt	60 g unsweetened coconut flakes, lightly toasted
55 g – 75 g loosely packed coconut sugar or brown sugar	30 g chopped macadamia nuts

1. Combine the coconut milk, 300 ml warm water, the oats, and a generous pinch of salt in the pot. 2. Close the lid, turn the pressure release valve to SEAL position, and then move the slider to PRESSURE. Select HI and set the cooking time to 13 minutes. Press START/STOP to begin cooking. When finished, release the pressure naturally. 3. Stir the sugar into the oats. The oats will thicken a bit upon standing. 4. Top the oats with the mango, coconut flakes, and nuts. Serve warm.
Per Serving: Calories 275; Fat: 11.91g; Sodium: 178mg; Carbs: 48.69g; Fibre: 8.8g; Sugar: 24.94g; Protein: 7.49g

Wheat Berry & Citrus Salad

Prep Time: 30 minutes | Cook Time: 30 minutes | Serves: 4-6

140 g wheat berries	2 tablespoons extra-virgin olive oil
½ cinnamon stick	
Salt	2 tablespoons cider vinegar
2 large oranges	150 g seedless red grapes, halved
100 g pitted Medjool dates	60 g chopped toasted pistachios

1. Combine the wheat berries, 960 ml water, the cinnamon stick, and ½ teaspoon salt in the pot. 2. Close the lid, turn the pressure release valve to SEAL position, and then move the slider to PRESSURE. Select HI and set the cooking time to 30 minutes. Press START/STOP to begin cooking. When finished, release the pressure naturally. 3. Drain the wheat berries and transfer them to a large bowl; discard the cinnamon stick. Let cool for 10 minutes. 4. Squeeze the juice of ½ orange into a blender. Add the dates, olive oil, and vinegar and let stand for 10 minutes to soften the dates. Blend them until smooth. 5. Cut the peels away from the remaining orange and orange half. Slice the oranges and cut them into quarters. 6. Combine the wheat berries with the dressing, orange pieces, grapes, and pistachios. Season the salad with salt. 7. Serve warm or at room temperature.
Per Serving: Calories 191; Fat: 7.3g; Sodium: 67mg; Carbs: 29.26g; Fibre: 5g; Sugar: 10.42g; Protein: 5.31g

Yogurt Parfait with Berry Crunch

Prep Time: 30 minutes | Cook Time: 8 hours | Serves: 4

For the yogurt

1.9 L whole milk or low fat milk	live active cultures
2 tablespoons plain yogurt with	

For the parfaits

55 g packed brown sugar	60 g freeze-dried raspberries, crushed
1 vanilla bean	
120 g fresh raspberries	

1. Pour the milk into the pot and lock on the lid. Move slider to AIR FRY/STOVETOP and use the dial to select YOGURT. Select "FEr" and adjust the cooking time to 8 hours. Press START/STOP to begin pasteurization. Unit will display "boiL" while pasteurizing. 2. When pasteurization temperature is reached, the unit will beep and display "COOL." Once the milk has cooled to 45°C, open the lid and skim the top of the milk. Add active cultures to milk and stir to combine. Close the lid and press START/STOP to begin incubation process. 3. When the cooking time is up, pour the yogurt into clean containers and store in the refrigerator for 8 hours before serving so the yogurt can continue to thicken. The yogurt can be stored in the refrigerator for up to 7 days. 4. In a medium bowl, Whisk together 960 g of the yogurt and the brown sugar in a medium bowl. Split the vanilla bean lengthwise with a sharp paring knife. Using the dull side of the knife, scrape the sticky black vanilla seeds into the yogurt; whisk them to combine. 5. Spoon half the yogurt into four sundae glasses or other serving dishes. Top the dish with the fresh raspberries and then the remaining yogurt. Sprinkle the dish with the freeze-dried berries and serve.

Per Serving: Calories 557; Fat: 15.35g; Sodium: 225mg; Carbs: 92.12g; Fibre: 2.2g; Sugar: 89.2g; Protein: 15.42g

Boiled Eggs with Prosciutto Slices

Prep Time: 10 minutes | Cook Time: 5 minutes | Serves: 2

240 ml water	1 tsp. truffle salt
4 large eggs	8 slices prosciutto

1. Pour the water into the pot and insert the rack. Carefully place the eggs on the rack. 2. Close the lid, turn the pressure release valve to SEAL position, and then move the slider to PRESSURE. Select HI and set the cooking time to 3 minutes. Press START/STOP to begin cooking. When finished, release the pressure quickly. 3. Run the eggs under cold water until cool, then peel. 4. Sprinkle the eggs with truffle salt. Serve the eggs with the prosciutto slices.
Per Serving: Calories 266; Fat: 16.87g; Sodium: 1722mg; Carbs: 3.29g; Fibre: 0g; Sugar: 1.66g; Protein: 24.02g

Egg Fried Rice

Prep Time: 15 minutes | Cook Time: 30 minutes | Serves: 4-6

295ml water	3 large eggs, beaten
190 g uncooked brown rice	65 g frozen peas
Salt	Freshly ground black pepper
1 tsp. sesame oil	Sriracha sauce, for topping (optional)
5 slices raw bacon, chopped	
1 tsp. soy sauce	4 green onions, sliced

1. Combine the water, rice and a pinch of salt in the pot. 2. Close the lid, turn the pressure release valve to SEAL position, and then move the slider to PRESSURE. Select HI and set the cooking time to 15 minutes. Press START/STOP to begin cooking. When finished, release the pressure naturally. 3. Use a fork to fluff the rice, and then transfer it to a large plate. Set aside. 4. Clean out the pot and then return it to the unit. 5. Select SEAR/SAUTÉ mode, and adjust the cooking temperature to Lo3. 6. When the pot is hot, add sesame oil and chopped bacon, and sauté them for 5 to 7 minutes until each piece is crispy; stir in the soy sauce, then push the bacon to one side of the pot; add the eggs to the opposite side of the pot, and gently push the eggs back and forth until they start to scramble slightly. Add the cooked rice and mix everything together quickly. 7. Stop the process and stir in the peas. Let the fried rice sit for a minute or two until the peas have thawed and warmed. 8. Season the dish with salt and pepper to taste, and top with sriracha sauce (if using) and the green onions. 9. Serve and enjoy.
Per Serving: Calories 258; Fat: 12.8g; Sodium: 181mg; Carbs: 26.37g; Fibre: 1.6g; Sugar: 1.03g; Protein: 8.85g

Pumpkin Pie Oatmeal with Cranberries & Pecans

Prep Time: 15 minutes | Cook Time: 4 minutes | Serves: 4

320 g steel-cut oats	2 tbsp (28 g) unsalted butter, at room temperature
1.1 L milk	
1 (411-g) can pure pumpkin puree	30 g dried cranberries
170 g light brown sugar	28 g chopped pecans
1 tsp ground cinnamon	60 ml pure maple syrup, for drizzling
½ tsp coarse salt	
1 tsp pure vanilla extract	

1. Combine the oats, milk and pumpkin in the pot of your pressure cooker, then whisk until smooth. Add the brown sugar, cinnamon and salt and stir well. 2. Close the lid and move slider to PRESSURE. Make sure the pressure release valve is in the SEAL position. The temperature will default to HIGH, which is the correct setting. Set time to 4 minutes. Select START/STOP to begin cooking. 3. Once the timer beeps, naturally release the pressure for 10 minutes. Then turn the pressure relief valve to the VENT position for quick pressure relief. Move slider to AIR FRY/ STOVETOP to unlock the lid, then carefully open it. 4. Stir in the vanilla, butter, cranberries and pecans. 5. Serve right away in bowls and drizzle the oatmeal with maple syrup.
Per Serving: Calories 576; Fat 27.21g; Sodium 433mg; Carbs 79.43g; Fibre 13.5g; Sugar 29.55g; Protein 23.5g

Steel-Cut Oats with Dried Apples

Prep time: 15 minutes | Cook time: 10 minutes | Serves: 6

2 tablespoons salted butter	½ teaspoon salt
120 g steel-cut oats	Maple syrup or brown sugar, to
½ teaspoon ground allspice	serve
95 g dried apples, chopped	Milk or cream, to serve

1. Add the butter to the Ninja XL Pressure Cooker. Move slider to AIR FRY/STOVETOP. Select SEAR/SAUTÉ and set to 3. Select START/STOP to begin preheating. Allow unit to preheat for 5 minutes. 2. Stir the butter occasionally until it begins to smell nutty and the milk solids at the bottom begin to brown, about 3 minutes. 3. Stir in the oats and allspice, then cook, stirring often, until fragrant and toasted, about 3 minutes. Add 1.3 L water, the apples and salt; stir to combine, then distribute in an even layer. 4. Press START/STOP to turn off the SEAR/SAUTÉ function, close the lid and move slider to PRESSURE. Ensuring the pressure release valve is in the SEAL position. The temperature will default to HIGH, which is the correct setting. Set time to 5 minutes. Select START/STOP to begin cooking. 5. When cooking is complete, release the pressure quickly by turning the pressure release valve to the VENT position. Move slider to the right to unlock the lid, then carefully open it. 6. Stir the mixture well, then re-cover without locking the lid in place. Let rest for 10 minutes. Stir vigorously until thick and creamy, about 30 seconds. 7. Serve with maple syrup and milk.
Per Serving: Calories 99; Fat 4.63g; Sodium 225mg; Carbs 18.71g; Fibre 3.9g; Sugar 3.11g; Protein 4.8g

Cheese Sausage and Egg Strata

Prep time: 10 minutes | Cook time: 21 minutes | Serves: 6

5 English muffins, toasted and torn into 2.5 cm pieces	300 ml milk
1 tablespoon olive oil	3 tablespoons chopped fresh chives
300 g pork or turkey breakfast sausage	Salt and freshly ground black pepper
6 large eggs	75 g grated cheddar cheese

1. Spray a round metal baking pan with that will fit in the pot with cooking spray. Place the English muffin pieces in the pan; set aside. 2. Put the oil in the pot, move slider to AIR FRY/STOVETOP. Select SEAR/SAUTÉ and set to 3. Select START/STOP to begin preheating. Allow unit to preheat for 5 minutes. 3. When the oil is hot, add the sausage and cook, breaking it up into large pieces with a spatula, until cooked through, 6 minutes. Press START/STOP to stop cooking. Pour out the sausage onto a paper towel–lined plate. Return the pot to the appliance. 4. In a bowl, combine the eggs, milk, chives, ½ teaspoon salt, and several grinds of pepper and whisk well. 5. Slowly pour the egg mixture over the English muffins, lightly pressing down on the bread so it absorbs the custard. Sprinkle the sausage and cheese evenly over the top; press again to submerge most of the bread in the custard. Cover with foil. 6. Pour 360 ml cold water into the pot. Then place the bottom layer of the Deluxe Reversible Rack in the lower position in the pot. Place the muffins with foil on the rack. Close the lid and move the slider to PRESSURE. Ensuring the pressure release valve is in the SEAL position. The temperature will default to HIGH, which is the correct setting. Set time to 15 minutes. Select START/STOP to begin cooking. 7. When cooking is complete, release the pressure quickly by turning the pressure release valve to the VENT position. Move slider to the right to unlock the lid. 8. Insert a butter knife into the centre of the strata; it should come out with no liquid custard coating the knife. 9. If the pudding is not done, lock on the lid and return to HIGH pressure for 1 minute more. Quick-release the pressure. 10. Remove the strata from the pot and serve right away.
Per Serving: Calories 348; Fat 18.93g; Sodium 818mg; Carbs 27.39g; Fibre 2.2g; Sugar 3.52g; Protein 17.29g

Creamy Polenta

Prep time: 10 minutes | Cook time: 6½ hours | Serves: 4

240g coarse stoneground yellow polenta	Salt and ground black pepper

1. Add 1.8 L water, the polenta and 2½ teaspoons salt to Ninja XL Pressure Cooker. 2. Close the lid and move slider to PRESSURE. Ensuring the pressure release valve is in the SEAL position. The temperature will default to HIGH, which is the correct setting. Set time to 20 minutes. Select START/STOP to begin cooking. 3. When pressure cooking is complete, let the pressure reduce naturally for 20 minutes, then release the remaining steam by moving the pressure valve to Venting. Move slider to the right to unlock the lid, then carefully open it. 4. Then Select SEAR/SAUTÉ and set to 3. Bring the mixture to a simmer, stirring often. Press START/STOP, lock the lid in place and move the pressure valve to Venting. 5. Select Slow Cook and set the temperature to Lo. Set the cooking time for 6 hours. Press START/STOP to begin cooking, then carefully open the pot. 6. Whisk the polenta until creamy, then taste and season with salt and pepper. Let stand for about 10 minutes to thicken slightly, then stir again and serve.
Per Serving: Calories 222; Fat 1.05g; Sodium 5mg; Carbs 47.84g; Fibre 2.5g; Sugar 1.52g; Protein 4.41g

Strawberry Oatmeal

Prep Time: 10 minutes | Cook Time: 3 minutes | Serves: 4

240 ml plain unsweetened almond milk	45 g cream cheese, softened
240 ml water	½ tsp pure vanilla extract
80 g old-fashioned rolled oats	170 g sliced strawberries
¼ tsp salt	25 g crumbled digestive biscuits
1 cinnamon stick	Honey, for drizzling

1. Add the almond milk, water, oats, cinnamon stick and salt to the pot and stir to mix well. Close the lid and move slider to PRESSURE. Make sure the pressure release valve is in the SEAL position. The temperature will default to HIGH, which is the correct setting. Set time to 3 minutes. Select START/STOP to begin cooking. 2. When cooking is complete, naturally release the pressure for 20 minutes. Then turn the pressure relief valve to the VENT position for quick pressure relief. Move slider to AIR FRY/ STOVETOP to unlock the lid, then carefully open it. 3. Stir in the oats and remove the cinnamon stick. 4. Add the cream cheese and vanilla. Stir until the cream cheese is completely melted into the oats. 5. Place the cooked oats in four serving bowls and top with strawberries, digestive biscuits and a drizzle of honey.
Per Serving: Calories 508; Fat 39.6g; Sodium 341mg; Carbs 36.11g; Fibre 11.2g; Sugar 11.02g; Protein 18.27g

Taco Huevos Rancheros

Prep Time: 10 minutes | Cook Time: 20 minutes | Serves: 4

220 g dried pinto beans, picked over and soaked overnight or quick-soaked	Salt and freshly ground black pepper
4 teaspoons taco seasoning, plus more for garnish	4 large eggs
235 g tomato salsa	4 (15 cm) corn tortillas, warmed, or 4 handfuls tortilla chips
Optional garnishes	
Sour cream	Grated pepper Jack cheese
Chopped fresh coriander	

1. Drain the beans. 2. Stir the beans, 360 ml water and the taco seasoning in the pot. 3. Close the lid, turn the pressure release valve to SEAL position, and then move the slider to PRESSURE. 4. Select HI and set the cooking time to 7 minutes. 5. Press START/STOP to begin cooking. 6. When finished, release the pressure quickly. 7. Drain off most of the cooking liquid from the beans and discard. Return the beans in the pot to the appliance, stir in the salsa, and then season them with salt and pepper. 8. Use a wooden spoon to create four indentations in the beans. Carefully crack the eggs into the indentations, and sprinkle the eggs with a few pinches of taco seasoning. 9. Cover the lid and use the dial to select SEAR/SAUTÉ. Select Lo2, and then press START/STOP to begin cooking. Cook them for 5 minutes until the egg whites are just set and the yolks are still runny. Remove the pot from the appliance. 10. Place the tortillas or tortilla chips on plates. Carefully scoop up the eggs and beans and place them on top of the tortillas or chips. Serve the dish immediately, and you can serve with the garnishes, if desired.
Per Serving: Calories 317; Fat: 6.7g; Sodium: 303mg; Carbs: 44.77g; Fibre: 10g; Sugar: 2.73g; Protein: 19.25g

Quinoa Chili with Feta cheese

Prep time: 30 minutes | Cook time: 6½ hours | Serves: 4 to 6

3 tablespoons rapeseed oil
1 medium yellow onion, finely chopped
4 medium garlic cloves, smashed and peeled
3 plum tomatoes, cored and chopped
Salt and ground black pepper
1 yellow pepper, stemmed, seeded and chopped
1 habanero chili, halved
2½ teaspoons sweet paprika
2½ teaspoons ground cumin
1 teaspoon dried oregano
255 g red, white or tricolour (rainbow) quinoa, rinsed and drained
100 g feta cheese, cut into 1 cm cubes
Chopped fresh coriander, to serve

1. Select sear/sauté function of your Ninja XL Pressure Cooker and set to lol, heat the oil until shimmering. 2. Add the onion, tomatoes, garlic, 1½ teaspoons salt and ¼ teaspoon pepper. Cook, stirring occasionally, until the moisture evaporates and the onion is softened and translucent, about 10 minutes. 3. Add the pepper, paprika, chili, cumin and oregano, then cook, stirring frequently, until the spices begin to stick to the bottom of the pot, 1 to 2 minutes. 4. Stir in the quinoa and 480 ml water, scraping up any browned bits; distribute the mixture in an even layer. 5. Close the lid and move slider to PRESSURE. Ensuring the pressure release valve is in the SEAL position. Adjust the pressure level to low. Set time to 12 minutes. Select START/STOP to begin cooking. 6. When pressure cooking is complete, let the pressure reduce naturally for 10 minutes, then release the remaining steam by moving the pressure valve to venting. Press START/STOP, then carefully open the pot. 7. Fluff the quinoa with a fork, removing and discarding the chili halves. Add the feta cheese and stir until it begins to melt. Stir in 480 ml water and re-cover without locking the lid in place, then let stand for 5 minutes. 8. Select SEAR/SAUTÉ function, bring the mixture to a boil. Press START/STOP to begin cooking, lock the lid in place and move the pressure valve to venting. Select slow cook and set the temperature to Lo. Set the cooking time for 6 hours; the mixture is done when the quinoa has absorbed the liquid. 9. Season with salt and pepper. Sprinkle with coriander and serve.
Per Serving: Calories 248; Fat 15.61g; Sodium 330mg; Carbs 23.65g; Fibre 2.3g; Sugar 15.2g; Protein 6.46g

Cream Coffee Cake

Prep time: 15 minutes | Cook time: 25 minutes | Serves: 6

165g plain flour, divided
200g granulated sugar
1 teaspoon salt, divided
½ teaspoon ground cinnamon
1 teaspoon baking powder
230g plus 1 tablespoon unsalted
butter, divided
120g full-fat sour cream
1 large egg
½ teaspoon vanilla extract
105g packed light brown sugar
360ml water

1. In a large bowl, whisk together 125g flour, granulated sugar, ½ teaspoon salt, cinnamon, and baking powder. 2. Soften 115g butter. Cut remaining butter into cubes and chill for later. 3. In a medium bowl, whisk 115g softened butter, sour cream, egg, and vanilla together until fluffy. 4. Fold wet ingredients into dry ingredients to make the coffee cake batter. 5. In a separate medium bowl, combine remaining cubed butter, 40g flour, and brown sugar. 6. Mix the mixture until it is crumbly and roughly the size of peas to make the streusel. 7. Pour half of the streusel into the basket. Pour half of the coffee cake batter on top of streusel in the basket. Repeat with remaining streusel and coffee cake batter. 8. Top the food with a paper towel and a piece of foil and crimp the edges of the pan. 9. Add the water to the cooking pot, place the Cook & Crisp Basket on top of diffuser and press down firmly, and then place the basket in the cooking pot. 10. Install the pressure lid and turn the pressure release valve to the SEAL position. 11. Select PRESSURE COOK, set the cooking temperature to HI and adjust the cooking time to 25 minutes. 12. When cooked, let the unit naturally release pressure. 13. Carefully remove coffee cake using the foil sling. Remove paper towel and foil. 14. Let the dish cool on a rack 10 minutes and then remove the coffee cake from the basket by turning it over onto a plate. Let cool fully. 15. Store the dish in an air-tight container at room temperature up to 3 days.
Per Serving: Calories 387; Fat 22.02g; Sodium 438mg; Carbs 42.69g; Fibre 0.9g; Sugar 16.88g; Protein 5.37g

Banana Chocolate Bread

Prep time: 15 minutes | Cook time: 65 minutes | Serves: 6

210g plain flour
100g granulated sugar
105g packed light brown sugar
1 teaspoon baking soda
½ teaspoon salt
½ teaspoon ground cinnamon
2 large eggs, lightly beaten
115g melted unsalted butter,
cooled slightly
120ml buttermilk
1 teaspoon vanilla extract
3 mashed banana
170g mini semisweet chocolate chips
240ml water

1. In a large bowl, whisk together flour, granulated sugar, brown sugar, baking soda, salt, and cinnamon. 2. Whisk together eggs, butter, buttermilk, and vanilla in a medium bowl. 3. Make a well in the centre of dry ingredients and mix in wet ingredients. The batter should still be lumpy with a few dry spots. 4. Fold in mashed banana and chocolate chips. 5. Add the water to the cooking pot, place the Cook & Crisp Basket on top of diffuser and press down firmly, and then pour the banana bread batter into the basket. 6. Place a paper towel on top of food and tightly cover with foil. 7. Install the pressure lid and turn the pressure release valve to the SEAL position. 8. Select PRESSURE COOK, set the cooking temperature to LO and adjust the cooking time to 65 minutes. 9. When cooked, turn the pressure release valve to the VENT position to quick release the steam. 10. Remove foil and paper towel. Use a clean paper towel to gently blot up any additional moisture that may have accumulated on top of the dish. 11. Let the dish cool on a cooling rack 10 minutes. 12. You can store the dish in an air-tight container up to 3 days.
Per Serving: Calories 356; Fat 13.25g; Sodium 483mg; Carbs 51.69g; Fibre 2.6g; Sugar 16.72g; Protein 8.26g

French Toast Casserole

Prep time: 10 minutes | Cook time: 30 minutes | Serves: 5

½ loaf (day-old) French bread, cut into 2.5cm chunks
8 large eggs
180ml whole milk
3 tablespoons granulated sugar
3 tablespoons packed light brown sugar
1 teaspoon vanilla extract
1 teaspoon ground cinnamon
½ teaspoon salt
2 tablespoons unsalted butter, cubed and chilled
360ml water
85g maple syrup

1. Arrange chunks of French bread in a single layer on bottom of a cake pan. 2. In a medium bowl, whisk together eggs, milk, granulated sugar, brown sugar, vanilla, cinnamon, and salt until fully combined. Pour egg mixture over French bread. 3. Sprinkle cubed butter on top of French bread. Refrigerate them for at least 2 hours or overnight. 4. Add the water to the cooking pot, place the Cook & Crisp Basket on top of diffuser and press down firmly, and then transfer the food into the basket. Place a paper towel on top of food and tightly cover with foil. 5. Install the pressure lid and turn the pressure release valve to the SEAL position. 6. Select PRESSURE COOK, set the cooking temperature to LO and adjust the cooking time to 30 minutes. 7. When cooked, let the unit naturally release pressure. 8. Remove foil and paper towel. Serve the dish topped with maple syrup.
Per Serving: Calories 340; Fat 13.35g; Sodium 517mg; Carbs 38.96g; Fibre 2.9g; Sugar 26.13g; Protein 15.55g

Gala Apple Pie Oatmeal

Prep time: 5 minutes | Cook time: 5 minutes | Serves: 4

720ml water
180g diced Gala apples, divided
80g steel cut oats
1 tablespoon packed light brown
sugar
3 teaspoons apple pie spice, divided
⅛ teaspoon salt

1. Combine water, 120g apples, oats, brown sugar, 2 teaspoons apple pie spice, and salt in the cooking pot. 2. Install the pressure lid and turn the pressure release valve to the SEAL position. 3. Select PRESSURE COOK, set the cooking temperature to HI and adjust the cooking time to 5 minutes. 4. When cooked, let the unit naturally release pressure. 5. Top the dish with remaining apples and apple pie spice, and serve.
Per Serving: Calories 291; Fat 1.7g; Sodium 98mg; Carbs 75.3g; Fibre 4.6g; Sugar 6g; Protein 4.23g

Cheese Polenta with Eggs

Prep Time: 10 minutes | Cook Time: 9 minutes | Serves: 4

175 g uncooked polenta (not instant)
946 ml water
1 tsp salt, plus more if needed
¼ tsp freshly ground black pepper, plus more if needed
1 tbsp (15 ml) extra-virgin olive

oil
4 large eggs
3 tbsp (43 g) unsalted butter
2 tbsp (30 ml) heavy whipping cream
55g grated Parmesan cheese, plus more for topping

1. Add the polenta, water, salt and pepper to the pot and stir until well combined. 2. Close the lid and move slider to PRESSURE. Make sure the pressure release valve is in the SEAL position. The temperature will default to HIGH, which is the correct setting. Set time to 9 minutes. Select START/STOP to begin cooking. 3. In the meantime, heat the olive oil in a small skillet over high heat. Once the oil is shimmering, crack the eggs into the hot oil. Fry the eggs for about 4 minutes, or until the white part is firm. 4. Once the timer beeps, turn the pressure relief valve to the VENT position for quick pressure relief. Move slider to the right to unlock the lid, then carefully open it. 5. Stir in the butter, cream and cheese. Taste the polenta and adjust the salt and pepper, if needed. 6. Transfer the polenta to four bowls and top each with a fried egg.
Per Serving: Calories 285; Fat 18.69g; Sodium 904mg; Carbs 23.25g; Fibre 2.4g; Sugar 17.68g; Protein 8.36g

Cinnamon-Apple & Butternut Squash Soup with Pecans

Prep Time: 10 minutes | Cook Time: 6 minutes | Serves: 4

430 g seeded, peeled and cut butternut squash (1.3-cm chunks)
1 apple, peeled, cored and cut into 1.3-cm chunks (I like Honeycrisp or Gala apples)
1 (400-ml) can full-fat coconut

milk
2 tsp (5 g) ground cinnamon
1 tbsp (15 ml) pure maple syrup
Pinch of salt
55 g roasted and chopped pecans

1. Add the butternut squash, apple pieces, cinnamon, coconut milk, maple syrup and salt to the pot and stir to mix well. 2. Close the lid and move slider to PRESSURE. Make sure the pressure release valve is in the SEAL position. The temperature will default to HIGH, which is the correct setting. Set time to 6 minutes. Select START/STOP to begin cooking. 3. When cooking is complete, turn the pressure relief valve to the VENT position for quick pressure relief. Move slider to the right to unlock the lid, then carefully open it. 4. Using an immersion blender or high-powered blender, blend until smooth. 5. Serve warm and top with pecans.
Per Serving: Calories 372; Fat 33.29g; Sodium 163mg; Carbs 20.85g; Fibre 6.1g; Sugar 13.52g; Protein 4.65g

Spanish Tortilla with Sauce

Prep Time: 25 minutes | Cook Time: 20 minutes | Serves: 4

2 tablespoons olive oil
½ medium yellow onion, thinly sliced
1 large (300 g) russet potato, peeled and cut into 1 cm
Salt and freshly ground black

pepper
8 large eggs
½ teaspoon smoked paprika
150 g drained jarred roasted red peppers

1. Spray a suitable baking pan with cooking spray and line the bottom with a round of parchment paper; spray the parchment with the cooking spray as well. 2. Add the oil to the pot; use the dial to select SEAR/SAUTÉ. Select Lo3, and then press START/STOP to begin cooking. 3. When the oil is hot, add the onion and cook for 3 minutes until beginning to soften; add the potato, 1 teaspoon salt, and several grinds of pepper and stir them to combine. Cover the lid loosely and cook them for 4 to 5 minutes until the potatoes are barely tender when pierced with a fork. Stop the process. 4. Scrape the onion and potato into the prepared baking pan. 5. In a small bowl, whisk together the eggs with ¼ teaspoon of the paprika. Pour the egg mixture into the baking pan over the potato mixture. 6. Pour 360 ml water into the pot and place the rack in the pot; place the baking

pan on the rack. 7. Close the lid, turn the pressure release valve to SEAL position, and then move the slider to PRESSURE. 8. Select HI and set the cooking time to 10 minutes. 9. Press START/STOP to begin cooking. 10. When finished, release the pressure naturally. 11. Blend the roasted peppers with the remaining ¼ teaspoon smoked paprika and a few grinds of pepper until smooth. Set aside. 12. Carefully remove the pan from the pot. 13. Run a knife around the edges of the pan, place a dinner plate over the pan, and carefully invert the tortilla onto the plate. 14. Cut the tortilla into wedges and serve with the sauce.
Per Serving: Calories 293; Fat: 16.47g; Sodium: 148mg; Carbs: 21.46g; Fibre: 2.1g; Sugar: 3.04g; Protein: 15.1g

Spinach Eggs Florentine

Prep Time: 10 minutes | Cook Time: 30 minutes | Serves: 4

1 tablespoon olive oil
2 medium garlic cloves, chopped
125 g baby spinach
Salt and freshly ground black pepper

360 g cottage cheese
5 large eggs
40 g – 75 g crumbled feta cheese
2 tablespoons chopped fresh dill

1. Spray a suitable baking pan with cooking spray and set aside. 2. Add the oil to the pot, then use the dial to select SEAR/SAUTÉ. Select Lo3, and then press START/STOP to begin cooking. 3. When the oil is hot, add the garlic and cook for 30 seconds until fragrant; add the spinach, 2 teaspoons water, a few pinches of salt, and several grinds of pepper, and then cook them for 2 minutes until wilted. 4. Stop the process, transfer the spinach and garlic to a mesh strainer and press with a wooden spoon to extract as much liquid as possible. 5. Stir the spinach mixture with the cottage cheese in a bowl until combined; add the eggs, feta cheese, dill, ½ teaspoon salt and a few grinds of pepper, and whisk them combine. 6. Transfer the egg mixture to the prepared baking pan and cover the pan tightly with foil. 7. Add 360 ml water to the pot, then place in the rack and place the baking pan on the rack. 8. Close the lid, turn the pressure release valve to SEAL position, and then move the slider to PRESSURE. 9. Select HI and set the cooking time to 25 minutes. 10. Press START/STOP to begin cooking. 11. When finished, release the pressure naturally. Blot the excess water from the top of the foil with paper towels. Remove the baking pan from the pot and carefully uncover. The eggs are done when a knife inserted into the centre comes out clean with no liquid egg clinging to the knife. 12. Let the dish sit for 5 minutes and then cut into wedges and serve.
Per Serving: Calories: 240; Fat: 15.15g; Sodium: 462mg; Carbs: 6.96g; Fibre: 1.5g; Sugar: 2.67g; Protein: 19.63g

Crescent Rolls

Prep Time: 40 minutes | Cook Time: 10 minutes | Serves: 8

370- 430 g plain flour
2 pkg. (5 g each) active dry yeast
1 tsp. salt
240 ml whole milk

110 g butter, cubed
60 g honey
3 large egg yolks
2 tbsp. butter, melted

1. Combine 180 g flour, yeast and salt in a bowl. 2. In a small saucepan, heat milk, cubed butter and honey to 50°C. 3. Add the liquid to dry ingredients; beat them on medium speed for 2 minutes; add the egg yolks, and beat them again on high for 2 minutes; stir in enough remaining flour to form soft dough. 4. Turn dough onto a floured surface; knead the dough for 6 to 8 minutes until smooth and elastic. 5. Place the kneaded dough in a greased bowl, turning once to grease the top. Cover the bowl with plastic wrap and let rise in a warm place for about 45 minutes or until doubled. 6. Punch down dough; place it in a resealable plastic bag. Seal and refrigerate it overnight. 7. Turn dough onto a lightly floured surface and divide in half. Roll each portion into a 36 cm. circle; cut each circle into 16 wedges. Lightly brush wedges with melted butter. Roll them up from wide ends, pinching pointed ends to seal. 8. Line a baking sheet with parchment paper, and transfer the rolls to it with point side down; cover the baking sheet with lightly greased plastic wrap, and then let them rise in a warm place for 45 minutes or until doubled. 9. After that, transfer the baking sheet to the pot. Close the lid and move slider to AIR FRY/STOVETOP, then use the dial to select BAKE/ROAST. Adjust the cooking temperature to 190°C and set the cooking time to 11 minutes. Press START/STOP to begin cooking. 10. Serve warm.
Per Serving: Calories: 427; Fat: 17.73g; Sodium: 424mg; Carbs:

58.36g; Fibre: 2.1g; Sugar: 12.82g; Protein: 8.87g

Easy Breads

Prep Time: 20 minutes | Cook Time: 5 minutes | Serves: 10

180 g plain flour
65 g whole wheat flour
1 tsp. salt

¼ tsp. garlic powder
180 ml hot water
2 tbsp. olive oil

1. Combine the flours, salt and garlic powder in a large bowl. Stir in water and oil. Turn onto a floured surface; knead them 10-12 times. 2. Divide dough into 10 portions, and then roll each portion into a 15 cm. circle on a lightly floured surface. 3. Add the breads to the pot. Move slider to AIR FRY/STOVETOP, and then use the dial to select SEAR/SAUTÉ. Select Lo3, and then press START/STOP to begin cooking. 4. Cook the breads for 1 minute on each side or until lightly browned. 5. Serve the breads warm.
Per Serving: Calories 113; Fat: 3.03g; Sodium: 234mg; Carbs: 18.68g; Fibre: 1.2g; Sugar: 0.08g; Protein: 2.74g

Beer-nana Loaf

Prep Time: 15 minutes | Cook Time: 55 minutes | Serves: 1 loaf

370 g self-rising flour
60 g quick-cooking oats
105 g packed brown sugar
3 medium mashed ripe bananas
1 bottle (300 ml.) wheat beer

60 g maple syrup
2 tbsp. olive oil
1 tbsp. sesame seeds
¼ tsp. salt

1. Mix the flour, oats and brown sugar in a large bowl. 2. Mix the bananas, beer and maple syrup in another bowl until blended. Add to the flour mixture; stir them just until moistened. 3. Transfer the mixture to a greased loaf pan; drizzle the mixture with oil and sprinkle with sesame seeds and salt. 4. Add the loaf pan to the pot. Close the lid and move slider to AIR FRY/STOVETOP, then use the dial to select BAKE/ROAST. Adjust the cooking temperature to 190°C and set the cooking time to 60 minutes. Press START/STOP to begin cooking. 5. A toothpick inserted in centre should come out clean when cooked. 6. Cool the load in pan for 10 minutes before removing to wire rack to cool.
Per Serving: Calories 678; Fat: 11.75g; Sodium: 1280mg; Carbs: 126.47g; Fibre: 4.4g; Sugar: 43.31g; Protein: 11.62g

Parmesan Bread

Prep Time: 10 minutes | Cook Time: 30 minutes | Serves: 6 to 8

115g unsalted butter, melted
¼ teaspoon salt
75g grated Parmesan cheese
3 to 4 cloves garlic, minced
1 tablespoon chopped fresh

parsley
455g frozen bread dough, defrosted
Olive oil
1 egg, beaten

1. Mix the melted butter, salt, Parmesan cheese, garlic and chopped parsley in a suitable bowl. 2. Roll the prepared dough out into a rectangle that measures 20 cm by 43 cm. 3. Spread the butter mixture over the prepared dough, leaving a 1 cm border un-buttered along one of the long edges. Roll the prepared dough from one long edge to the other, ending with the un-buttered border. Pinch the seam shut tightly. Shape the log into a circle sealing the ends by pushing one end into the other and stretching the prepared dough around it. 4. Cut out a circle of aluminum foil that is the same size as the Ninja Foodi Pressure Steam Fryer basket. Brush the foil circle with oil and place an oven safe ramekin or glass in the centre. 5. Transfer the prepared dough ring to the aluminum foil circle, around the ramekin. This will help you make sure the prepared dough will fit in the basket and maintain its ring shape. Use kitchen shears to cut 8 slits around the outer edge of the prepared dough ring halfway to the centre. Brush the prepared dough ring with egg wash. 6. Brush the sides of the Cook & Crisp Basket with oil and transfer the prepared dough ring, foil circle and ramekin into the basket. 7. Slide the Cook & Crisp Basket back into the Pressure Steam Fryer, but do not turn it on. Let the prepared dough rise inside the Pressure Steam Fryer for around 30 minutes. 8. After the bread has proofed in the Ninja Foodi Pressure Steam Fryer for around 30 minutes. 9. Put on the Smart Lid on top of the Ninja Foodi Steam Fryer. 10. Move the Lid Slider to the "Air Fry/Stovetop". Select the "Air Fry" mode for cooking. 11. Cook the bread ring on the "Air Fry" mode at 170°C for 15 minutes. Flip the bread over by inverting it onto a plate or cutting board and sliding it back into the cook & crisp Basket. 12. Air-fry for another 15 minutes. Serve Warm.
Per serving: Calories: 334; Fat: 10.9g; Sodium: 354mg; Carbs: 20.5g; Fibre: 4.1g; Sugar 8.2g; Protein 06g

Chapter 2 Vegetable and Sides Recipes

Parmesan Potatoes

Prep Time: 10 minutes | Cook Time: 20 minutes | Serves: 3

340g potatoes, diced
1 tablespoon olive oil
1 teaspoon smoked paprika
1 teaspoon red pepper flakes,
crushed
Sea salt and black pepper, to taste
50g parmesan cheese, grated

1. Place the Cook & Crisp Basket in your Pressure Cooker Steam Fryer. 2. Mix the potatoes with the olive oil and spices until well coated on all sides. 3. Arrange the potatoes in the Ninja Foodi Pressure Steam Fryer basket. 4. Put on the Smart Lid on top of the Ninja Foodi Steam Fryer. 5. Move the Lid Slider to the "Air Fry/Stovetop". Select the "Air Fry" mode for cooking. 6. Cook the potatoes at 200°C for about 15 minutes, shaking the basket halfway through the cooking time. 7. Top the warm potatoes with cheese and serve immediately. Enjoy!

Per serving: Calories: 361; Fat: 10.9g; Sodium: 454mg; Carbs: 10g; Fibre: 3.1g; Sugar 5.2g; Protein 10g

Mashed Potatoes with Kale

Prep Time: 25 minutes | Cook Time: 10 minutes | Serves: 4-6

4 medium russet potatoes, peeled and quartered
Salt
1 medium (200 g) bunch lacinato kale, tough centre rib discarded, leaves chopped
4 tablespoons unsalted butter, at room temperature
4 green onions, thinly sliced
60 g to 120 g whole milk or heavy cream

1. Place the potatoes in the pot and add 240 ml of water. Sprinkle them with ½ teaspoon salt. Put the kale on top of the potatoes, but don't stir it in. 2. Close the lid, turn the pressure release valve to SEAL position, and then move the slider to PRESSURE. Select HI and set the cooking time to 8 minutes. Press START/STOP to begin cooking. When finished, release the pressure quickly. 3. Set a colander in the sink and pour the potatoes and kale into the colander. Let the vegetables sit and cool for a few minutes; letting the steam evaporate will make the potatoes fluffier when you mash them. 4. While the vegetables cool, return the pot to the unit, add the butter, then select SEAR/SAUTÉ mode, and adjust to lo3. 5. When the butter has melted, add the green onions and cook them for 1 minute until tender; add the milk or cream and cook them for 1 minute to bring to a simmer. 6. Stop the process, and return the potatoes and kale to the pot and mash with a potato masher until the potatoes are mostly smooth. 7. Season the dish with salt and pepper. Enjoy.

Per Serving: Calories 270; Fat: 6.64g; Sodium: 54mg; Carbs: 45.39g; Fibre: 3.3g; Sugar: 2.31g; Protein: 8.88g

Cauliflower Mash

Prep Time: 15 minutes | Cook Time: 20 minutes | Serves: 6

1 large head cauliflower, chopped
120 ml chicken stock
2 garlic cloves, crushed
1 tsp. whole peppercorns
1 bay leaf
½ tsp. salt

1. Place cauliflower in the pot, and add water to cover. Bring to a boil at Hi5 on SEAR/SAUTÉ mode and then reduce the cooking temperature to Lo2; cover the saucepan and simmer them for 10 to 12 minutes until tender. Drain the cauliflower and then return to pot. 2. Combine remaining ingredients in a small saucepan, and bring to a boil. 3. Immediately remove the saucepan from heat and strain, discarding garlic, peppercorns and bay leaf. 4. Add stock to cauliflower. Mash them until reaching desired consistency. Serve and enjoy.

Per Serving: Calories 45; Fat: 1.54g; Sodium: 290mg; Carbs: 2.72g; Fibre: 0.9g; Sugar: 0.9g; Protein: 5.26g

Vegetable Bowls

Prep Time: 20 minutes | Cook Time: 60 minutes | Serves: 6

455 g sweet potatoes cut into 2.5 cm chunks
Extra-virgin olive oil, for drizzling
Fine sea salt and freshly ground black pepper
455 g Brussels sprouts, cleaned and halved
1 bunch asparagus, cut into 2.5 cm pieces with woody stems removed (optional)
130 g quinoa, rinsed
300 ml water
6 tablespoons tahini
60 ml freshly squeezed lemon
juice
2 cloves garlic, minced
1 teaspoon ground cumin
60 g chopped kale
150 g cherry tomatoes, halved
1 cucumber, chopped

1. Arrange the sweet potatoes on a large baking pan and drizzle with olive oil. Toss the potatoes to coat with the oil, then season with salt and pepper. 2. Add the baking pan to the pot. Close the lid and move slider to AIR FRY/STOVETOP, then use the dial to select BAKE/ROAST. Adjust the cooking temperature to 220°Cand set the cooking time to 25 minutes. Press START/STOP to begin cooking. 3. When cooked, transfer the sweet potatoes to a plate and clean the baking pan. 4. Arrange the Brussels sprouts and asparagus on the baking pan and drizzle with olive oil. Toss the sprouts and asparagus to coat with the oil, then season with salt and pepper; add the cooked sweet potatoes to them. 5. Cook them on BAKE/ROAST mode for 15 to 20 minutes until the vegetables are tender and golden. 6. Transfer the vegetables to a large plate and clean the pot. 7. Mix quinoa and 240 ml of water in the pot. 8. Close the lid, turn the pressure release valve to SEAL position, and then move the slider to PRESSURE. Select HI and set the cooking time to 1 minute. Press START/STOP to begin cooking. When finished, release the pressure naturally. Fluff the quinoa. 9. Combine the tahini, lemon juice, garlic, cumin, remaining 60 ml water, ¼ teaspoon salt, and several grinds of pepper in a small bowl. 10. To serve, fill each bowl with some chopped kale, cooked quinoa, roasted vegetables, cherry tomatoes, and cucumber. Drizzle the creamy tahini dressing over the top. 11. You can store the leftovers in four separate airtight containers—for the quinoa, the roasted vegetables, the raw vegetables, and the dressing—in the fridge for 5 days.

Per Serving: Calories 285; Fat: 10.66g; Sodium: 50mg; Carbs: 41.13g; Fibre: 11.4g; Sugar: 5.72g; Protein: 11.97g

Honey Peas & Carrots

Prep Time: 15 minutes | Cook Time: 5¼ hours | Serves: 12

455 g carrots, sliced
1 large onion, chopped
60 ml water
55 g butter, cubed
60 g honey
4 garlic cloves, minced
1 tsp. salt
1 tsp. dried marjoram
⅛ tsp. white pepper
1 pkg frozen peas

1. Combine the first nine ingredients in the pot. 2. Move slider to AIR FRY/STOVETOP. Select SLOW COOK. Set the temperature to low and set the time to 5 hours. Press START/STOP to begin cooking. 3. Stir in peas. Cook, covered, turn the heat to high and cook for 15-25 minutes longer or until vegetables are tender.

Per Serving: Calories 88; Fat 4.02g; Sodium 252mg; Carbs 12.72g; Fibre 2.1g; Sugar 8.14g; Protein 1.3g

Creamy Fiesta Corn

Prep Time: 15 minutes | Cook Time: 16 minutes | Serves: 8

225 g bacon strips, chopped
675 g fresh or frozen super sweet corn
1 medium sweet red pepper, finely chopped
1 medium sweet yellow pepper, finely chopped
200 g reduced-fat cream cheese
120 g cream
100 g chopped green chilies, optional
2 tsp. sugar
1 tsp. pepper
¼ tsp. salt

1. Move slider to AIR FRY/STOVETOP. Select SEAR/SAUTÉ and set to 3. Select START/STOP to begin preheating. Allow unit to preheat for 2 minutes. After 2 minutes, cook the bacon over medium heat until crisp, stirring occasionally. Remove with a slotted spoon; drain on paper towels. Discard drippings, reserving 1 tbsp. in the pot. 2. Add corn, red pepper and yellow pepper to drippings; cook and stir for 5-6 minutes or until tender. Stir in the remaining ingredients until well blended; bring to a boil. Reduce the heat to Lo1; simmer, covered, 8-10 minutes or until mixture is thickened. Serve.

Per Serving: Calories 296; Fat 15.21g; Sodium 846mg; Carbs 37.27g; Fibre 7g; Sugar 4.57g; Protein 10.71g

Crispy Courgette Fries

Prep Time: 25 minutes | Cook Time: 20 minutes | Serves: 4

2 medium courgette	¼ tsp. ground chipotle pepper
110 g panko (Japanese) bread crumbs	¼ tsp. salt
75 g grated Parmesan cheese	¼ tsp. pepper
2 tsp. smoked paprika	40 g plain flour
½ tsp. garlic powder	2 large eggs, beaten
	3 tbsp. olive oil

1. Cut each courgette in half lengthwise and then in half crosswise. Cut each piece lengthwise into ½ cm slices. 2. Mix bread crumbs, cheese and seasonings in a shallow bowl. Place flour and eggs in separate shallow bowls. 3. Dip courgette slices in flour, egg and then in crumb mixture, patting to help coating adhere. Place them on a foil-lined rimmed baking pan and drizzle them with oil. 4. Place the baking pan on the rack in the lower position and then place the rack in the pot. Move slider to STEAMCRISP and then use the dial to select STEAM BAKE. Adjust the cooking temperature to 220°C and set the cooking time to 25 minutes. Press START/STOP to begin cooking. 5. Serve and enjoy.
Per Serving: Calories 273; Fat: 18.3g; Sodium: 564mg; Carbs: 16.61g; Fibre: 1.1g; Sugar: 1.05g; Protein: 10.8g

Sweet-Sour Red Cabbage

Prep Time: 15 minutes | Cook Time: 20 minutes | Serves: 6

1 medium red cabbage	3 tablespoons red wine vinegar
2 tablespoons olive oil	1 tablespoon brown sugar
½ medium red onion, sliced	Salt and freshly ground black pepper
1½ teaspoons caraway seeds	
½ teaspoon baking soda	

1. Cut the cabbage into quarters. Cut out the hard, white core at the base of each quarter and discard. Shred the cabbage into ½ cm-wide strips. Set aside. 2. Select SEAR/SAUTÉ. Select Hi5, and then press START/STOP to begin cooking. 3. When the pot is hot, heat the oil; add onion, caraway seeds, and baking soda to the pot, and cook them for 4 minutes until tender. 4. Add vinegar and brown sugar to the pot, and stop the process; stir in the cabbage, ½ teaspoon salt, and several grinds of black pepper. 5. Close the lid, turn the pressure release valve to SEAL position, and then move the slider to PRESSURE. Select HI and set the cooking time to 5 minutes. Press START/STOP to begin cooking. When finished, release the pressure quickly. 6. Season the dish with salt and pepper. Serve and enjoy.
Per Serving: Calories 93; Fat: 4.81g; Sodium: 144mg; Carbs: 12.24g; Fibre: 3.2g; Sugar: 6.7g; Protein: 2.16g

Tomato & Ricotta Risotto

Prep Time: 5 minutes | Cook Time: 15 minutes | Serves: 4

4 tablespoons unsalted butter	½ teaspoon salt
960 ml chicken stock, divided	¼ teaspoon ground black pepper
300 g Arborio rice	40 g ricotta cheese
2 tablespoons tomato paste	10 g julienned fresh basil leaves

1. Select SEAR/SAUTÉ. Select Hi5, and then press START/STOP to begin cooking. 2. When the pot is hot, heat the butter for 30 seconds until melted; add 240 ml stock and rice, and cook them for 3 minutes until stock is absorbed by rice. 3. Add the remaining 720 ml stock, tomato paste, salt, and pepper to the pot, and stop the process. 4. Close the lid, turn the pressure release valve to SEAL position, and then move the slider to PRESSURE. Select HI and set the cooking time to 10 minutes. Press START/STOP to begin cooking. When finished, release the pressure naturally. 5. Gently fold in ricotta cheese. 6. Ladle risotto into four bowls, garnish the dish with basil, and serve warm.
Per Serving: Calories 259; Fat: 19.52g; Sodium: 1240mg; Carbs: 25.34g; Fibre: 9.7g; Sugar: 2.63g; Protein: 10.11g

Cheese Roasted Broccoli

Prep Time: 10 minutes | Cook Time: 20 minutes | Serves: 4

2 small broccoli crowns	½ tsp. salt
3 tbsp. olive oil	½ tsp. pepper
¼ tsp. crushed red pepper flakes	2 tbsp. grated Parmesan cheese
4 garlic cloves, thinly sliced	1 tsp. grated lemon zest

1. Close the lid and move slider to the AIR FRY/ STOVETOP. Preheat the pot by selecting BAKE/ ROAST, setting temperature to 400°F, and setting time to 5 minutes. Select START/STOP to begin preheating. 2. Cut broccoli crowns into quarters from top to bottom. Place in a parchment paper-lined pan that fits the pot. Drizzle with oil; sprinkle with seasonings. 3. Place the bottom layer of the Deluxe Reversible Rack in the lower position in the pot. Then place the pan on the rack. Close the lid. 4. Roast until crisp-tender, 10-12 minutes. Sprinkle with garlic; roast 5 minutes. Sprinkle with cheese; roast until the cheese is melted and the stalks of broccoli are tender, 2 to 4 minutes more. Sprinkle with the lemon zest.
Per Serving: Calories 133; Fat 11.41g; Sodium 375mg; Carbs 5.46g; Fibre 3.3g; Sugar 0.93g; Protein 4.67g

Cheese Snap Pea Pasta

Prep Time: 10 minutes | Cook Time: 30 minutes | Serves: 12

455 g fresh sugar snap peas, trimmed	3 garlic cloves, minced
400 g angel hair pasta	½ tsp. salt
5 tbsp. olive oil, divided	¼ tsp. crushed red pepper flakes
1 medium red onion, finely chopped	⅛ tsp. coarsely ground pepper
	125 g grated Parmesan cheese, divided

1. Add 3.8 L water to the pot. Move slider to AIR FRY/STOVETOP. Select SEAR/SAUTÉ and set to Hi5. Select START/STOP to begin cooking. Bring the water to a boil. 2. Add peas; cook, uncovered, just until crisp-tender, 3-4 minutes. Using a strainer, remove peas from the pot. 3. In the same pot, add the pasta to the boiling water and cook according to the package directions. Drain and reserve 240 ml cooking water; return to the pot. Toss with 3 tbsp. oil. 4. In a frying-pan, heat the remaining oil over medium heat; sauté the onion until tender, 2-3 minutes. Add garlic and seasonings; cook and stir 1 minute. Stir in peas; heat through. 5. Toss with pasta, adding 100 g cheese and reserved cooking water as desired. Sprinkle with remaining cheese.
Per Serving: Calories 144; Fat 8.82g; Sodium 287mg; Carbs 11.9g; Fibre 2.5g; Sugar 0.45g; Protein 4.8g

Creamy Butternut Squash Soup

Prep Time: 20 minutes | Cook Time: 26 minutes | Serves: 6

55 g unsalted butter	¼ teaspoon ground cinnamon
1 medium yellow onion, peeled and finely chopped	¼ teaspoon ground cumin
1 medium carrot, peeled and finely chopped	720 ml vegetable stock or chicken stock
2 cloves garlic, peeled and minced	2 tablespoons maple syrup
375 g cubed butternut squash	240 g heavy cream
½ teaspoon dried thyme	60 g sour cream
	3 tablespoons chopped fresh chives

1. Move slider to AIR FRY/STOVETOP. Select SEAR/SAUTÉ and set to 3. Select START/STOP to begin preheating. Allow unit to preheat for 2 minutes. After 2 minutes, melt butter in the pot. Add the onion and carrot and cook until tender, about 5 minutes. Add garlic, squash, cinnamon, thyme, and cumin and cook until fragrant, about 1 minute. Press the START/STOP button. 2. Add stock and maple syrup and stir well. Close the lid and move slider to PRESSURE. Make sure the pressure release valve is in the SEAL position. The temperature will default to HIGH, which is the correct setting. Set time to 15 minutes. Select START/STOP to begin cooking. 3. When cooking is complete, naturally release the pressure for 15 minutes. Then turn the pressure relief valve to the VENT position for quick pressure relief. Move slider to AIR FRY/ STOVETOP to unlock the lid, then carefully open it. Stir well. 4. Use an immersion blender, or work in batches with a blender, to purée soup until smooth. 5. Mix cream and sour cream in a small bowl, then stir into soup. Close the lid to warm cream, about 5 minutes. Serve hot with chives for garnish.
Per Serving: Calories 262; Fat 17.17g; Sodium 278mg; Carbs 24.66g; Fibre 2.9g; Sugar 10.28g; Protein 5.02g

Healthy Carrot Apple Soup

Prep Time: 20 minutes | Cook Time: 17 minutes | Serves: 6

55 g unsalted butter
4 medium carrots, peeled and finely chopped
2 medium Granny Smith apples, cored and chopped
½ medium sweet onion, peeled and finely chopped
1 clove garlic, peeled and minced
1 teaspoon grated fresh ginger
½ teaspoon dried tarragon
⅛ teaspoon ground nutmeg
720 ml Vegetable Stock or Chicken Stock
180 g heavy cream
½ teaspoon salt
½ teaspoon ground black pepper
3 tablespoons chopped fresh chives

1. Move slider to AIR FRY/STOVETOP. Select SEAR/SAUTÉ and set to 3. Select START/STOP to begin preheating. Allow unit to preheat for 2 minutes. After 2 minutes, melt butter in the pot. Add carrots and cook until tender, about 5 minutes. Add apples, onion, ginger, garlic, tarragon, and nutmeg and cook until fragrant, about 2 minutes. Press the START/STOP button. 2. Add stock and stir well. Close the lid and move slider to PRESSURE. Make sure the pressure release valve is in the SEAL position. The temperature will default to HIGH, which is the correct setting. Set time to 10 minutes. Select START/STOP to begin cooking. 3. When cooking is complete, naturally release the pressure for 15 minutes. Then turn the pressure relief valve to the VENT position for quick pressure relief. Move slider to AIR FRY/ STOVETOP to unlock the lid, then carefully open it. Stir well. 4. Use an immersion blender, or work in batches with a blender, to purée soup until smooth. Stir in cream, salt, and pepper. Sprinkle with chives and serve hot.
Per Serving: Calories 230; Fat 14.42g; Sodium 481mg; Carbs 22.21g; Fibre 3.9g; Sugar 12.13g; Protein 4.47g

Cheesy Cauliflower Casserole

Prep Time: 15 minutes | Cook Time: 13 minutes | Serves: 6

Grass-fed butter, ghee or avocado oil, for casserole dish
115 g cream cheese, softened
60 ml milk or heavy cream
60 g shredded Gruyère cheese, divided
40 g shredded Parmesan cheese, divided
30 g shredded Swiss cheese, divided
1 tsp sea salt
½ tsp garlic granules or garlic powder
½ tsp dried thyme
2 tbsp (8 g) chopped fresh flat-leaf parsley, plus more for garnish (optional)
1 large head cauliflower, chopped into bite-size florets
355 ml water

1. Grease a casserole dish that fits in the pot with butter. Set aside. 2. In a large bowl, combine the cream cheese and stir well. Add three-quarters of the cheeses (reserving the rest) and the salt, thyme, garlic, parsley and cauliflower florets and gently toss until everything is combined. 3. Transfer to the prepared casserole dish and sprinkle with the remaining quarter of the cheeses. Cover the casserole dish with its glass lid. If your casserole dish doesn't come with a glass lid, you can cover the top of the dish with unbleached parchment paper, top it with foil and secure it around the edges. 4. Pour the water into the pot and place the bottom layer of the Deluxe Reversible Rack in the lower position in the pot. 5. Carefully set the covered casserole dish on the rack. 6. Close the lid and move slider to PRESSURE. Make sure the pressure release valve is in the SEAL position. The temperature will default to HIGH, which is the correct setting. Set time to 10 minutes. Select START/STOP to begin cooking. 7. When cooking is complete, naturally release the pressure for 15 minutes. Then turn the pressure relief valve to the VENT position for quick pressure relief. 8. Cook on BROIL function for 2-3 minutes, just until the cheese becomes light golden brown, then remove from the pot and allow to rest for 15 minutes before serving. 9. Serve as is or garnished with chopped fresh flat-leaf parsley.
Per Serving: Calories 208; Fat 17.12g; Sodium 778mg; Carbs 5.29g; Fibre 1g; Sugar 2.14g; Protein 9.16g

Delicious Summer Ratatouille

Prep Time: 15 minutes | Cook Time: 11 minutes | Serves: 6

80 ml avocado oil or olive oil, divided
1 large white onion, diced
80 ml fresh lemon juice
3 cloves garlic, minced
32 g tomato paste
40 g loosely packed fresh basil, plus more for garnish
2 tbsp (30 ml) white wine vinegar
1 tsp sea salt, plus more to taste
1 small aubergine, diced (see note)
2 medium courgette, diced
2 medium yellow summer squash, diced
455 g cherry or grape tomatoes
3 tbsp (15 g) grated fresh Parmesan, for garnish (optional)

1. Move slider to AIR FRY/STOVETOP. Select SEAR/SAUTÉ and set to 3. Select START/STOP to begin cooking. Coat the bottom of the pot with 2 tablespoons (30 ml) of the oil, then add the onion. Sauté for 3 minutes, or until translucent and fragrant. Press START/STOP to turn off the SEAR/SAUTÉ function. 2. In the meantime, prepare the lemon-basil sauce: In a food processor, combine the remaining oil, garlic, tomato paste, lemon juice, basil, vinegar and salt. Pulse until smooth. 3. Place the courgette, aubergine, squash and tomatoes in the pot. Pour the lemon-basil sauce over the vegetable mixture. 4. Close the lid and move slider to PRESSURE. Make sure the pressure release valve is in the SEAL position. The temperature will default to HIGH, which is the correct setting. Set time to 8 minutes. Select START/STOP to begin cooking. 5. When cooking is complete, turn the pressure relief valve to the VENT position for quick pressure relief. Move slider to the right to unlock the lid, then carefully open it. 6. Serve hot with Parmesan cheese (if using) and more basil for garnish, and additional salt to taste.
Per Serving: Calories 218; Fat 12.67g; Sodium 425mg; Carbs 25.66g; Fibre 5.9g; Sugar 16.47g; Protein 4.36g

Bacon Brussels Sprouts Hash

Prep time: 5 minutes | Cook time: 10 minutes | Serves: 4

4 slices bacon, quartered
1 medium red onion, peeled and sliced
1 medium sweet potato, peeled and small-diced
455g Brussels sprouts, trimmed and halved
240ml water
2 tablespoons maple syrup
2 tablespoons fresh orange juice
⅛ teaspoon hot sauce
1 tablespoon chopped fresh chives

1. Add the bacon to the cooking pot; press FUNCTION and turn the dial to select SEAR/SAUTÉ. 2. Press TEMP and turn the dial to select HI, and press START/STOP to begin cooking. 3. Cook the bacon for 5 minutes until crisp and the fat is rendered. Transfer bacon to a paper towel–lined plate and crumble when cooled. 4. Add onion, sweet potato, and Brussels sprouts to the cooking pot and stir-fry them for an additional 2 minutes in bacon drippings. Remove veggies from pot. 5. Add the water to the cooking pot, place the reversible rack in the pot in the lower position and drop the lower rack through the reversible rack handles. 6. Arrange the veggies onto the rack. 7. Install pressure lid and turn the pressure release valve to the SEAL position. 8. Select PRESSURE COOK, set the cooking temperature to HI and adjust the cooking time to 3 minutes. 9. When cooked, let the unit naturally release pressure. 10. Transfer cooked veggies to a serving dish. Toss with maple syrup, orange juice, and hot sauce. Garnish the dish with crumbled bacon and chives. Serve warm.
Per Serving: Calories 214; Fat 10.63g; Sodium 167mg; Carbs 24.9g; Fibre 5.3g; Sugar 11.68g; Protein 7.71g

Mushrooms in Beef Stock

Prep time: 5 minutes | Cook time: 15 minutes | Serves: 4

3 tablespoons unsalted butter
4 cloves garlic, peeled and minced
455g whole button mushrooms, cleaned
480ml beef stock
2 teaspoons Worcestershire sauce
1 tablespoon fresh thyme leaves
⅛ teaspoon salt

1. Melt the butter in the cooking pot at MD:HI for 30 seconds on SEAR/SAUTÉ mode; add garlic and sauté for 1 minute; add mushrooms and sauté for 1 minute more. 2. Stop the machine, and add stock and Worcestershire sauce to the pot. 3. Install the pressure lid and turn the pressure release valve to the SEAL position. 4. Select PRESSURE COOK, set the cooking temperature to HI and adjust the cooking time to 13 minutes. 5. When cooked, let the unit naturally release pressure. 6. Transfer mushrooms to a serving dish. Garnish the dish with fresh thyme leaves and salt, and serve.
Per Serving: Calories 93; Fat 6.46g; Sodium 562mg; Carbs 5.44g; Fibre 1.3g; Sugar 2.56g; Protein 5.44g

Pressure-Cooked Russet Potatoes

Prep time: 5 minutes | Cook time: 10 minutes | Serves: 4

240ml water
4 medium russet potatoes, scrubbed

1. Add the water to the cooking pot, place the reversible rack in the pot in the lower position and drop the lower rack through the reversible rack handles. 2. Arrange the potatoes onto the rack. 3. Install the pressure lid and turn the pressure release valve to the SEAL position. 4. Select PRESSURE COOK, set the cooking temperature to HI and adjust the cooking time to 10 minutes. 5. When cooked, let the unit naturally release pressure. 6. Serve warm.
Per Serving: Calories 292; Fat 0.3g; Sodium 20mg; Carbs 66.68g; Fibre 4.8g; Sugar 2.29g; Protein 7.9g

Parmesan Fingerling Potatoes

Prep time: 5 minutes | Cook time: 11 minutes | Serves: 6

2 tablespoons unsalted butter, divided
675g fingerling potatoes, scrubbed
4 cloves garlic, peeled and chopped
480ml water
1 teaspoon salt
½ teaspoon ground black pepper
2 tablespoons sour cream
50g grated Parmesan cheese
2 tablespoons chopped fresh chives

1. Pierce each potato three times. 2. Melt the butter in the cooking pot at MD:HI for 30 seconds on SEAR/SAUTÉ mode; add potatoes and sauté them for 4 minute; add garlic and heat for 1 minute more. 3. Add water to the pot. 4. Install the pressure lid and turn the pressure release valve to the SEAL position. 5. Select PRESSURE COOK, set the cooking temperature to HI and adjust the cooking time to 6 minutes. 6. When cooked, let the unit naturally release pressure. 7. Transfer potatoes to a serving dish. Toss the potatoes with remaining butter, salt, pepper, sour cream, and Parmesan cheese. Garnish with chopped chives. Serve warm.
Per Serving: Calories 155; Fat 5.44g; Sodium 552mg; Carbs 22.09g; Fibre 2.6g; Sugar 0.94g; Protein 5.13g

Bacon-Corn Casserole

Prep time: 5 minutes | Cook time: 17 minutes | Serves: 4

6 slices bacon, quartered
1 small red pepper, seeded and diced
60ml whole milk
2 tablespoons gluten-free plain flour
2 tablespoons unsalted butter, melted
50g cream cheese, room temperature
½ teaspoon salt
½ teaspoon ground black pepper
2 (380g) cans corn, drained
2 tablespoons Parmesan cheese
240ml water

1. Add the bacon to the cooking pot; press FUNCTION and turn the dial to select SEAR/SAUTÉ. 2. Press TEMP and turn the dial to select HI, and press START/STOP to begin cooking. 3. Cook the bacon for 5 minutes until crisp. Transfer bacon to a paper towel–lined plate. Crumble when cooled. 4. Add pepper to pot and cook for 5 minutes in bacon drippings until tender. 5. In medium bowl, whisk together milk and flour. Add butter, cream cheese, salt, and pepper. Add crumbled bacon, pepper, and corn. Transfer the mixture to a suitable glass dish and sprinkle them with Parmesan cheese. 6. Add the water to the cooking pot, place the reversible rack in the pot in the lower position and drop the lower rack through the reversible rack handles. 7. Arrange the dish onto the rack. 8. Install the pressure lid and turn the pressure release valve to the SEAL position. 9. Select PRESSURE COOK, set the cooking temperature to HI and adjust the cooking time to 7 minutes. 10. When cooked, let the unit naturally release pressure. 11. Remove dish from the cooking pot and let cool for 10 minutes. Serve warm.
Per Serving: Calories 360; Fat 24.95g; Sodium 875mg; Carbs 27.35g; Fibre 1.9g; Sugar 7.34g; Protein 9.87g

Cauliflower Florets with Cheddar Sauce

Prep time: 5 minutes | Cook time: 7 minutes | Serves: 4

240ml water
1 large head cauliflower, cut into florets
1 tablespoon unsalted butter
50g grated Cheddar cheese
180ml whole milk
1 tablespoon gluten-free plain flour
½ teaspoon salt
½ teaspoon ground black pepper

1. Add the water to the cooking pot, place the reversible rack in the pot in the lower position and drop the lower rack through the reversible rack handles. 2. Arrange the cauliflower florets onto the rack. 3. Install the pressure lid and turn the pressure release valve to the SEAL position. 4. Select PRESSURE COOK, set the cooking temperature to HI and adjust the cooking time to 5 minutes. 5. When cooked, let the unit naturally release pressure. 6. Transfer cauliflower to a serving dish and drain the pot. 7. Melt the butter in the cooking pot at MD for 30 seconds on SEAR/SAUTÉ mode; add cheese, milk, flour, salt, and pepper, and whisk them for 2 minutes until smooth. 8. Pour sauce over cauliflower in the dish and serve warm.
Per Serving: Calories 152; Fat 9.13g; Sodium 440mg; Carbs 11.44g; Fibre 1.5g; Sugar 7.48g; Protein 7.03g

Smashed Purple Potatoes

Prep time: 10 minutes | Cook time: 10 minutes | Serves: 6

4 tablespoons unsalted butter, divided
675g baby purple potatoes, scrubbed
3 cloves garlic, peeled and minced
480ml water
2 tablespoons Parmesan cheese
60ml whole milk
1 teaspoon salt
½ teaspoon ground black pepper

1. Use a fork to pierce each potato four times. 2. Melt the butter in the cooking pot at MD:HI for 30 seconds on SEAR/SAUTÉ mode; add potatoes and garlic, and sauté them for 3 minutes. 3. Stop the machine and add water to the pot. 4. Install the pressure lid and turn the pressure release valve to the SEAL position. 5. Select PRESSURE COOK, set the cooking temperature to HI and adjust the cooking time to 7 minutes. 6. When cooked, let the unit naturally release pressure. 7. Transfer the potatoes to a serving bowl. Toss with remaining butter, Parmesan, milk, salt, and pepper. 8. Using an immersion blender or the back of a fork, gently mash potatoes until desired consistency. Serve warm.
Per Serving: Calories 153; Fat 6.04g; Sodium 434mg; Carbs 21.98g; Fibre 2.6g; Sugar 2.21g; Protein 3.49g

English Cucumber & Quinoa Tabbouleh

Prep time: 10 minutes | Cook time: 20 minutes | Serves: 4

180g quinoa
420ml water
1 tablespoon olive oil
3 tablespoons lemon juice
½ teaspoon salt
1 English cucumber, peeled and diced
2 Roma tomatoes, seeded and diced
1 tablespoon lemon zest
2 spring onions, thinly sliced
½ teaspoon ground black pepper
10g chopped fresh parsley
10g chopped fresh mint leaves

1. Add quinoa, water, olive oil, lemon juice, and salt to the cooking pot, and stir them well. 2. Install the pressure lid and turn the pressure release valve to the SEAL position. 3. Select PRESSURE COOK, set the cooking temperature to HI and adjust the cooking time to 20 minutes. 4. When cooked, let the unit naturally release pressure. 5. Transfer quinoa to a serving dish and fluff with a fork. Toss in cucumber, tomatoes, lemon zest, spring onions, black pepper, parsley, and mint. 6. Cover the dish and refrigerate the food for at least 1 hour or up to overnight. Serve chilled.
Per Serving: Calories 214; Fat 6.28g; Sodium 304mg; Carbs 33.34g; Fibre 4.6g; Sugar 3.2g; Protein 7.45g

Lemon Quinoa

Prep time: 5 minutes | Cook time: 20 minutes | Serves: 4

180g quinoa
420ml water
2 tablespoons unsalted butter
2 tablespoons lemon juice
2 tablespoons lime juice
½ teaspoon salt

1. Combine the quinoa, water, butter, lemon juice, lime juice, and salt in the cooking pot. 2. Install the pressure lid and turn the pressure release valve to the SEAL position. 3. Select PRESSURE COOK, set the cooking temperature to HI and adjust the cooking time to 20 minutes. 4. When cooked, let the unit naturally release pressure. 5. Transfer quinoa to a serving dish and fluff with a fork. Serve warm.
Per Serving: Calories 195; Fat 6.46g; Sodium 298mg; Carbs 28.43g; Fibre 3g; Sugar 0.32g; Protein 6.29g

Creamy Cheese Mushroom Risotto

Prep Time: 15 minutes | Cook Time: 15 minutes | Serves: 8

4 tbsp (55 g) grass-fed butter or ghee, divided
1 medium yellow onion, diced
680 g mushrooms, woody ends removed, thinly sliced
5 cloves garlic, finely chopped
120 ml dry white wine
195 g uncooked arborio or other short-grain white rice
1 large celery rib with leaves, thinly sliced
1 tsp sea salt
475 ml chicken or vegetable stock
60 ml heavy cream
40 g shredded Parmesan cheese, plus more for garnish
15 g finely chopped fresh flat-leaf parsley, plus more for garnish
1 tsp finely chopped fresh thyme leaves

1. Place 2 tablespoons butter in the pot. Move slider to AIR FRY/ STOVETOP. Select SEAR/SAUTÉ and set to 3. Select START/STOP to begin cooking. and press sauté. Once the butter has melted, add the onion and mushrooms and sauté, stirring occasionally, for 7 minutes, or until caramelized. 2. Then, add the garlic and sauté for 1 minute, stirring occasionally. Add the wine and deglaze the pot, scraping up any browned bits with a wooden spoon. 3. Add the rice, then give everything a stir to combine, stirring for 1 minute. Press START/ STOP to turn off the SEAR/SAUTÉ function. 4. Add the celery, salt and stock, then give everything a quick stir. 5. Close the lid and move slider to PRESSURE. Make sure the pressure release valve is in the SEAL position. The temperature will default to HIGH, which is the correct setting. Set time to 6 minutes. Select START/STOP to begin cooking. 6. When cooking is complete, naturally release the pressure for 10 minutes. Then turn the pressure relief valve to the VENT position for quick pressure relief. Move slider to AIR FRY/ STOVETOP to unlock the lid, then carefully open it. 7. Add the cream, the remaining 2 tablespoons of butter, Parmesan, thyme and parsley, then quickly stir until the cream and Parmesan are fully mixed in. Allow the mixture to rest for 10 minutes. 8. Serve right away, garnished with shredded Parmesan and chopped fresh flat-leaf parsley.
Per Serving: Calories 484; Fat 11.92g; Sodium 855mg; Carbs 88.59g; Fibre 11.2g; Sugar 3.83g; Protein 16.69g

Simple Artichokes with Lemon-Garlic Butter

Prep Time: 15 minutes | Cook Time: 13 minutes | Serves: 4

4 medium to large globe artichokes
Juice of 1 lemon, divided
240 ml water
1 tsp Dijon mustard
1 clove garlic
¼ tsp sea salt, plus more to taste
4 tbsp (55 g) unsalted butter or ghee, melted

1. Remove the outer leaves of the artichokes, trim about 1.3 cm from the top and remove the stem so each artichoke can sit upright. Brush each artichoke with lemon juice, reserve the remaining lemon juice and set aside. 2. Pour the water into the pot and place the bottom layer of the Deluxe Reversible Rack in the lower position in the pot. Place the artichokes, stem side down, on the rack so they sit upright. 3. Close the lid and move slider to PRESSURE. Make sure the pressure release valve is in the SEAL position. The temperature will default to HIGH, which is the correct setting. Set time to 13 minutes. Select START/ STOP to begin cooking. 4. In the meantime, prepare the lemon-garlic butter. In a small bowl, stir the Dijon, garlic, remaining lemon juice and salt into the butter. 5. Serve warm with the lemon-garlic butter on the side for dipping. Sprinkle with additional salt to taste.
Per Serving: Calories 178; Fat 10.9g; Sodium 621mg; Carbs 19.33g; Fibre 13.1g; Sugar 1.83g; Protein 4.99g

Loaded Mashed Cheese Potatoes

Prep Time: 15 minutes | Cook Time: 10 minutes | Serves: 6

240 ml water
5 medium russet potatoes, peeled and cut into 5-cm cubes
4 tbsp (55 g) grass-fed butter
230 g sour cream
120 ml milk or heavy cream
1 tsp sea salt
115 g shredded cheddar cheese
80 g shredded Italian cheese blend (equal parts provolone, Romano and Parmesan)
170 g precooked crispy bacon or turkey bacon, crumbled
1 spring onion, white and light green parts only, sliced

1. Pour the water into the pot and place the bottom layer of the Deluxe Reversible Rack in the lower position in the pot. 2. Layer the potatoes on the rack. 3. Close the lid and move slider to PRESSURE. Make sure the pressure release valve is in the SEAL position. The temperature will default to HIGH, which is the correct setting. Set time to 10 minutes. Select START/STOP to begin cooking. 4. When cooking is complete, turn the pressure relief valve to the VENT position for quick pressure relief. Move slider to the right to unlock the lid, then carefully open it. 5. Carefully remove the potatoes and the rack, setting the potatoes aside. Pour out and discard the water that remains in the pot, then return the potatoes to the pot; alternatively, transfer the potatoes to a large bowl. 6. Add the butter, allowing it to melt over the potatoes. Once the butter has melted, add the sour cream, milk and salt, then use a potato masher to start mixing everything together—do not overmix, just mash until there are no more lumps. 7. Gently fold in the cheeses, 115 g of the crumbled crispy bacon bits and the spring onions until all of the cheese has melted into the hot potatoes and everything is incorporated; do not overmix. 8. Serve immediately, garnished with the remaining 2 ounces (55 g) of crumbled crispy bacon bits.
Per Serving: Calories 674; Fat 35.73g; Sodium 1225mg; Carbs 62.35g; Fibre 4.7g; Sugar 2.34g; Protein 29.33g

Flavourful Citrus Beetroots

Prep Time: 15 minutes | Cook Time: 23 minutes | Serves: 6

240 ml water
5 medium beetroot, about 5 cm in diameter, leaves removed
2 tbsp (28 g) grass-fed butter,
ghee or avocado oil
¾ tsp sea salt
Zest of 1 orange
Juice of 1 orange

1. Pour the water into the pot and place the bottom layer of the Deluxe Reversible Rack in the lower position in the pot. Place the beetroot on the rack. 2. Close the lid and move slider to PRESSURE. Make sure the pressure release valve is in the SEAL position. The temperature will default to HIGH, which is the correct setting. Set time to 20 minutes. Select START/STOP to begin cooking. 3. Once the timer sounds, naturally release the pressure for 15 minutes. Then turn the pressure relief valve to the VENT position for quick pressure relief. Move slider to AIR FRY/ STOVETOP to unlock the lid, then carefully open it. 4. Carefully remove the beetroot and rack, setting the beetroot aside on a cutting board. Pour out and discard the water that remains in the pot. 5. Slice off the tops of the beetroot and carefully slide or cut off the skin—it should come off very easily—then discard the tops and peeled-off skin. Using a sharp knife, slice the beetroot into round slices about 6 mm thick. 6. Add butter to the pot. Move slider to AIR FRY/STOVETOP. Select SEAR/SAUTÉ and set to 3. Select START/ STOP to begin cooking. Once the butter has melted, add the beetroot back to the pot along with the salt and the orange zest and juice, gently stirring occasionally for 2 minutes to warm the citrus. Press START/ STOP to turn off the SEAR/SAUTÉ function. 7. Serve immediately.
Per Serving: Calories 80; Fat 4.03g; Sodium 375mg; Carbs 10.64g; Fibre 3.1g; Sugar 4.62g; Protein 1.48g

Ginger-Garlic Bok Choy

Prep Time: 15 minutes | Cook Time: 6 minutes | Serves: 4

3 tbsp (43 g) grass-fed butter or ghee	120 ml filtered water
1 2-cm piece fresh ginger, peeled and finely minced	7 baby bok choy, cut in half down the middle
3 cloves garlic, minced	1 spring onion, white and light green parts only, sliced on a bias
¾ tsp sea salt	1 tsp toasted sesame oil, for garnish
3 tbsp (45 ml) coconut aminos	

1. Add butter to the pot. Move slider to AIR FRY/STOVETOP. Select SEAR/SAUTÉ and set to 3. Select START/STOP to begin cooking. Once the butter has melted, add the ginger and garlic and sauté for 2 minutes, stirring occasionally. Press START/STOP to turn off the SEAR/SAUTÉ function. 2. Add the salt, coconut aminos and water to the pot, then add the bok choy and spring onion and stir gently. 3. Close the lid and move slider to PRESSURE. Make sure the pressure release valve is in the SEAL position. The temperature will default to HIGH, which is the correct setting. Set time to 3 minutes. Select START/STOP to begin cooking. 4. Once the timer sounds, naturally release the pressure for 5 minutes. Then turn the pressure relief valve to the VENT position for quick pressure relief. Move slider to AIR FRY/ STOVETOP to unlock the lid, then carefully open it. 5. Serve immediately, drizzled with the toasted sesame oil.

Per Serving: Calories 187; Fat 12.62g; Sodium 501mg; Carbs 2.15g; Fibre 0.7g; Sugar 0.74g; Protein 16.11g

Barbecue Tofu Sandwiches

Prep Time: 20 minutes | Cook Time: 15 minutes | Serves: 6

1 tablespoon olive oil	wine vinegar
1 medium yellow onion, sliced through root end	Freshly ground black pepper
1 red pepper, thinly sliced	455 g extra-firm tofu, patted dry and cut into 1 x 5 cm sticks
160 g thick barbecue sauce	4 hamburger buns, toasted
2 tablespoons balsamic or red	

1. Add the oil to the pot. Select SEAR/SAUTÉ. Select Lo3, and then press START/STOP to begin cooking. 2. When the oil is hot, add onion and pepper, and cook them for 4 minutes until they begin to brown. 3. Stop the process, and stir in barbecue sauce, 60 ml water, the vinegar, and several grinds of pepper, then add the tofu and stir them gently. 4. Close the lid, turn the pressure release valve to SEAL position, and then move the slider to PRESSURE. Select HI and set the cooking time to 3 minutes. Press START/STOP to begin cooking. When finished, release the pressure quickly. 5. Transfer the tofu and vegetables to a large bowl; cover the bowl with foil. 6. Simmer the left food in the pot at Hi5 on SEAR/SAUTÉ mode for 3 minutes until the sauce has thickened. 7. Mound the tofu and veggies on the bottom half of the buns. Drizzle with some of the sauce and sandwich with the bun tops. Serve immediately.

Per Serving: Calories 141; Fat: 7.18g; Sodium: 73mg; Carbs: 12.21g; Fibre: 1g; Sugar: 4.21g; Protein: 8.98g

Middle Eastern Lentils & Rice

Prep Time: 25 minutes | Cook Time: 20 minutes | Serves: 4-6

190 g dark green lentils du Puy	stock, or water
960 ml boiling water	Salt and freshly ground black pepper
2 tablespoons olive oil	
1 large yellow onion, thinly sliced	200 g basmati rice, rinsed and drained
3 medium garlic cloves, finely chopped	240 g plain Greek yogurt or 4 fried eggs
1¼ teaspoons ground cumin	
720 ml store-bought vegetable	

1. Pour the lentils into a large bowl and add the boiling water; set aside. 2. Add the oil to the pot. Select SEAR/SAUTÉ. Select Hi5, and then press START/STOP to begin cooking. 3. When the oil is hot, add the onion and sauté them for 10 to 12 minutes until they are well browned; add 60 ml water and simmer for 30 seconds until evaporated, scraping up any browned bits from the bottom of the pot; add the garlic and cumin, ad cook them for 30 seconds until fragrant. 4.

Stop the process and set aside 30 g of the onion mixture for garnish. 5. Drain the lentils and add them to the pot with the onion. Add 480 ml of the stock, 1¼ teaspoons salt, and several grinds of pepper. Place the rack in the pot. 6. Combine the rice, the remaining 240 ml stock, and a generous pinch of salt in a suitable baking pan. 7. Place the baking pan on the rack. 8. Close the lid, turn the pressure release valve to SEAL position, and then move the slider to PRESSURE. Select HI and set the cooking time to 4 minutes. Press START/STOP to begin cooking. When finished, release the pressure naturally. 9. Fluff the rice with a fork. Remove the rack and gently stir the lentils and rice together. Garnish the dish with the reserved fried onions and serve with yogurt or fried eggs.

Per Serving: Calories 156; Fat: 9.61g; Sodium: 138mg; Carbs: 16.57g; Fibre: 5.1g; Sugar: 2.89g; Protein: 7.51g

Japanese-Style Vegetable Curry

Prep Time: 15 minutes | Cook Time: 15 minutes | Serves: 4

1 tablespoon rapeseed oil	2.5 cm chunks
1 large onion, sliced through the root end	2 large carrots, peeled and cut at an angle into 2.5 cm -thick slices
4 cubes mild Japanese curry sauce mix	455 g extra-firm tofu, cut into 2.5 cm cubes
455 g winter squash or Yukon Gold potatoes, peeled and cut into	Cooked udon noodles or steamed rice, for serving

1. Add the oil to the pot. Select SEAR/SAUTÉ. Select Hi5, and then press START/STOP to begin cooking. 2. When the oil is hot, add the onions and cook them for 4 minutes until they are tender. 3. Stop the process, add the curry mix and 360 ml water to the pot, and break up the curry cubes; add the squash and carrots and stir them very gently to combine; place the tofu cubes on top, but do not stir them in. 4. Close the lid, turn the pressure release valve to SEAL position, and then move the slider to PRESSURE. Select HI and set the cooking time to 8 minutes. Press START/STOP to begin cooking. When finished, release the pressure quickly. 5. Stir the dish gently to combine the tofu and other ingredients without breaking up the tofu. 6. Serve the dish with hot noodles or rice.

Per Serving: Calories 305; Fat: 12.95g; Sodium: 477mg; Carbs: 36.87g; Fibre: 3.4g; Sugar: 3.7g; Protein: 14.43g

Chapter 3 Poultry Mains Recipes

Crispy Fried Chicken

Prep Time: 10 minutes | Cook Time: 20 minutes | Serves: 4

1 teaspoon cayenne pepper	1 beaten egg
2 tablespoon mustard powder	25g cauliflower
2 tablespoon oregano	20g gluten-free oats
2 tablespoon thyme	8 chicken drumsticks
3 tablespoon coconut milk	

1. Place the Cook & Crisp Basket in your Pressure Cooker Steam Fryer. 2. Lay out chicken and season with pepper and salt on all sides. 3. Add all other ingredients to a blender, blending till a smooth-like breadcrumb mixture is created. Place in a suitable bowl and add a beaten egg to another bowl. 4. Dip chicken into breadcrumbs, then into egg, and breadcrumbs once more. 5. Place coated drumsticks into basket. Put on the Smart Lid on top of the Ninja Foodi Steam Fryer. Move the Lid Slider to the "Air Fry/Stovetop". Select the "Air Fry" mode for cooking. 6. Adjust the cooking temperature to 175°C. 7. Cook for 20 minutes. Bump up the temperature to 200°C. Cook for another 5 minutes till crispy.
Per serving: Calories: 489; Fat: 11g; Sodium: 501mg; Carbs: 8.9g; Fibre: 4.6g; Sugar 8g; Protein 26g

Air Fried Turkey Breast

Prep Time: 10 minutes | Cook Time: 60 minutes | Serves: 6-8

Pepper and salt	Turkey seasonings of choice
1 oven-ready turkey breast	

1. Place the Cook & Crisp Basket in your Pressure Cooker Steam Fryer. 2. Season turkey with pepper, salt, and other desired seasonings. 3. Place turkey in "cook & crisp basket". 4. Put on the Smart Lid on top of the Ninja Foodi Steam Fryer. 5. Move the Lid Slider to the "Air Fry/Stovetop". Select the "Air Fry" mode for cooking. 6. Adjust the cooking temperature to 175°C. 7. Cook 60 minutes. The meat should be at 75°C when done. 8. Allow to rest 10 to 15 minutes before slicing. Enjoy!
Per serving: Calories: 237; Fat: 10.9g; Sodium: 354mg; Carbs: 20.5g; Fibre: 4.1g; Sugar 8.2g; Protein 26g

Chicken Mushroom Kabobs

Prep Time: 10 minutes | Cook Time: 20 minutes | Serves: 4

2 diced chicken breasts	80ml low-sodium soy sauce
3 peppers	110g raw honey
6 mushrooms	Olive oil
Sesame seeds	Salt and pepper, to taste

1. Place the Cook & Crisp Basket in your Pressure Cooker Steam Fryer. 2. Chop up chicken into cubes, seasoning with a few sprays of olive oil, pepper, and salt. 3. Dice up peppers and cut mushrooms in half. 4. Mix soy sauce and honey till well mixed. Add sesame seeds and stir. 5. Skewer chicken, peppers, and mushrooms onto wooden skewers. 6. Coat kabobs with honey-soy sauce. 7. Place coated kabobs in "cook & crisp basket". Put on the Smart Lid on top of the Ninja Foodi Steam Fryer. Move the Lid Slider to the "Air Fry/Stovetop". Select the "Air Fry" mode for cooking. 8. Adjust the cooking temperature to 200°C. Cook for 15 to 20 minutes.
Per serving: Calories: 219; Fat: 10g; Sodium: 891mg; Carbs: 22.9g; Fibre: 4g; Sugar 4g; Protein 13g

Chicken Tenders

Prep Time: 10 minutes | Cook Time: 15 minutes | Serves: 4-6

55g coconut flour	2 beaten eggs
1 tablespoon spicy brown mustard	455g of chicken tenders

1. Place the Cook & Crisp Basket in your Pressure Cooker Steam Fryer. 2. Season tenders with pepper and salt. 3. Place a thin layer of mustard onto tenders and then dredge in flour and dip in egg. 4. Place tenders in the Cook & Crisp Basket. Put on the Smart Lid on top of the Ninja Foodi Steam Fryer. Move the Lid Slider to the "Air Fry/ Stovetop". Select the "Air Fry" mode for cooking. 5. Cook for 10 to 15 minutes at 200°C till crispy.

Per serving: Calories: 478; Fat: 12.9g; Sodium: 414mg; Carbs: 11g; Fibre: 5g; Sugar 9g; Protein 11g

KFC Chicken

Prep Time: 10 minutes | Cook Time: 20 minutes | Serves: 6

1 teaspoon chili flakes	½ tablespoon basil
1 teaspoon curcumin	½ teaspoon thyme
1 teaspoon white pepper	2 garlic cloves
1 teaspoon ginger powder	1 egg
1 teaspoon garlic powder	6 boneless, skinless chicken
1 teaspoon paprika	thighs
1 teaspoon powdered mustard	2 tablespoons unsweetened
1 teaspoon pepper	almond milk
1 tablespoon celery salt	35g whey protein isolate powder
⅓ teaspoon oregano	

1. Place the Cook & Crisp Basket in your Pressure Cooker Steam Fryer. 2. Wash and pat dry chicken thighs. Slice into small chunks. 3. Mash cloves and add them along with all spices in a blender. Blend until smooth and pour over chicken, adding milk and egg. Mix thoroughly. 4. Cover chicken and chill for around 1 hour. Add whey protein to a suitable bowl and dredge coated chicken pieces. Shake excess powder. Place coated chicken in the Cook & Crisp Basket. 5. Put on the Smart Lid on top of the Ninja Foodi Steam Fryer. Move the Lid Slider to the "Air Fry/Stovetop". Select the "Air Fry" mode for cooking. Adjust the cooking temperature to 200°C. 6. Cook for 20 minutes till crispy, making sure to turn halfway through cooking.
Per serving: Calories: 184; Fat: 5g; Sodium: 441mg; Carbs: 17g; Fibre: 4.6g; Sugar 5g; Protein 9g

Meatballs & Spaghetti Squash

Prep Time: 20 minutes | Cook Time: 40 minutes | Serves: 4

455 g turkey mince	60 ml red wine vinegar
35 g almond flour	120 ml water
2 tsp Italian seasoning	1 (800-g) can San Marzano whole
1 tsp. garlic powder	tomatoes
1 large egg, beaten	1 (410-g) can pureed tomatoes
½ tsp. sea salt	1½ tsp salt
Nonstick cooking spray, for pan	1 medium spaghetti squash
Sauce:	40 g shredded Parmesan cheese,
1 tbsp. avocado oil or olive oil	for garnish (optional)
1 medium yellow onion, diced	Fresh basil, for garnish
3 cloves garlic, minced	Salt
60 ml red wine	

1. Mix all the meatball ingredients in a medium bowl, except for the nonstick cooking spray. Roll the mixture into 2.5 cm balls. 2. Lightly spray a baking pan with nonstick cooking spray and place the meatballs on it. 3. Place the rack in the pot in the higher broil position and then place the baking pan on it. Close the lid and move slider to AIR FRY/STOVETOP, then use the dial to select BROIL. Set the cooking time to 4 minutes and then press START/STOP to begin cooking. 4. The meatballs need to be browned on the outside. Transfer them to a plate and set aside. 5. Select SEAR/SAUTÉ. Select Hi5, and then press START/STOP to begin cooking. 6. When the pot is hot, coat the bottom of the pan with the oil, and cook the onion and garlic until fragrant and lightly browned. 7. Stop the process, pour in the wine, vinegar and water and deglaze the pot with the liquid; add the whole and pureed tomatoes and salt to the pot. 8. Close the lid, turn the pressure release valve to SEAL position, and then move the slider to PRESSURE. Select HI and set the cooking time to 30 minutes. Press START/STOP to begin cooking. When finished, release the pressure quickly. 9. Remove the spaghetti squash and set aside to cool for about 10 minutes. 10. Once cool, slice in half. Scoop out and discard the seeds, and use a fork to pull out the spaghetti squash strands. 11. Pour the sauce and meatballs on top of the squash strands. Top the dish with Parmesan cheese (if using), fresh basil and additional salt to taste. Enjoy.
Per Serving: Calories 730; Fat: 59.03g; Sodium: 1631mg; Carbs: 20.1g; Fibre: 3.8g; Sugar: 7.95g; Protein: 29.46g

Chicken Fritters

Prep Time: 10 minutes | Cook Time: 20 minutes | Serves: 16-18 fritters

Chicken Fritters:

½ teaspoon salt	35g coconut flour
⅛ teaspoon pepper	80g vegan mayo
1 ½ tablespoon fresh dill	2 eggs
150g shredded mozzarella cheese	675g chicken breasts

Garlic Dip:

⅛ teaspoon pepper	1 pressed garlic cloves
¼ teaspoon salt	80g vegan mayo
½ tablespoon lemon juice	

1. Place the Cook & Crisp Basket in your Pressure Cooker Steam Fryer. 2. Slice chicken breasts into ⅓ pieces and place in a suitable bowl. Add all remaining fritter ingredients to the bowl and stir well. Cover and chill 2 hours or overnight. 3. Spray "cook & crisp basket" with a bit of olive oil. 4. Add marinated chicken to basket. Put on the Smart Lid on top of the Ninja Foodi Steam Fryer. Move the Lid Slider to the "Air Fry/Stovetop". Select the "Air Fry" mode for cooking. 5. Adjust the cooking temperature to 175°C. 6. Cook for 20 minutes, making sure to turn halfway through cooking process. 7. To make the dipping sauce, mix all the dip ingredients until smooth.
Per serving: Calories: 334; Fat: 12.9g; Sodium: 414mg; Carbs: 11g; Fibre: 5g; Sugar 9g; Protein 31g

Chicken Wing Stir-Fry

Prep Time: 10 minutes | Cook Time: 25 minutes | Serves: 14-20 wings

80g cornflour	1 egg white
¼ teaspoon pepper	14-20 chicken wing pieces
½ teaspoon salt	

Stir-fry:

¼ teaspoon pepper	2 trimmed spring onions
1 teaspoon sea salt	2 jalapeno peppers
2 tablespoons avocado oil	

1. Place the Cook & Crisp Basket in your Pressure Cooker Steam Fryer. 2. Coat the Cook & Crisp Basket with oil. 3. Mix pepper, salt, and egg white till foamy. 4. Pat wings dry and add to the bowl of egg white mixture. Coat well. Let marinate at least 20 minutes. 5. Place coated wings in a big bowl and add cornflour. Dredge wings well. Shake off and add to "cook & crisp basket". 6. Put on the Smart Lid on top of the Ninja Foodi Steam Fryer. 7. Move the Lid Slider to the "Air Fry/Stovetop". Select the "Air Fry" mode for cooking. 8. Cook 25 minutes at 195°C. When timer sounds, bump up the temperature to 200°C. Cook for an additional 5 minutes till browned. 9. For stir fry, remove seeds from jalapenos and chop up spring onions. Add both to bowl and set to the side. Heat a wok with oil and add pepper, salt, spring onions, and jalapenos. Cook 1 minute. 10. Add air fried chicken to frying pan and toss with stir-fried veggies. Cook 1 minute and devour!
Per serving: Calories: 489; Fat: 11g; Sodium: 501mg; Carbs: 8.9g; Fibre: 4.6g; Sugar 8g; Protein 26g

Chicken Parmesan

Prep Time: 10 minutes | Cook Time: 9 minutes | Serves: 4

120g keto marinara	6 tablespoon gluten-free seasoned breadcrumbs
6 tablespoon mozzarella cheese	2 (200g) chicken breasts
1 tablespoon melted ghee	Olive oil
2 tablespoon grated parmesan cheese	

1. Place the Cook & Crisp Basket in your Pressure Cooker Steam Fryer. 2. Grease the "cook & crisp basket" with olive oil. 3. Mix parmesan cheese and breadcrumbs together. 4. Brush melted ghee onto the chicken and dip into breadcrumb mixture. 5. Place the coated chicken in the basket and top with olive oil. 6. Put on the Smart Lid on top of the Ninja Foodi Steam Fryer. 7. Move the Lid Slider to the "Air Fry/Stovetop". Select the "Air Fry" mode for cooking. 8. Adjust the cooking temperature to 180°C. 9. Cook 2 breasts for around 6 minutes and top each breast with a tablespoon of sauce and 1 ½ tablespoons of mozzarella cheese. Cook another 3 minutes to melt cheese. 10. Keep cooked pieces warm as you repeat the process with remaining breasts.
Per serving: Calories: 584; Fat: 15g; Sodium: 441mg; Carbs: 17g; Fibre: 4.6g; Sugar 5g; Protein 29g

Orange Chicken Thighs

Prep Time: 15 minutes | Cook Time: 25 minutes | Serves: 4

240 ml water or chicken stock	2 tbsp light brown sugar
1.4 kg chicken thighs, skin on	2 tsp white wine vinegar
240 ml fresh orange juice	2 tsp. hot sauce
180 g ketchup	20 g chopped fresh corinader
1 tbsp. Worcestershire sauce	

1. Pour the water or chicken stock into the pot, and then add the chicken thighs. 2. Close the lid, turn the pressure release valve to SEAL position, and then move the slider to PRESSURE. Select HI and set the cooking time to 9 minutes. Press START/STOP to begin cooking. When finished, release the pressure quickly. 3. Remove the chicken from the pot and place on a baking pan. 4. Clean the pot. Place the rack in the pot in the higher broil position and then place the pan on it. Close the lid and move slider to AIR FRY/STOVETOP, then use the dial to select BROIL. Set the cooking time to 5 minutes and then press START/STOP to begin cooking. 5. Clean the pot and wipe clean. Select SEAR/SAUTÉ. Select Hi5, and then press START/STOP to begin cooking. 6. When the pot is hot, add orange juice, ketchup, Worcestershire sauce, brown sugar, vinegar and hot sauce, bring to a liquid and then simmer the sauce at Lo1 for 7 to 8 minutes until thick and slightly reduced. 7. Pour the sauce over the chicken thighs in the plate, sprinkle them with corinader and enjoy.
Per Serving: Calories 877; Fat: 57.04g; Sodium: 860mg; Carbs: 31.26g; Fibre: 0.5g; Sugar: 22.21g; Protein: 57.74g

Lemon Pulled Turkey

Prep Time: 20 minutes | Cook Time: 30 minutes | Serves: 6

1 tablespoon lemon pepper seasoning blend	2 tablespoons fresh lemon juice
1.1 kg boneless turkey tenderloins	2 tablespoons red wine vinegar
160 ml chicken stock	2 tablespoons packed fresh oregano leaves, minced
50 g ginger jam	½ teaspoon red pepper flakes

1. Pat and massage the lemon pepper seasoning into the turkey tenderloins. 2. Mix the stock, jam, lemon juice, vinegar, oregano, and red pepper flakes in the pot until the jam dissolves into the sauce. 3. Place the turkey tenderloins into this sauce without turning the meat over. 4. Close the lid, turn the pressure release valve to SEAL position, and then move the slider to PRESSURE. Select HI and set the cooking time to 25 minutes. Press START/STOP to begin cooking. When finished, release the pressure naturally. 5. Shred the meat with two forks in the pot, and then stir well to coat with sauce. Set the lid askew over the pot for 5 to 10 minutes to blend the flavours and allow the meat to continue to absorb the sauce. 6. Serve and enjoy.
Per Serving: Calories: 961; Fat: 85.93g; Sodium: 195mg; Carbs: 1.87g; Fibre: 0.3g; Sugar: 0.4g; Protein: 41.96g

Chicken with Peas & Mushroom

Prep time: 10 minutes | Cook time: 10 minutes | Serves: 4

4 boneless skinless chicken breast halves (150g each)	sliced
1 envelope onion mushroom soup mix	1 medium onion, chopped
225g baby Portobello mushrooms,	180ml water
	4 garlic cloves, minced
	200g frozen peas, thawed

1. Coat the chicken with soup mix in the cooking pot, and then add the mushrooms, onion, water and garlic to the pot. 2. Install the pressure lid and turn the pressure release valve to the SEAL position. 3. Select PRESSURE COOK, set the cooking temperature to HI and adjust the cooking time to 6 minutes. 4. When cooked, let the unit naturally release pressure. 5. A thermometer inserted in chicken should read at least 75°C. 6. Add peas and simmer the food at LO on SEAR/SAUTÉ mode for 3 to 5 minutes without covering the pot, stirring occasionally. 7. Serve warm.
Per Serving: Calories 273; Fat 5.05g; Sodium 287mg; Carbs 12.85g; Fibre 4.2g; Sugar 2.59g; Protein 42.83g

Chicken Enchilada Casserole

Prep Time: 5 minutes | Cook Time: 15 minutes | Serves: 4-6

4 tablespoons salted butter	(fajita size is the best for this)
30 g plain flour	240 g sour cream
480 ml chicken stock	1 (175 g) can diced green chilies,
900 g boneless, skinless chicken	with their juices
thighs (or chicken breasts if you	50 g crumbled crumbled feta (or
prefer)	grated Parmesan)
200 g shredded Monterey Jack or	1½ tablespoons cornflour
Pepper Jack cheese	200 g shredded Mexican cheese
10–12 small flour or corn tortillas	blend

1. Select SEAR/SAUTÉ. Select Lo2, and then press START/STOP to begin cooking. 2. When the pot is hot, melt the butter; whisk in the flour and whisk for 1 minute or until just lightly browned; stir in chicken stock and scrape up any browned bits from the bottom of the pot. 3. Stop the process and place in the chicken thighs. 4. Close the lid, turn the pressure release valve to SEAL position, and then move the slider to PRESSURE. Select HI and set the cooking time to 8 minutes. Press START/STOP to begin cooking. When finished, release the pressure quickly. 5. Transfer the chicken thighs to a mixing bowl along with 2 tablespoons of the stock from the pot, and shred the meat. 6. Let them cool slightly, and then add 200 g of the Monterey Jack or Pepper Jack cheese. Mix them well. 7. Scoop the chicken-cheese mixture onto the tortillas and roll them up, leaving the ends open, and place them in a casserole dish with seam side down. 8. In a small bowl, mix the cornflour with 1½ tablespoons cold water to form slurry. Set aside. 9. Whisk the sour cream into the stock until a smooth mixture forms in the pot until well-combined, and then whisk in the green chilies and cotija cheese. 10. Select SEAR/SAUTÉ. Select Hi5, and then press START/STOP to begin cooking. 11. Once the stock mixture is bubbling, immediately stir in the cornflour slurry and let cook for another minute until the sauce has thickened. 12. Let the sauce stand for a while after cooking. 13. Pour the sauce over the enchiladas and top with the shredded Mexican cheese. 14. Serve and enjoy.

Per Serving: Calories 1128; Fat: 56.89g; Sodium: 2438mg; Carbs: 92.21g; Fibre: 10.9g; Sugar: 12.85g; Protein: 63.9g

Turkey Bolognese with "Spaghetti"

Prep Time: 5 minutes | Cook Time: 25 minutes | Serves: 4

1 tablespoon extra-virgin olive oil	vinegar
1 yellow onion, chopped	1 teaspoon pure maple syrup
2 cloves garlic, minced	½ teaspoon dried oregano
455 g turkey mince	1 teaspoon dried basil
Fine sea salt	1 (1.3 kg) spaghetti squash
1 can diced tomatoes	60 g full-fat coconut milk
2 celery stalks, diced	(optional)
2 carrots, diced	Freshly ground black pepper
1 tablespoon aged balsamic	Fresh basil, for garnish (optional)

1. Pour the diced tomatoes with their juices into a blender and blend them until smooth. Set aside. 2. Wash the spaghetti squash and carefully pierce the skin once with a sharp knife to vent. 3. Select SEAR/SAUTÉ. Select Lo2, and then press START/STOP to begin cooking. 4. When the pot is hot, add olive oil, onion, garlic, turkey, and 1 teaspoon salt to the pot, and sauté them for 8 minutes until the turkey is browned. 5. Stop the process, and add blended tomatoes, the celery, carrots, vinegar, maple syrup, oregano, basil, and ½ teaspoon salt to the pot; stir them well. Place the whole squash directly into the sauce, pierced side up. 6. Close the lid, turn the pressure release valve to SEAL position, and then move the slider to PRESSURE. Select HI and set the cooking time to 15 minutes. Press START/STOP to begin cooking. When finished, release the pressure naturally. 7. Lift the spaghetti squash out of the pot. Transfer it to a cutting board to cool slightly. Stir the coconut milk into the sauce and season with salt and pepper, to taste. 8. Cut the cooked squash in half crosswise and use a spoon to remove the seeds from the centre. Use a fork to scrape out "noodles" from the squash and place them on plates. 9. Spoon the Bolognese sauce on top of the noodles and serve. 10. You can store the leftovers in an airtight container in the fridge for 3 or 4 days.

Per Serving: Calories 725; Fat: 58.57g; Sodium: 398mg; Carbs: 26.68g; Fibre: 7.4g; Sugar: 9.99g; Protein: 25.17g

Cream Chicken & Ziti Casserole

Prep Time: 5 minutes | Cook Time: 10 minutes | Serves: 4

30 g sliced almonds	¼ teaspoon table salt
1 tablespoon butter	600 ml chicken stock
1 small yellow onion, chopped	200 g dried ziti
455 g unseasoned chicken breast	160 ml regular or low-fat
cut for stir-fry, any flavouring	evaporated milk
packets discarded; or 455 g	70 g packed sun-dried tomatoes,
boneless skinless chicken breast,	sliced into very thin strips
cut into 1 x 1 cm strips	120 g heavy cream
1¼ teaspoons dried sage	1½ tablespoons flour
1 teaspoon dried thyme	25 g finely grated Parmigiano-
½ teaspoon dried oregano	Reggiano
¼ teaspoon grated nutmeg	

1. Cook the sliced almonds in a medium dry frying pan over medium-low heat for 2 minutes until lightly toasted. Pour the almonds into a small bowl and set aside. 2. Select SEAR/SAUTÉ. Select Lo3, and then press START/STOP to begin cooking. 3. When the pot is hot, melt the butter; add onion and cook for 3 minutes until softened; add chicken, sage, thyme, oregano, nutmeg, and salt, and cook them for 2 minutes juts until the chicken loses its raw colour. 4. Stop the process, and stir in the stock, ziti, evaporated milk, and sun-dried tomatoes until uniform. 5. Close the lid, turn the pressure release valve to SEAL position, and then move the slider to PRESSURE. Select HI and set the cooking time to 7 minutes. Press START/STOP to begin cooking. When finished, release the pressure naturally. 6. Whisk the cream and flour in a small bowl until the flour dissolves. 7. Keep stirring the sauce in the pot at Lo2 on SEAR/SAUTÉ mode until comes to a simmer. Whisk the cream mixture one time to make sure the flour is thoroughly combined. Stir this slurry into the pot and continue cooking for 2 minutes until thickened, stirring almost constantly. 8. Stir in the cheese and set the lid askew over the insert for a couple of minutes to blend the flavours. 9. Sprinkle the toasted almonds over individual servings.

Per Serving: Calories 346; Fat: 13.01g; Sodium: 1077mg; Carbs: 54.38g; Fibre: 8.4g; Sugar: 37.9g; Protein: 10.58g

Cider & Mustard–Braised Chicken

Prep Time: 10 minutes | Cook Time: 35 minutes | Serves: 4

2 slices thick-cut bacon, chopped	300 g quartered cremini
8 bone-in chicken thighs, skin	mushrooms
removed and fat trimmed	2 large shallots, thinly sliced
Salt and freshly ground black	360 ml bottled hard apple cider
pepper	2 tablespoons grainy mustard

1. Season the chicken all over with salt and pepper. 2. Select SEAR/SAUTÉ. Select Lo3, and then press START/STOP to begin cooking. 3. When the pot is hot, cook the bacon for 3 to 4 minutes until browned. Transfer the bacon to a bowl with a slotted spoon; leave the drippings in the pot. 4. Add the chicken thighs to the pot and cook for 3 minutes until browned on one side. Transfer them to a plate. 5. Add the mushrooms and shallots to the pot and sauté them for 3 minutes until the shallots are tender; add the cider and mustard and bring to a simmer, scraping up any browned bits on the bottom of the pot. 6. Stop the process, and add all the chicken, any accumulated juices, and the bacon to the pot. 7. Close the lid, turn the pressure release valve to SEAL position, and then move the slider to PRESSURE. Select HI and set the cooking time to 20 minutes. Press START/STOP to begin cooking. When finished, release the pressure quickly. 8. Transfer the chicken and vegetables to a serving dish with a slotted spoon. Cover the dish with foil and set aside. 9. Bring the liquid in the pot to a simmer at Lo2 at SEAR/SAUTÉ mode; skim any liquid fat that pools on top of the sauce and discard; cook the sauce for 5 minutes until the sauce is reduced by half. 10. Stop the process, and pour the sauce over the chicken thighs. 11. Serve warm.

Per Serving: Calories 975; Fat: 69.92g; Sodium: 468mg; Carbs: 15.12g; Fibre: 1.6g; Sugar: 10.66g; Protein: 68.87g

Bacon Chicken Salad

Prep Time: 10 minutes | Cook Time: 10 minutes | Serves: 4

225 g bacon
240 ml water or chicken stock
680 g boneless, skinless chicken breast, cut into bite-size pieces
150 g cherry tomatoes, halved
115 g mayonnaise
Coarse salt
Freshly ground pepper
220 g spring mix lettuce

1. Select SEAR/SAUTÉ. Select Lo3, and then press START/STOP to begin cooking. 2. When the pot is hot, cook the bacon until browned and crispy, then transfer the bacon to a paper towels to drain any excess fat. Discard the drippings but do not wipe clean. 3. Add the water or chicken stock to the pot, taking care to scrape up any browned bits from the bottom of the pot. Add the chicken. 4. Close the lid, turn the pressure release valve to SEAL position, and then move the slider to PRESSURE. Select HI and set the cooking time to 6 minutes. Press START/STOP to begin cooking. When finished, release the pressure quickly. 5. Remove the chicken and allow cooling completely. 6. Mix the chicken, tomatoes and mayonnaise in a large bowl. 7. Crumble the bacon and gently fold into the chicken mixture. Season them with salt and pepper. 8. Place 55 g of lettuce on each of the four plates. Evenly divide the chicken salad and place on top of the lettuce. Enjoy.
Per Serving: Calories 618; Fat: 36.52g; Sodium: 1679mg; Carbs: 50.57g; Fibre: 6g; Sugar: 15.55g; Protein: 25.28g

Cheese Chicken-Broccoli Casserole

Prep Time: 15 minutes | Cook Time: 20 minutes | Serves: 4

237 ml water
228 g broccoli florets, cut into bite-size pieces
2 tbsp (28 g) grass-fed butter or ghee
1 medium yellow onion, finely diced
5 cloves garlic, chopped
2 large celery ribs with leaves, thinly sliced
2 medium carrots, peeled and finely diced
1 tsp sea salt
15 g finely chopped fresh flat-leaf parsley, plus more for garnish
1 tbsp (4 g) finely chopped fresh dill
1 tsp finely chopped fresh thyme leaves
2 boneless, skinless chicken breasts
237 ml chicken or vegetable stock
345 g sour cream
173 g shredded cheddar cheese

1. Place the water in the pot and place the Cook & Crisp Basket in the pot. Layer the broccoli florets in the basket. 2. Close the lid and move slider to PRESSURE. Make sure the pressure release valve is in the SEAL position. The temperature will default to HIGH, which is the correct setting. Set time to 1 minute. Select START/STOP to begin cooking. 3. When cooking is complete, turn the pressure relief valve to the VENT position for quick pressure relief. Move slider to the right to unlock the lid, then carefully open it. 4. Immediately remove the basket and broccoli, using caution because both are very hot. Set aside. Discard the water in the pot. 5. Place your healthy fat of choice in the pot and move slider to AIR FRY/STOVETOP. Select SEAR/SAUTÉ and set to 3. Select START/STOP to begin cooking. Once the fat has melted, add the onion and sauté for 5 minutes, stirring occasionally. Then, add the garlic and sauté for 1 minute, stirring occasionally. Press START/STOP to turn off the SEAR/SAUTÉ function. 6. Add the carrots, celery, salt, parsley, thyme, dill, chicken and stock to the pot, making sure the chicken is submerged in the liquid. Close the lid and cook on high pressure for 9 minutes. 7. Once the timer sounds, turn the pressure relief valve to the VENT position for quick pressure relief. Move slider to the right to unlock the lid, then carefully open it. 8. With tongs, transfer the chicken to a plate or cutting board. Chop the chicken into bite-size chunks, then set aside. 9. Cook on SEAR/SAUTÉ function and set the heat to 4. Allow the liquid in the pot to come to a simmer; allow it to simmer for about five minutes, or until the liquid reduces. Return the chicken to the pot and add the broccoli, sour cream and cheese, quickly stirring until the sour cream and cheese are fully mixed in. 10. Press START/STOP to turn off the SEAR/SAUTÉ function. Taste for seasoning and adjust the salt to taste. Allow the casserole to rest for 10 minutes. 11. Serve immediately, garnished with chopped fresh parsley.
Per Serving: Calories 551; Fat 33.44g; Sodium 1363mg; Carbs 17.68g; Fibre 3.4g; Sugar 4.61g; Protein 45.3g

Savory Turkey Tacos

Prep Time: 15 minutes | Cook Time: 18 minutes | Serves: 6

2 tbsp (30 ml) avocado oil or olive oil
1 yellow onion, diced
905 g turkey mince
1 tbsp (8 g) chili powder
2 tsp (5 g) ground cumin
2 tsp (5 g) paprika
1½ tsp (8 g) sea salt
1 tsp dried oregano
1 tsp chipotle powder (optional)
1 (411-g) can fire-roasted tomatoes
1 (115-g) can diced green chiles
2 tbsp (32 g) tomato paste
2 tbsp (30 ml) cider vinegar
175 ml water
10 g fresh coriander, for garnish
1 avocado, peeled, pitted and diced, for garnish
Tortillas, cooked rice or cauliflower rice, for serving (optional)

1. Move slider to AIR FRY/STOVETOP. Select SEAR/SAUTÉ and set to 3. Select START/STOP to begin preheating. Allow unit to preheat for 1 minute. After 1 minute, coat the bottom of the pot with the oil. Add the onion and sauté for 2 to 3 minutes, then add the turkey mince. Cook until the turkey is mostly cooked through, about another 8 minutes. Press START/STOP to turn off the SEAR/SAUTÉ function. 2. In a small bowl, mix together the cumin, paprika, chili powder, salt, oregano and chipotle powder (if using). Add the spice mixture to the turkey stir to coat well. 3. Add the fire-roasted tomatoes, vinegar tomato paste, green chiles, and water to the pot and stir. 4. Close the lid and move slider to PRESSURE. Make sure the pressure release valve is in the SEAL position. The temperature will default to HIGH, which is the correct setting. Set time to 7 minutes. Select START/STOP to begin cooking. 5. When cooking is complete, turn the pressure relief valve to the VENT position for quick pressure relief. Move slider to the right to unlock the lid, then carefully open it. 6. Serve hot with fresh coriander, avocado and tortillas, rice or cauliflower rice (if using).
Per Serving: Calories 862; Fat 77.44g; Sodium 835mg; Carbs 10.91g; Fibre 5.5g; Sugar 4.01g; Protein 31.21g

Honey-Garlic Shredded Chicken

Prep Time: 15 minutes | Cook Time: 25 minutes | Serves: 6

2 tbsp (28 g) grass-fed butter, ghee or avocado oil
1 medium yellow onion, thinly sliced
7 cloves garlic, finely chopped
½ tsp sea salt
1 tsp chili powder
1 tsp ground ginger
15 g finely chopped fresh flat-leaf parsley, plus more for garnish (optional)
1 tsp finely chopped fresh thyme leaves
80 ml honey
60 ml coconut aminos
2 tbsp (30 ml) cider vinegar
905 g boneless, skinless chicken breast
175 ml chicken or veggie stock
1 spring onion, white and light green parts only, thinly sliced, for garnish (optional)

1. Place your healthy fat of choice in the pot. Move slider to AIR FRY/STOVETOP. Select SEAR/SAUTÉ and set to 3. Select START/STOP to begin cooking. Once the fat has melted, add the onion and sauté, stirring occasionally, for 5 minutes, or until fragrant. Then, add the garlic and sauté for 1 minute, stirring occasionally. Press START/STOP. 2. Add the salt, chili powder, ginger, thyme, parsley, honey, vinegar, coconut aminos, chicken and stock to the pot, stirring well, making sure the chicken is submerged in the liquid. 3. Close the lid and move slider to PRESSURE. Make sure the pressure release valve is in the SEAL position. The temperature will default to HIGH, which is the correct setting. Set time to 10 minutes. Select START/STOP to begin cooking. 4. When cooking is complete, naturally release the pressure for 15 minutes. Then turn the pressure relief valve to the VENT position for quick pressure relief. Move slider to AIR FRY/ STOVETOP to unlock the lid, then carefully open it. 5. With tongs or a large slotted spoon, transfer the chicken to a plate or cutting board. Shred the chicken into bite-size chunks, then set aside. 6. Move slider to AIR FRY/STOVETOP. Select SEAR/SAUTÉ and set to 4. Select START/STOP to begin cooking. Allow the liquid in the pot to come to a simmer, then simmer for about 5 minutes, or until the liquid slightly thickens. Press START/STOP. Add back the shredded chicken, give the mixture a stir and allow it to rest for 10 minutes. 7. Serve immediately, garnished with chopped fresh flat-leaf parsley and/or thinly sliced spring onion (if using).
Per Serving: Calories 378; Fat 12.96g; Sodium 701mg; Carbs 50.55g; Fibre 2.9g; Sugar 24.38g; Protein 15.53g

Bacon Wrapped-Chicken With Dates

Prep Time: 15 minutes | Cook Time: 10 minutes | Serves: 4

4 boneless, skinless chicken cutlets
Salt
Freshly ground black pepper
Big pinch of crushed red pepper flakes
4 to 6 slices prosciutto
2 tbsp (30 ml) extra-virgin olive oil

1 tsp red wine vinegar
120 ml low-sodium chicken stock
1 clove garlic, grated
1 tsp balsamic vinegar
½ tsp light brown sugar
150 g chopped pitted dates
3 sprigs thyme
Chili-garlic bow ties, to serve (optional)

1. Season the chicken with salt, black pepper and red pepper flakes. Wrap the chicken in prosciutto. 2. Move slider to AIR FRY/ STOVETOP. Select SEAR/SAUTÉ and set to 3. Select START/ STOP to begin preheating. Allow unit to preheat for 2 minutes. After 2 minutes, add the oil to the pot. Sauté the chicken for 3 minutes on each side. 3. When both sides of the chicken are crisped, remove from the pot and transfer to a plate. 4. Deglaze the pan with the red wine vinegar and chicken stock. Scrape any bits off the bottom of the pot. 5. Press START/STOP to turn off the SEAR/SAUTÉ function. Add the garlic to the pot. Stir to combine. Stir in the brown sugar, balsamic vinegar, dates and thyme. Nestle the chicken breasts back into the pot. 6. Close the lid and move slider to PRESSURE. Make sure the pressure release valve is in the SEAL position. The temperature will default to HIGH, which is the correct setting. Set time to 5 minutes. Select START/STOP to begin cooking. 7. When the timer beeps, quick release the pressure. Remove the thyme sprigs. Transfer the chicken to plates, then top with the dates and sauce. Add more salt, black pepper or red pepper flakes, if needed. Serve with chili-garlic bow ties, if desired.
Per Serving: Calories 637; Fat 19.99g; Sodium 1761mg; Carbs 33.63g; Fibre 3.3g; Sugar 27.91g; Protein 85.02g

Creamy Chicken with Mashed Cauliflower

Prep Time: 20 minutes | Cook Time: 16 minutes | Serves: 4

240 ml full-fat canned coconut milk
455 g fresh or frozen cauliflower florets
455 g boneless, skinless chicken breasts
Fine sea salt and freshly ground

black pepper
40 g chopped sun-dried tomatoes
½ teaspoon dried basil
½ teaspoon dried oregano
3 cloves garlic, minced
Heaping 30 g baby spinach or chopped kale

1. Pour the coconut milk into the pot and add the cauliflower florets. Place the chicken breasts directly on top of the cauliflower, then sprinkle with ½ teaspoon salt and a few grinds of pepper. Close the lid and move slider to PRESSURE. Make sure the pressure release valve is in the SEAL position. The temperature will default to HIGH, which is the correct setting. Set time to 10 minutes. Select START/STOP to begin cooking. 2. When cooking is complete, turn the pressure relief valve to the VENT position for quick pressure relief. Move slider to the right to unlock the lid, then carefully open it. 3. Use tongs to transfer the chicken to a cutting board to rest. Use oven mitts to lift out the pot and drain the cauliflower, reserving the liquid for the sauce. Pour the drained cauliflower into a separate bowl and set aside. 4. Return the pot to the pressure cooker housing and add the reserved liquid. Move slider to AIR FRY/STOVETOP. Select SEAR/SAUTÉ and set to 3. Select START/STOP to begin cooking. Add the sun-dried tomatoes, oregano, basil, and garlic and simmer, stirring constantly, for about 5 minutes, until the sauce reduces by about one-third. 5. Taste and add more salt as needed, then stir in the spinach until it wilts, about 1 minute more. Remove the pot for the housing and set it aside so the sauce can cool and thicken a bit more (though it is still a relatively thin sauce that packs a lot of flavor). 6. Use a fork to mash the cauliflower, then season it with salt and pepper to taste. To serve, slice the chicken and place several slices on a plate with some mash. 7. Top them both with a spoonful of the cream sauce, tomatoes, and spinach. 8. Store leftovers in an airtight container in the fridge for 3 or 4 days.
Per Serving: Calories 377; Fat 21.22g; Sodium 582mg; Carbs 35.43g; Fibre 6.3g; Sugar 11.99g; Protein 14.99g

Root Beer-Braised Pulled Chicken

Prep Time: 15 minutes | Cook Time: 25 minutes | Serves: 6

180 ml root beer (do not use diet)
1.2 kg boneless skinless chicken breasts, preferably two or three giant breasts
2 small red onions, thinly sliced and broken into rings
6 tablespoons barbecue sauce

of any sort, just not a chunky or creamy sauce
2 tablespoons Worcestershire sauce
1 teaspoon ground black pepper
½ teaspoon garlic powder

1. Pour the root beer into the pot. Add the chicken and stir well. Scatter the onions over the top, then dollop or sprinkle the barbecue sauce, black pepper, Worcestershire sauce, and garlic powder over everything. 2. Close the lid and move slider to PRESSURE. Make sure the pressure release valve is in the SEAL position. The temperature will default to HIGH, which is the correct setting. Set time to 25 minutes. Select START/STOP to begin cooking. 3. When cooking is complete, naturally release the pressure for 20 minutes. Then turn the pressure relief valve to the VENT position for quick pressure relief. Move slider to AIR FRY/ STOVETOP to unlock the lid, then carefully open it. 4. Shred the chicken with two forks in the pot. Stir well, then close the lid for 5 minutes to allow the meat to continue to absorb the sauce.
Per Serving: Calories 263; Fat 4.98g; Sodium 835mg; Carbs 7.86g; Fibre 0.2g; Sugar 6.47g; Protein 43.71g

Thai-Style Pulled Chicken

Prep Time: 15 minutes | Cook Time: 25 minutes | Serves: 6

120 ml chicken stock
120 ml regular coconut milk
2 medium shallots, thinly sliced and separated into rings
4 medium garlic cloves, peeled and slivered
2 tablespoons thinly sliced thin lemongrass (peeled if necessary)

2 tablespoons hot red pepper sauce, preferably Sriracha
2 tablespoons light brown sugar
½ teaspoon ground dried turmeric
½ teaspoon table salt
1.2 kg boneless skinless chicken breasts, preferably two or three giant breasts

1. Add the stock, coconut milk, shallots, garlic, lemongrass, pepper sauce, brown sugar, turmeric, and salt to the pot and stir until the brown sugar dissolves. Set the chicken breasts into this sauce, turning the pieces to coat them on all sides. 2. Close the lid and move slider to PRESSURE. Make sure the pressure release valve is in the SEAL position. The temperature will default to HIGH, which is the correct setting. Set time to 25 minutes. Select START/STOP to begin cooking. 3. When cooking is complete, naturally release the pressure for 15 minutes. Then turn the pressure relief valve to the VENT position for quick pressure relief. Move slider to AIR FRY/ STOVETOP to unlock the lid, then carefully open it. 4. Use two forks to shred the chicken right in the pot. Stir well, then set the lid askew over the pot and set aside for 5 to 10 minutes to blend the flavors and allow the meat to absorb some of the sauce.
Per Serving: Calories 320; Fat 7.05g; Sodium 403mg; Carbs 12.61g; Fibre 1.3g; Sugar 4.35g; Protein 48.96g

Spicy Chicken Breast Halves

Prep time: 10 minutes | Cook time: 10 minutes | Serves: 6

4 boneless skinless chicken breast halves (150g each)
480ml chicken stock
3 tablespoon lime juice

1 tablespoon chili powder
1 teaspoon grated lime zest
Fresh coriander leaves, optional

1. Mix up the stock, lime juice and chili powder. 2. Place the chicken in the cooking pot and pour the stock mixture over the chicken. 3. Install the pressure lid and turn the pressure release valve to the SEAL position. 4. Select PRESSURE COOK, set the cooking temperature to HI and adjust the cooking time to 6 minutes. 5. When cooked, let the unit naturally release pressure. 6. A thermometer inserted in chicken should read at least 75°C. 7. Remove the chicken. When cool enough to handle, shred meat with 2 forks; return to the pot. Stir in lime zest. 8. If desired, serve the dish with coriander.
Per Serving: Calories 1029; Fat 47.29g; Sodium 1326mg; Carbs 10.53g; Fibre 3.1g; Sugar 4.52g; Protein 131.89g

Teriyaki Chicken Wings

Prep time: 10 minutes | Cook time: 10 minutes | Serves: 6

1.3 kg "party" chicken wings (separated at the joints)	2 tablespoons cider vinegar or rice vinegar
120 ml plus 2 tablespoons low-sodium soy sauce	4 teaspoons finely chopped fresh ginger
Salt and freshly ground black pepper	4 medium garlic cloves, finely chopped
75 g packed brown sugar	1 tablespoon cornflour

1. Pour 360 ml water into the pot and place a Cook & Crisp Basket inside. In a large bowl, toss the wings with 2 tablespoons of the soy sauce and season with salt and pepper. Place the wings on the basket. 2. Close the lid and move slider to PRESSURE. Ensuring the pressure release valve is in the SEAL position. The temperature will default to HIGH, which is the correct setting. Set time to 5 minutes. Select START/STOP to begin cooking. 3. Preheat the grill er and move an oven rack so that it is 10 cm below the grill er element. Cover a baking sheet with foil and grease with cooking spray. 4. When the cooking time is up, quick-release the pressure. Transfer the chicken wings to the prepared baking sheet. Discard the cooking liquid and remove the basket from the pot. 5. Add the remaining soy sauce, vinegar, the brown sugar, ginger, and garlic to the pot. 6. Move slider to AIR FRY/ STOVETOP. Select SEAR/SAUTÉ and set to 3. Select START/STOP to begin cooking. Bring to a simmer, stirring often, until the sugar has dissolved, 3 minutes. 7. In a small bowl, mix the cornflour with 1 tablespoon water. 8. Add the cornflour mixture to the pot and cook, stirring constantly, until the sauce has thickened, 1 minute. 9. Spoon the sauce over the wings, turning them so both sides are covered. Cook until the wings are browned and crispy on the edges, 3 minutes.
Per Serving: Calories 354; Fat 8.11g; Sodium 1340mg; Carbs 15.22g; Fibre 0.2g; Sugar 11.91g; Protein 51.92g

Tasty Barbecue Chicken–Stuffed Sweet Potatoes

Prep time: 10 minutes | Cook time: 18 minutes | Serves: 4

240 g thin barbecue sauce	Salt and freshly ground black pepper
455 g boneless, skinless chicken thighs, fat trimmed	240 g sour cream
4 small sweet potatoes, pricked with a fork	2 green onions, thinly sliced

1. Combine the barbecue sauce and chicken in the pot. 2. Then place the bottom layer of the Deluxe Reversible Rack in the lower position in the pot over the chicken and arrange the sweet potatoes on top. 3. Close the lid and move slider to PRESSURE. Ensuring the pressure release valve is in the SEAL position. The temperature will default to HIGH, which is the correct setting. Set time to 18 minutes. Select START/STOP to begin cooking. 4. When the cooking time is up, let the pressure come down naturally for 10 minutes and then quick-release the remaining pressure. 5. Split the sweet potatoes open lengthwise, season with salt and pepper, and set aside. 6. Remove the rack from the pot. Pull the chicken into shreds with two forks, return it to the sauce, and stir to combine. (The sauce will have browned in places on the bottom of the pot; just scrape them up and stir into the sauce.)7. Divide the chicken among the sweet potatoes; you may not need all of the sauce. Spread the sour cream on top sprinkle with green onions. Serve.
Per Serving: Calories 468; Fat 13.15g; Sodium 913mg; Carbs 72.99g; Fibre 5g; Sugar 15g; Protein 14.71g

Indian Curried Chicken

Prep time: 10 minutes | Cook time: 15 minutes | Serves: 4

3 tablespoons butter or ghee, at room temperature	paste (such as Patak's)
1 medium yellow onion, halved and sliced through the root end	675 g boneless, skinless chicken thighs, fat trimmed, cut into 5 cm to 8cm pieces
1 (250 g) can tomatoes with green chilies, with juice	2 tablespoons flour
2 tablespoons mild Indian curry	Salt and freshly ground black pepper

1. Add 1 tablespoon of the butter or ghee to the pot, Move slider to AIR FRY/STOVETOP. Select SEAR/SAUTÉ and set to 3. Select START/STOP to begin cooking. Once hot, add onion and cook, stirring often, until browned, 6 minutes. Press START/STOP. 2. Add the tomatoes to the pot, stir, and scrape up any browned bits on the base of the pot. Add the curry paste and stir to combine. Nestle the chicken into the sauce. 3. Close the lid and move slider to PRESSURE, Ensuring the pressure release valve is in the SEAL position. The temperature will default to HIGH, which is the correct setting. Set time to 8 minutes. Select START/STOP to begin cooking. 4. When the cooking time is up, quick-release the pressure. In a small bowl, mix the remaining 2 tablespoons butter or ghee with the flour until smooth. 5. Move slider to AIR FRY/STOVETOP. Select SEAR/ SAUTÉ and set to 3. Add the flour mixture to the pot in two additions, Press START/STOP to begin cooking. Stirring between additions, and cook until the sauce is thickened, 1 minute. Press START/STOP. 6. Season with salt and pepper and serve.
Per Serving: Calories 402; Fat 18.43g; Sodium 974mg; Carbs 42.31g; Fibre 2.7g; Sugar 9.96g; Protein 16.84g

Cheese and Courgette Stuffed Chicken

Prep time: 20 minutes | Cook time: 15 minutes | Serves: 4

1 slice sturdy sandwich bread, finely chopped	pepper
1 small (125 g) courgette, grated	4 medium boneless, skinless chicken breasts
50 g grated Italian cheese blend	1 jar thin marinara sauce (such as Rao's)
1 teaspoon Italian seasoning	
Salt and freshly ground black	

1. In a medium bowl, combine the breadcrumbs, cheese, courgette, and Italian seasoning. Season with salt and pepper. 2. Cut a horizontal slit into each chicken breast to form a 13 - to 15 cm long pocket. Stuff the chicken breasts with the breadcrumb mixture. Season the chicken with salt and pepper. 3. Pour the sauce into the pot. Add 60 ml water to the marinara jar, screw on the lid, and shake. Add the water to the pot. Place the bottom layer of the Deluxe Reversible Rack in the lower position in the pot and place the chicken breasts on the rack. 4. Close the lid and move slider to PRESSURE, Ensuring the pressure release valve is in the SEAL position. Set the temperature to LOW and set the time to 8 minutes. 5. When the cooking time is up, let the pressure come down naturally for 5 minutes and then quick-release the remaining pressure. 6. Make sure the chicken is cooked through; you should use an instant-read thermometer to check the temperature of the thickest part of the biggest chicken piece, and the thermometer should show a minimum of 75°C. 7. If the chicken isn't done, select SEAR/SAUTÉ and set to Lo1. Remove the rack, nestle the chicken into the sauce, press START/STOP to begin cooking. Simmer a few minutes more, uncovered, until the chicken is done. Press START/ STOP. 8. Serve the chicken with the sauce.
Per Serving: Calories 434; Fat 10.02g; Sodium 671mg; Carbs 25.84g; Fibre 1.3g; Sugar 17.98g; Protein 58.38g

Italian Turkey with Vegetables

Prep time: 25 minutes | Cook time: 25 minutes | Serves: 14

455g. carrots cut into 5cm pieces	3.2kg.), thawed and skin removed
2 medium onions cut into wedges	2 tablespoon olive oil
3 celery ribs, cut into 5cm pieces	1½ teaspoon seasoned salt
1 can (360ml) chicken stock	1 teaspoon Italian seasoning
1 bone-in turkey breast (2.7kg –	½ teaspoon pepper

1. Add the carrots, onions, celery ribs and stock to the cooking pot. 2. Brush turkey with oil; sprinkle with seasonings and place over vegetables. 3. Install the pressure lid and turn the pressure release valve to the SEAL position. 4. Select PRESSURE COOK, set the cooking temperature to HI and adjust the cooking time to 25 minutes. 5. When cooked, let the unit naturally release pressure. 6. A thermometer inserted in turkey breast should read at least 75°C. 7. Remove turkey from the cooker and tent with foil. Let stand 10 minutes before slicing.
Per Serving: Calories 533; Fat 25.06g; Sodium 1122mg; Carbs 4.51g; Fibre 1.3g; Sugar 1.94g; Protein 67.9g

Cranberry Hot Chicken Wings

Prep time: 45 minutes | Cook time: 35 minutes | Serves: 6

1 can jellied cranberry sauce	2 tsp. garlic powder
120 ml orange juice	1 tsp. dried minced onion
60 g hot pepper sauce	1 garlic clove, minced
2 tbsp. soy sauce	24. chicken wings
2 tbsp. honey	1 tsp. salt
1 tbsp. brown sugar	4 tsp. cornflour
1 tbsp. Dijon mustard	2 tbsp. cold water

1. Whisk together first 10 ingredients. For the chicken, use a sharp knife to cut through two wing joints; discard wing tips. 2. Place wing pieces in the pot; sprinkle with salt. Pour cranberry mixture over top. 3. Close the lid and move slider to PRESSURE. Ensuring the pressure release valve is in the SEAL position. The temperature will default to HIGH, which is the correct setting. Set time to 10 minutes. Select START/STOP to begin cooking. 4. When cooking is complete, release the pressure quickly by turning the pressure release valve to the VENT position. Move slider to the right to unlock the lid, then carefully open it. 5. Remove wings to a plate. Skim fat from cooking juices in the pressure cooker. Place the deluxe reversible rack in the pot in the higher grill position. Place the wings on the rack, then close the lid. 6. Move slider to AIR FRY/STOVETOP. Select GRILL. Press START/STOP to begin cooking, stirring occasionally, until mixture is reduced by half, 20-25 minutes. 7. In a small bowl, mix cornflour and water until smooth; stir into juices. Return to a boil, stirring constantly; cook and stir until glaze is thickened, 1-2 minutes. 8. Grill wings 8 – 10 cm from heat until lightly browned, 2-3 minutes. Brush with glaze before serving. 9. Serve with remaining glaze.
Per Serving: Calories 729; Fat 14.54g; Sodium 966mg; Carbs 61.3g; Fibre 1.1g; Sugar 28.42g; Protein 84.42g

Lemony Chicken with Artichoke Avocado

Prep time: 10 minutes | Cook time: 15 minutes | Serves: 4

2 tbsp extra-virgin olive oil	60 ml white wine
Juice of ½ lemon	1 can quartered artichoke hearts, drained
1 tbsp white wine vinegar	
Salt	1 avocado, peeled, pitted and cubed
Freshly ground black pepper	
4 large boneless, skinless chicken breasts	1 tsp chopped fresh parsley
	Lemon wedges, for serving

1. In a gallon-size resealable plastic bag, combine the olive oil, vinegar, lemon juice, salt, pepper and chicken. 2. Seal the bag and shake to evenly coat the chicken. Marinate the chicken for at least 30 minutes and up to an hour in the refrigerator. 3. Move slider to AIR FRY/STOVETOP. Select SEAR/SAUTÉ and set to 3. Select START/STOP to begin preheating. 4. Place the chicken and its marinade in the pot. Sauté for about 5 minutes on the first side. Flip the chicken, press cancel and then add the white wine. Stir the wine into the marinade. 5. Add the artichoke hearts to the pot. Press START/STOP. 6. Close the lid and move slider to PRESSURE. Ensuring the pressure release valve is in the SEAL position. The temperature will default to HIGH, which is the correct setting. Set time to 10 minutes. Select START/STOP to begin cooking. 7. When cooking is complete, release the pressure quickly by turning the pressure release valve to the VENT position. Move slider to the right to unlock the lid, then carefully open it. 8. Use tongs to transfer the chicken and artichoke hearts to a serving platter. 9. Add the avocado to the platter along with 3 tablespoons of the cooking liquid left in the pot. 10. Top with fresh parsley and add lemon wedges to the platter.
Per Serving: Calories 632; Fat 37.31g; Sodium 519mg; Carbs 10.12g; Fibre 5.7g; Sugar 1.35g; Protein 62.99g

Juicy Chicken Sliders

Prep time: 10 minutes | Cook time: 30 minutes | Serves: 4

2 large boneless, skinless chicken breasts	¼ tsp freshly ground black pepper
	Juice of 1 lime
60 ml water or chicken stock	½ red onion, thinly sliced
1 tsp salt	1 clove garlic, grated
½ tsp ground cumin	35 g mild-medium sliced pickled

jalapeño peppers	4 brioche slider buns
1 tbsp honey	125 g Gouda cheese, shredded

1. Add the chicken, water or stock, lime juice, salt, cumin, black pepper, red onion, garlic, jalapeños and honey to the pot. 2. Move slider to AIR FRY/STOVETOP. Select SEAR/SAUTÉ and set to 3. Select START/STOP to begin cooking. Once done, press START/STOP to turn off the SEAR/SAUTÉ function. 3. Move slider to PRESSURE, Ensuring the pressure release valve is in the SEAL position. The temperature will default to HIGH, which is the correct setting. Set time to 15 minutes. Select START/STOP to begin cooking. 4. Meanwhile, preheat the oven to 190°C. Line a half sheet pan with foil. Slice the slider buns in half horizontally, placing the bun bottoms on the prepared sheet pan. 5. When cooking is complete, release the pressure quickly by moving the pressure release valve to the VENT position. Move slider to the right to unlock the lid, then carefully open it. 6. Use two forks to shred the chicken and mix together all the contents of the pot. 7. Use tongs to transfer equal amounts of the chicken mixture to each bun bottom. 8. Top each little pile of chicken with a pinch of shredded cheese and then cover with the top bun. 9. Bake the sliders for 15 minutes, or until the cheese melts. Let cool slightly for 2 minutes before serving.
Per Serving: Calories 721; Fat 42.47g; Sodium 1225mg; Carbs 39.55g; Fibre 1.2g; Sugar 22.75g; Protein 44.06g

Cajun Beans & Sausage

Prep time: 25 minutes | Cook time: 5 minutes | Serves: 8

1 pkg. (300g) fully cooked spicy chicken sausage links, halved lengthwise and cut into 1 cm slices	1 large onion, chopped
	1 large green pepper, chopped
	70g chopped roasted sweet red peppers
180ml reduced-sodium chicken stock	3 garlic cloves, minced
	1 teaspoon Cajun seasoning
2 cans (400g each) red beans, rinsed and drained	1 teaspoon dried oregano
	½ teaspoon dried thyme
2 cans (360g each) diced tomatoes, undrained	½ teaspoon pepper
	1.1kg cooked brown rice
3 medium carrots, chopped	

1. Brown the sausage in the cooking pot at MD on SEAR/SAUTÉ mode; add stock and cook them for 1 minute, stirring to loosen browned bits. 2. Stop the cooker, and stir in beans, tomatoes, vegetables, garlic and seasonings. 3. Install the pressure lid and turn the pressure release valve to the SEAL position. 4. Select PRESSURE COOK, set the cooking temperature to HI and adjust the cooking time to 5 minutes. 5. When cooked, let the unit naturally release pressure. 6. Serve the dish with hot brown rice.
Per Serving: Calories 283; Fat 3.18g; Sodium 369mg; Carbs 54.19g; Fibre 9.4g; Sugar 8.55g; Protein 11.27g

Apple Chicken

Prep time: 25 minutes | Cook time: 20 minutes | Serves: 4

4 bone-in chicken thighs (about 675g) skin removed	1 medium onion, chopped
	80g barbecue sauce
¼ teaspoon salt	1 tablespoon honey
¼ teaspoon pepper	1 garlic clove, minced
1 tablespoon rapeseed oil	2 medium Fuji or Gala apples, coarsely chopped
120ml apple cider or juice	

1. Sprinkle chicken with salt and pepper. 2. Heat oil in the cooking pot at MD on SEAR/SAUTÉ mode; when oil is hot, brown chicken; remove and keep warm. 3. Stop the cooker and add apple cider, stirring to loosen browned bits from pot; stir in the onion, barbecue sauce, honey, garlic and chicken. 4. Install the pressure lid and turn the pressure release valve to the SEAL position. 5. Select PRESSURE COOK, set the cooking temperature to HI and adjust the cooking time to 10 minutes. 6. When cooked, let the unit naturally release pressure. 7. A thermometer inserted in chicken should read at least 75°C. 8. Remove chicken; keep warm. 9. Add apples to the pot and simmer at LO on SEAR/SAUTÉ mode for 10 minutes until apples are tender, stirring constantly. 10. Serve warm.
Per Serving: Calories 591; Fat 35.89g; Sodium 548mg; Carbs 32.78g; Fibre 2.8g; Sugar 25.73g; Protein 32.75g

Turkey Breasts in Chicken Stock

Prep time: 25 minutes | Cook time: 30 minutes | Serves: 12

1 can (360ml chicken stock
120ml lemon juice
55g packed brown sugar
10g fresh sage
10g fresh thyme leaves
60ml lime juice
60ml cider vinegar
60ml olive oil
1 envelope onion soup mix
2 tablespoons Dijon mustard

1 tablespoon minced fresh marjoram
1½ teaspoons paprika
1 teaspoon garlic powder
1 teaspoon pepper
½ teaspoon salt
2 boneless skinless turkey breast halves (900g each)
Lemon wedges, optional

1. Add all of the ingredients except the meat and lemon wedges to a blender and blend them until blended. 2. Place turkey in a bowl or shallow dish; pour marinade over turkey and turn to coat. 3. Cover the dish and refrigerate the food for 8 hours or overnight, turning occasionally. 4. Transfer the food to the cooking pot. 5. Install the pressure lid and turn the pressure release valve to the SEAL position. 6. Select PRESSURE COOK, set the cooking temperature to HI and adjust the cooking time to 20 minutes. 7. When cooked, let the unit naturally release pressure. 8. A thermometer inserted in turkey breasts should read at least 75°C. 9. Remove the turkey from the cooker; tent with foil. Let stand 10 minutes before slicing. 10. If desired, top with additional fresh thyme and marjoram and serve with lemon wedges.
Per Serving: Calories 424; Fat 9.88g; Sodium 537mg; Carbs 7.87g; Fibre 0.8g; Sugar 5.15g; Protein 72.15g

Creamy Herbed Chicken with Mushroom

Prep Time: 15 minutes | Cook Time: 23 minutes | Serves: 3

2 tbsp (28 g) grass-fed butter or ghee
1 medium yellow onion, thinly sliced
680 g mushrooms, cut into thirds, woody ends removed
5 cloves garlic, chopped
120 ml dry white wine
2 large celery ribs with leaves, thinly sliced
1 tsp sea salt
15 g finely chopped fresh flat-leaf parsley, plus more for garnish
1 tbsp (2 g) finely chopped fresh

rosemary
1 tbsp (4 g) finely chopped fresh dill
2 tsp (2 g) finely chopped fresh thyme leaves
2 boneless, skinless chicken breasts
175 ml chicken or vegetable stock
175 ml heavy cream
2 tbsp (15 g) gluten-free plain flour
20 g shredded Parmesan cheese, plus more for garnish

1. Add butter to the pot. Move slider to AIR FRY/STOVETOP. Select SEAR/SAUTÉ and set to 3. Select START/STOP to begin cooking. Once the fat butter melted, add the onion and mushrooms and sauté, stirring occasionally, for 7 minutes, or until caramelised. 2. Then, add the garlic and sauté for 1 minute, stirring occasionally. Add the wine and deglaze the pot, scraping up any browned bits with a wooden spoon. Press START/STOP to turn off the SEAR/SAUTÉ function. 3. Add the celery, salt, parsley, dill, thyme, rosemary, chicken and stock, ensuring the chicken is submerged in the liquid. 4. Close the lid and move slider to PRESSURE. Make sure the pressure release valve is in the SEAL position. The temperature will default to HIGH, which is the correct setting. Set time to 9 minutes. Select START/STOP to begin cooking. 5. Meanwhile, place the cream in a big measuring cup or medium bowl, then sprinkle the flour on the top, whisking until the flour is mostly incorporated. Set aside. 6. Once the timer beeps, turn the pressure relief valve to the VENT position for quick pressure relief. Move slider to the right to unlock the lid, then carefully open it. 7. With tongs, transfer the chicken to a plate or cutting board. Chop the chicken into bite-size chunks, then set aside. 8. Move slider to AIR FRY/STOVETOP. Select SEAR/SAUTÉ and set to 3. Select START/STOP to begin cooking. Add the cream mixture and the Parmesan to the pot, allowing the cream to come to a simmer, then quickly stir until the cream and Parmesan are fully mixed in. Simmer for about 5 minutes, or until the liquid slightly thickens. Press START/STOP. 9. Add the chicken and stir well. Taste for seasoning and adjust the salt to taste. Allow it to rest for 10 minutes. 10. Serve immediately, garnished with shredded Parmesan and chopped fresh parsley.

Per Serving: Calories 1234; Fat 35.35g; Sodium 1642mg; Carbs 185.63g; Fibre 28.2g; Sugar 7.19g; Protein 72.32g

Chicken Pieces with Broccoli Florets

Prep time: 15 minutes | Cook time: 5 minutes | Serves: 8

900g. boneless skinless chicken breasts cut into 2.5 cm. pieces
360g fresh broccoli florets
4 medium carrots, julienned
1 can (200g) sliced water chestnuts, drained
6 garlic cloves, minced
720ml reduced-sodium chicken stock

60ml reduced-sodium soy sauce
2 tablespoon brown sugar
2 tablespoon sesame oil
2 tablespoon rice vinegar
½ teaspoon salt
½ teaspoon pepper
40g cornflour
80ml water
Hot cooked rice

1. Mix the stock, soy sauce, brown sugar, sesame oil, vinegar, salt and pepper in a large bowl. 2. Add the chicken pieces, broccoli florets, carrots, water chestnuts, and garlic cloves to the cooking pot, and then pour the stock mixture over them. 3. Install the pressure lid and turn the pressure release valve to the SEAL position. 4. Select PRESSURE COOK, set the cooking temperature to HI and adjust the cooking time to 3 minutes. 5. When cooked, let the unit naturally release pressure. 6. A thermometer inserted in chicken should read at least 75°C. 7. Remove chicken and vegetables; keep warm. In a small bowl, mix cornflour and water until smooth; stir into cooking juices. 8. Simmer them in the cooking pot at LO on SEAR/SAUTÉ mode for 1 to 2 minutes until thickened. 9. Serve chicken and vegetables with hot cooked rice.
Per Serving: Calories 598; Fat 27.94g; Sodium 872mg; Carbs 47.98g; Fibre 6.2g; Sugar 3.83g; Protein 42.25g

Juicy Chicken & Broccoli

Prep Time: 15 minutes | Cook Time: 15 minutes | Serves: 4

680 g chicken, cut into bite-size pieces
1½ tbsp (12 g) cornflour
120 ml coconut aminos or gluten-free tamari
80 ml fresh orange juice
2 tsp (4 g) orange zest
60 ml rice vinegar
2 tsp (10 ml) sesame oil
3 cloves garlic, crushed, divided
1 tbsp (8 g) finely chopped fresh ginger, divided

1 tsp crushed red pepper flakes (optional)
1 tbsp (15 ml) avocado oil
273 g chopped broccoli
740 g cooked quinoa, 744 g rice or 440 g cauliflower rice, for serving
2 tsp (5 g) sesame seeds, for garnish (optional)
2 tbsp (12 g) chopped green onion, for garnish (optional)

1. Place the chicken and cornflour in a resealable plastic bag or lidded plastic container. Shake around until the chicken is well coated. 2. In a bowl, mix together the coconut aminos, vinegar, sesame oil, orange juice and zest, two-thirds of the garlic, two-thirds of the ginger and the red pepper flakes (if using). 3. Move slider to AIR FRY/STOVETOP. Select SEAR/SAUTÉ and set to 3. Select START/STOP to begin preheating. Allow unit to preheat for 2 minutes. After 2 minutes, add the avocado oil and the remaining garlic and ginger. Stir, then add the chicken. Cook for 1 to 2 minutes, or until the chicken is slightly browned. Press START/STOP to turn off the SEAR/SAUTÉ function. 4. Pour the orange sauce on top of the chicken. 5. Close the lid and move slider to PRESSURE. Make sure the pressure release valve is in the SEAL position. The temperature will default to HIGH, which is the correct setting. Set time to 7 minutes. Select START/STOP to begin cooking. 6. When cooking is complete, turn the pressure relief valve to the VENT position for quick pressure relief. Move slider to the right to unlock the lid, then carefully open it. 7. Toss in the chopped broccoli. Stir, then cook on SEAR/SAUTÉ function and set the heat to 4. Stir and cook the broccoli for another 3 to 4 minutes. 8. Serve over quinoa, rice or cauliflower rice, garnished with the sesame seeds and green onion (if using).
Per Serving: Calories 543; Fat 18.29g; Sodium 155mg; Carbs 48.63g; Fibre 7.4g; Sugar 4.53g; Protein 44.65g

Raisin Chicken with Capers

Prep time: 25 minutes | Cook time: 10 minutes | Serves: 8

2 tablespoon olive oil, divided	thinly sliced
8 boneless skinless chicken thighs	1 medium onion, thinly sliced
(100g each)	1 can (360g) diced tomatoes,
1 teaspoon salt	undrained
1 teaspoon pepper	75g golden raisins
120ml Marsala wine	2 tablespoon capers, drained
225g sliced fresh mushrooms	10g chopped fresh basil
1 medium sweet red pepper,	Hot cooked couscous

1. Sprinkle the chicken with salt and pepper. 2. Heat 1 teaspoon of oil in the cooking pot at MD on SEAR/SAUTÉ mode; when oil is hot, brown chicken in batches and transfer to a plate; add wine and cook them for 1 minute more, stirring to loosen browned bits from pot. 3. Stop the cooker and return the chicken to the pot. 4. Install the pressure lid and turn the pressure release valve to the SEAL position. 5. Select PRESSURE COOK, set the cooking temperature to HI and adjust the cooking time to 6 minutes. 6. When cooked, let the unit naturally release pressure. 7. A thermometer inserted in chicken should read at least 75°C. 8. Sprinkle the dish with basil before serving, and serve with hot cooked couscous.
Per Serving: Calories 243; Fat 6.74g; Sodium 461mg; Carbs 17.39g; Fibre 2.5g; Sugar 9.2g; Protein 28.33g

Peanut Butter Chicken

Prep Time: 15 minutes | Cook Time: 8 minutes | Serves: 6

130 g smooth peanut butter	558 to 744 g cooked rice or 330
60 ml soy sauce or gluten-free	to 440 g cauliflower rice, for
tamari	serving
60 ml honey	3 tbsp (8 g) chopped fresh
60 ml rice vinegar	coriander (optional)
160 ml chicken stock	3 tbsp (27 g) chopped peanuts
3 cloves garlic, minced	(optional)
905 g chicken breast	Salt
80 ml full-fat canned coconut	Freshly ground black pepper
milk	

1. Mix together the peanut butter, honey, vinegar, soy sauce, chicken stock and garlic in a bowl. 2. Place the chicken in the pot. Pour the peanut butter sauce on top. 3. Close the lid and move slider to PRESSURE. Make sure the pressure release valve is in the SEAL position. The temperature will default to HIGH, which is the correct setting. Set time to 8 minutes. Select START/STOP to begin cooking. 4. When cooking is complete, turn the pressure relief valve to the VENT position for quick pressure relief. Move slider to the right to unlock the lid, then carefully open it. 5. Pour in the coconut milk. You can cut or shred the chicken into smaller pieces, or keep as a larger breast. 6. Serve warm over rice or cauliflower rice. Garnish with fresh coriander and peanuts (if using). Sprinkle with salt and pepper to taste.
Per Serving: Calories 562; Fat 30.91g; Sodium 1166mg; Carbs 29.99g; Fibre 4.3g; Sugar 17.19g; Protein 43.75g

Lemony Chicken with Artichoke

Prep Time: 15 minutes | Cook Time: 10 minutes | Serves: 4

½ tsp sea salt, plus more to taste	drained
½ tsp freshly ground black pepper	1 (170 g) jar artichoke hearts,
680 g boneless, skinless chicken	drained
breast or thighs	3 sprigs thyme
237 ml dry white wine, e.g.,	1 lemon, sliced
chardonnay; or chicken stock	2 tsp (4 g) lemon pepper
Juice of 1 large lemon (about 60	3 tbsp (24 g) cornflour
ml)	2 tbsp (30 ml) water
2 tsp (4 g) garam masala	Cooked rice, cauliflower rice,
1 tsp ground turmeric	pasta or cooked vegetables, for
1 clove garlic, crushed	serving
1 (170 g) can hearts of palm,	

1. Season the chicken with salt and pepper. Place in the pot. 2. In a small bowl, mix together the wine, garam masala, lemon juice, turmeric and garlic. Pour on top of the chicken. 3. Cover the chicken with the hearts of palm, artichoke hearts, thyme and lemon slices and sprinkle with the lemon pepper. 4. Close the lid and move slider to PRESSURE. Make sure the pressure release valve is in the SEAL position. The temperature will default to HIGH, which is the correct setting. Set time to 9 minutes. Select START/STOP to begin cooking. 5. When cooking is complete, turn the pressure relief valve to the VENT position for quick pressure relief. Move slider to the right to unlock the lid, then carefully open it. 6. In a small bowl, whisk together the cornflour and the water and add to the sauce. Continue to stir until thickened. Remove the thyme sprigs. 7. Serve the chicken on top of rice, cauliflower rice or pasta, or with vegetables.
Per Serving: Calories 407; Fat 10.18g; Sodium 780mg; Carbs 61.26g; Fibre 6.9g; Sugar 18.92g; Protein 18.7g

Cheese Beef and Quinoa Bowls

Prep Time: 15 minutes | Cook Time: 12 minutes | Serves: 6

4 slices raw bacon, diced	240 ml water
1 yellow onion, diced	1 tbsp (14 g) mayonnaise
455 g 90% lean minced beef	1 tbsp (16 g) barbecue sauce
½ tsp ground mustard powder	1 tbsp (11 g) prepared yellow
½ tsp onion powder	mustard
1 tsp salt	2 tbsp (30 g) ketchup
½ tsp freshly ground black pepper	115 g shredded cheddar cheese
1 (410 g) can fire-roasted diced	75 g diced kosher dill pickles
tomatoes	90 g diced Roma tomatoes
173 g uncooked quinoa	

1. Move slider to AIR FRY/STOVETOP. Select SEAR/SAUTÉ and set to 3. Select START/STOP to begin preheating. Allow unit to preheat for 2 minutes. After 2 minutes, add the bacon and cook until crisp. Remove and transfer to a paper towel-lined plate. 2. Add the onion, beef, onion powder, mustard powder, salt and pepper. Break apart the beef using a wooden spoon. Once the onion begins to turn translucent, about 3 minutes, press START/STOP. 3. Stir in the can of tomatoes, quinoa and water. 4. Close the lid and move slider to PRESSURE. Make sure the pressure release valve is in the SEAL position. The temperature will default to HIGH, which is the correct setting. Set time to 1 minute. Select START/STOP to begin cooking. 5. When cooking is complete, naturally release the pressure for 10 minutes. Then turn the pressure relief valve to the VENT position for quick pressure relief. Move slider to AIR FRY/ STOVETOP to unlock the lid, then carefully open it. 6. Move slider to AIR FRY/STOVETOP. Select SEAR/SAUTÉ and set to 4. Select START/STOP to begin. Stir in the barbecue sauce, mayonnaise, mustard and ketchup. Sauté for 2 minutes while stirring. 7. Press START/STOP. Transfer the quinoa to a serving bowl and top with the cheese, pickles and tomatoes.
Per Serving: Calories 457; Fat 24.47g; Sodium 954mg; Carbs 26.76g; Fibre 4.2g; Sugar 5.49g; Protein 32.16g

Indian Chicken & Vegetables

Prep time: 15 minutes | Cook time: 5 minutes | Serves: 8

900g boneless skinless chicken	2 jars (375g each) tikka masala
thighs, cubed	curry sauce
2 medium sweet potatoes, peeled	120ml water
and cut into 3.5cm pieces	¾ teaspoon salt
2 medium sweet red peppers cut	Minced fresh coriander, optional
into 2.5cm pieces	Naan flatbreads, warmed
270g fresh cauliflowerets	

1. Combine the chicken and vegetables; add sauce, water and salt in the cooking pot. 2. Install the pressure lid and turn the pressure release valve to the SEAL position. 3. Select PRESSURE COOK, set the cooking temperature to HI and adjust the cooking time to 3 minutes. 4. When cooked, let the unit naturally release pressure. 5. A thermometer inserted in chicken should read at least 75°C. 6. If desired, top with coriander; serve the dish with warmed naan.
Per Serving: Calories 257; Fat 4.32g; Sodium 1211mg; Carbs 24.76g; Fibre 5.2g; Sugar 9.42g; Protein 30.32g

Barbecued Chicken with Simple Slaw

Prep Time: 15 minutes | Cook Time: 20 minutes | Serves: 4

Barbecued Chicken:
½ yellow onion, chopped
1 clove garlic, minced
60 ml raw apple cider vinegar
55 g pure maple syrup
60 ml water
1 tablespoon soy sauce or tamari
455 g boneless, skinless chicken breasts
1 teaspoon fine sea salt
Freshly ground black pepper
60 g tomato paste
1 teaspoon blackstrap molasses
1 teaspoon spicy brown mustard
½ teaspoon chili powder
½ teaspoon paprika
⅛ teaspoon cayenne pepper (optional)
200 g green cabbage, shredded
Simple Slaw:
2 tablespoons freshly squeezed lemon juice
2 tablespoons pure maple syrup
1 tablespoon extra-virgin olive oil
½ teaspoon fine sea salt
Freshly ground black pepper
200 g green cabbage, shredded
1 large shredded carrot (about 1 large carrot)
10 g chopped fresh flat-leaf parsley
Butter lettuce or buns, for serving

1. To make the barbecued chicken, add the onion, garlic, maple syrup, vinegar, water, and soy sauce to the pot and stir to combine well. 2. Then place the bottom layer of the Deluxe Reversible Rack in the lower position in the pot. Place the chicken breasts on the rack. Season the breasts with ¼ teaspoon of the salt and black pepper. 3. Close the lid and move slider to PRESSURE. Make sure the pressure release valve is in the SEAL position. The temperature will default to HIGH, which is the correct setting. Set time to 12 minutes. Select START/STOP to begin cooking. 4. Meanwhile, prepare the slaw. Mix together the lemon juice, maple syrup, olive oil, salt, and several grinds of pepper in a large bowl. Add the carrot, cabbage, and parsley and toss to coat. Refrigerate the slaw to let the flavours meld while you finish preparing the chicken. 5. When cooking is complete, turn the pressure relief valve to the VENT position for quick pressure relief. Move slider to the right to unlock the lid, then carefully open it. 6. Transfer the chicken to a cutting board to rest. Use oven mitts to remove the rack. 7. Move slider to AIR FRY/STOVETOP. Select SEAR/SAUTÉ and set to 3. Select START/STOP to begin cooking. add the tomato paste, mustard, molasses, paprika, cayenne, chili powder, and the remaining ¾ teaspoon salt to the sauce. Stir well, then add the cabbage. Simmer the cabbage in the sauce until very tender, about 8 minutes. 8. Once the cabbage is tender, use two forks to shred the chicken. Add it to the pot and stir well. Taste and adjust the seasonings as needed; add more cayenne if you like it spicy. 9. To serve, scoop the barbecued chicken into lettuce cups or onto your favourite buns, with the chilled slaw on top. Serve any additional slaw on the side. 10. Store leftovers in two separate airtight containers in the fridge. The chicken will keep for 3 or 4 days, but the slaw is best used within 1 day.
Per Serving: Calories 387; Fat 10.43g; Sodium 1353mg; Carbs 62.5g; Fibre 6.1g; Sugar 34.89g; Protein 13.81g

Small Potato & Chicken Stew

Prep time: 25 minutes | Cook time: 10 minutes | Serves: 4

455g small red potatoes, halved
1 large onion, finely chopped
90g shredded carrots
6 garlic cloves, minced
2 teaspoons grated lemon zest
2 teaspoons dried thyme
½ teaspoon salt
¼ teaspoon pepper
675g boneless skinless chicken thighs, cut 2.5cm pieces
480ml reduced-sodium chicken stock, divided
2 bay leaves
3 tablespoons plain flour
2 tablespoons minced fresh parsley

1. Place potatoes, onion and carrots in the cooking pot, and top them with garlic, lemon zest, thyme, salt and pepper; place the chicken on the vegetables, add 400ml of stock and bay leaves. 2. Install the pressure lid and turn the pressure release valve to the SEAL position. 3. Select PRESSURE COOK, set the cooking temperature to HI and adjust the cooking time to 5 minutes. 4. When cooked, let the unit naturally release pressure. 5. A thermometer inserted in chicken should read at least 75°C. 6. Remove chicken; keep warm. Discard bay leaves. In a small bowl, mix flour and remaining 60ml stock until smooth; stir into the cooking pot. 7. Simmer them at LO on SEAR/SAUTÉ mode for 1 to 2 minutes until slightly thickened. 8. Return chicken to the pot; heat through. 9. Sprinkle servings with parsley.
Per Serving: Calories 346; Fat 5.1g; Sodium 868mg; Carbs 30.89g; Fibre 3.6g; Sugar 4.85g; Protein 42.87g

Chapter 4 Beef, Pork, and Lamb Recipes

Beef Meatloaf Cups

Prep Time: 10 minutes | Cook Time: 25 minutes | Serves: 4

Meatloaves:

455g beef
25g seasoned breadcrumbs
25g parmesan cheese, grated
1 small onion. minced

2 garlic cloves, pressed
1 egg, beaten
Sea salt and black pepper, to taste

Glaze:

4 tablespoons tomato sauce
1 tablespoon brown sugar

1 tablespoon Dijon mustard

1. Place the Cook & Crisp Basket in your Pressure Cooker Steam Fryer. 2. Mix all the recipe ingredients for the meatloaves until everything is well mixed. 3. Scrape the beef mixture into oiled silicone cups and transfer them to the Cook & Crisp Basket. 4. Put on the Smart Lid on top of the Ninja Foodi Steam Fryer. 5. Move the Lid Slider to the "Air Fry/Stovetop". Select the "Air Fry" mode for cooking. 6. Cook the beef cups at 195°C for around 20 minutes. 7. In the meantime, mix the remaining recipe ingredients for the glaze. Then, spread the glaze on top of each muffin; continue to cook for another 5 minutes. 8. Serve.
Per serving: Calories: 355; Fat:18.6g; Carbs: 14.2g; Fibre: 2.3g; Sugars: 6.2g; Proteins: 27.5g

Cheese Ribeye Steak

Prep Time: 10 minutes | Cook Time: 15 minutes | Serves: 4

455g ribeye steak, bone-in
Sea salt and black pepper, to taste
2 tablespoons olive oil

½ teaspoon onion powder
1 teaspoon garlic powder
245g blue cheese, crumbled

1. Place the Cook & Crisp Basket in your Pressure Cooker Steam Fryer. 2. Toss the ribeye steak with the salt, black pepper, olive oil, onion powder, and garlic powder; place the ribeye steak in the Cook & Crisp Basket. 3. Put on the Smart Lid on top of the Ninja Foodi Steam Fryer. 4. Move the Lid Slider to the "Air Fry/Stovetop". Select the "Air Fry" mode for cooking. 5. Cook the ribeye steak at 200°C for around 15 minutes, turning it over halfway through the cooking time. 6. Top the ribeye steak with the cheese and serve warm. Serve.
Per serving: Calories: 399; Fat:29.4g; Carbs: 4.6g; Fibre: 0.3g; Sugars: 0.7g; Proteins: 29.2g

Rump Roast

Prep Time: 10 minutes | Cook Time: 50 minutes | Serves: 4

675g rump roast
Black pepper and salt, to taste
1 teaspoon paprika

2 tablespoons olive oil
60ml brandy
2 tablespoons cold butter

1. Place the Cook & Crisp Basket in your Pressure Cooker Steam Fryer. 2. Brush the basket with oil. 3. Toss the rump roast with the black pepper, salt, paprika, olive oil, and brandy; place the rump roast in Cook & Crisp Basket. 4. Put on the Smart Lid on top of the Ninja Foodi Steam Fryer. 5. Move the Lid Slider to the "Air Fry/Stovetop". Select the "Air Fry" mode for cooking. 6. Cook the rump roast at 200°C for around 50 minutes, turning it over halfway through the cooking time. 7. Serve with the cold butter and enjoy!
Per serving: Calories: 390; Fat:22.4g; Carbs: 1.4g; Fibre: 0.4g; Sugars: 0.6g; Proteins: 35.2g;

Coulotte Roast

Prep Time: 10 minutes | Cook Time: 55 minutes | Serves: 5

900g Coulotte roast
2 tablespoons olive oil
1 tablespoon fresh parsley, finely chopped

1 tablespoon fresh coriander, finely chopped
2 garlic cloves, minced
Salt and black pepper, to taste

1. Place the Cook & Crisp Basket in your Pressure Cooker Steam Fryer. 2. Toss the roast beef with the remaining ingredients; place the roast beef in the Cook & Crisp Basket Put on the Smart Lid on top of the Ninja Foodi Steam Fryer. 3. Move the Lid Slider to the "Air Fry/Stovetop". Select the "Air Fry" mode for cooking. 4. Cook the roast beef at 200°C for around 55 minutes, turning over halfway through the cooking time. 5. Enjoy!
Per serving: Calories: 306; Fat:16.7g; Carbs: 1.3g; Fibre: 0.2g; Sugars: 0.4g; Proteins: 37.7g

Beef mince & Pasta Casserole

Prep Time: 15 minutes | Cook Time: 17 minutes | Serves: 4

2 tablespoons olive oil
1 small yellow onion, chopped
2 jarred anchovy fillets, minced (optional)
2 teaspoons finely grated lemon zest
2 medium garlic cloves, peeled and minced
½ teaspoon ground black pepper

455 g lean beef mince
240 ml dry white wine, such as Chardonnay
2 medium plum or Roma tomatoes, chopped
10 g fresh dill fronds, chopped
½ teaspoon ground cinnamon
200 g dried ziti
360 ml beef or chicken stock

1. Select SEAR/SAUTÉ. Select Lo3, and then press START/STOP to begin cooking. 2. When the pot is hot, heat the oil for 1 to 2 minutes; add onion and cook for 2 minutes until softened. If using, add the anchovies and stir for 1 minute until the bits begin to melt. Stir in the lemon zest, garlic, and pepper until fragrant, a few seconds. 3. Crumble in the beef mince and cook for 3 minutes until the meat loses its raw and pink colour, stirring often to break up any clumps. Stir in the wine, tomatoes, dill, and cinnamon. Scrape up every speck of browned stuff on the pot's bottom. 4. Stop the process, and stir in the pasta and stock until uniform. 5. Close the lid, turn the pressure release valve to SEAL position, and then move the slider to PRESSURE. Select HI and set the cooking time to 7 minutes. Press START/STOP to begin cooking. When finished, release the pressure quickly. 6. Stir the dish well before serving.
Per Serving: Calories 562; Fat: 25.89g; Sodium: 983mg; Carbs: 46.75g; Fibre: 5.7g; Sugar: 39.21g; Protein: 28.36g

Mushroom Beef Patties

Prep Time: 10 minutes | Cook Time: 15 minutes | Serves: 4

455g chuck
2 garlic cloves, minced
1 small onion, chopped
100g mushrooms, chopped

1 teaspoon cayenne pepper
Sea salt and black pepper, to taste
4 brioche rolls

1. Place the Cook & Crisp Basket in your Pressure Cooker Steam Fryer. 2. Mix the chuck, garlic, onion, mushrooms, cayenne pepper, salt, and black pepper until everything is well mixed. Form the mixture into four patties. 3. Put on the Smart Lid on top of the Ninja Foodi Steam Fryer. 4. Move the Lid Slider to the "Air Fry/Stovetop". Select the "Air Fry" mode for cooking. 5. Cook the patties at 195°C for about 15 minutes or until cooked through; make sure to turn them over halfway through the cooking time. 6. Serve your patties on the prepared brioche rolls and enjoy!
Per serving: Calories: 305; Fat:10.4g; Carbs: 25.3g; Fibre: 1.7g; Sugars: 4.5g; Proteins: 27.7g

Soy Dipped Beef Tenderloin

Prep Time: 10 minutes | Cook Time: 20 minutes | Serves: 4

675g beef tenderloin, sliced
2 tablespoons sesame oil
1 teaspoon Five-spice powder
2 garlic cloves, minced

1 teaspoon fresh ginger, peeled and grated
2 tablespoons soy sauce

1. Place the Cook & Crisp Basket in your Pressure Cooker Steam Fryer. 2. Toss the beef tenderloin with the remaining ingredients; place the beef tenderloin in the Cook & Crisp Basket Put on the Smart Lid on top of the Ninja Foodi Steam Fryer. 3. Move the Lid Slider to the "Air Fry/Stovetop". Select the "Air Fry" mode for cooking. 4. Cook the beef tenderloin at 200°C for around 20 minutes, turning it over halfway through the cooking time. 5. Enjoy!
Per serving: Calories: 326; Fat:18.7g; Carbs: 3g; Fibre: 0.3g; Sugars: 1.6g; Proteins: 35.7g

Buttered Rump Roast

Prep Time: 25 minutes | Cook Time: 65 minutes | Serves: 6-8

8 tbsp. grass-fed butter, divided
905 g to 1.4 kg grass-fed beef rump roast
1 large yellow onion, thickly sliced
3 large celery ribs, thinly sliced
5 cloves garlic, chopped
1 tsp. chopped fresh thyme leaves
1 tsp. chopped fresh rosemary leaves
175 ml filtered water, or beef or chicken stock
60 ml coconut aminos
15 g finely chopped fresh parsley
1 tsp. sea salt

1. Select SEAR/SAUTÉ. Select Lo3, and then press START/STOP to begin cooking. 2. When the pot is hot, melt 2 tablespoons of butter; add the roast and brown for about 3½ minutes per side. 3. Transfer the roast to a plate and set aside. 4. Add the remaining 6 tablespoons of butter and the onion, celery, garlic, thyme and rosemary to the pot and sauté them, for 5 minutes, or until fragrant; add the filtered water or stock and coconut aminos, giving the mixture a quick stir and scraping up any browned bits with a wooden spoon. Add the parsley and salt, and then give the mixture another stir. 5. Stop the process, and return the browned roast to the pot. 6. Close the lid, turn the pressure release valve to SEAL position, and then move the slider to PRESSURE. Select HI and set the cooking time to 40 minutes. Press START/STOP to begin cooking. When finished, release the pressure naturally. 7. Carefully remove the roast, place on a large plate or cutting board and cut into shredded chunks. Add the shredded beef back to the pot. 8. Cook them at HI on PRESSURE mode for 5 minutes, and then release the pressure quickly. 9. To reduce the sauce, press sauté and allow the sauce and shredded beef to simmer for 5 to 10 minutes to thicken. 10. Once the sauce has reduced, allow the shredded beef to rest in the pot for about 15 minutes before serving. 11. Serve the dish immediately or refrigerate for later use.
Per Serving: Calories 192; Fat: 7.41g; Sodium: 405mg; Carbs: 3.52g; Fibre: 0.9g; Sugar: 1.35g; Protein: 28.04g

Lamb with Chickpea & Pitas

Prep Time: 15 minutes | Cook Time: 25 minutes | Serves: 4-6

1 tbsp. extra-virgin olive oil
4 (115-g) bone-in lamb shoulder chops
Salt
Freshly ground black pepper
1 yellow onion, diced
½ tsp. ground fennel seeds
1 tsp. smoked paprika
½ tsp. dried oregano
¼ tsp. crushed red pepper flakes
½ lemon
2 (440-g) cans chickpeas, drained and rinsed
175 ml chicken or beef stock
1 (410-g) can fire-roasted diced tomatoes
1 (170-g) can tomato paste
12 (18.5-cm) pitas
Tzatziki, for serving (optional)

1. Select SEAR/SAUTÉ. Select Lo3, and then press START/STOP to begin cooking. 2. When the pot is hot, heat the oil; add the lamb and season the top side with salt and black pepper, and then sear the first side for 3 to 4 minutes; flip the lamb and season that top side with salt and black pepper, then add the onion and sauté for 2 more minutes. Add the fennel, more salt and black pepper, paprika, oregano, red pepper flakes and lemon half to the pot. Stir everything to combine. 3. Stop the process, and stir in the chickpeas, stock and diced tomatoes. 4. Close the lid, turn the pressure release valve to SEAL position, and then move the slider to PRESSURE. Select HI and set the cooking time to 15 minutes. Press START/STOP to begin cooking. When finished, release the pressure quickly. 5. Transfer the lamb chops to a cutting board, then remove the bones and dice the meat. 6. Return the meat to the pot. Squeeze out the juice from the lemon half and discard the half. 7. Stir in the tomato paste and adjust the salt and black pepper, if needed. Serve with pita bread and tzatziki drizzled on top, if desired.
Per Serving: Calories 366; Fat: 7.21g; Sodium: 715mg; Carbs: 62.6g; Fibre: 12.9g; Sugar: 10.73g; Protein: 18.09g

Braised Pork Chops with Vegetables

Prep Time: 15 minutes | Cook Time: 30 minutes | Serves: 4

2 tablespoons solid or liquid fat
Choose from butter, lard, schmaltz, duck fat, or goose fat; or vegetable, corn, safflower, olive, avocado, or any nut oil—or choose a 50/50 combo of a solid and a liquid fat.
Four 250 g to 300 g bone-in pork loin chops
½ teaspoon table salt
½ teaspoon ground black pepper
205 g chopped quick-cooking vegetables
Choose at least two from carrots, celery, frozen artichoke heart quarters (do not thaw), leeks (white and pale green parts only, well washed), brown or white button mushrooms, onions (of any sort), shallots, shelled edamame (if frozen, do not thaw), shelled peas (if frozen, do not thaw), stemmed and cored pepper, trimmed spring onions, trimmed fennel, yellow summer squash, and/or courgette.
2 tablespoons minced fresh herbs
Choose one or two from marjoram, parsley, oregano, rosemary, sage, savory, and/or thyme.
Up to 1 teaspoon dried spices (optional)
Choose one or two from decorticated cardamom seeds, grated nutmeg, ground allspice, ground cardamom, ground coriander, ground cinnamon, ground fenugreek, and/or ground mace.
360 ml liquid
Choose a stock of any sort, or a combination of stock and white wine, dry vermouth, or dry sherry—most likely in a ratio of 240 ml stock and 120 ml wine or perhaps in a ratio of 300 ml stock and 60 ml wine for a more savory dish.

1. Move slider to AIR FRY/STOVETOP. Select SEAR/SAUTÉ and set to 3. Select START/STOP to begin preheating. Allow unit to preheat for 2 minutes. 2. After 2 minutes, melt the fat or warm the oil in the pot. Season the pork chops with salt and pepper, then put two in the cooker. Brown well on both sides, turning a couple of times, about 6 minutes. Transfer the chops to a nearby bowl and brown the other two in the same way before transferring them to the bowl. 3. Add the chopped vegetable and cook, stirring frequently, until a little softened, about 3 minutes. Stir in the herbs and spices (if using) until aromatic, just a few seconds. Pour in the liquid and scrape up any browned bits on the pot's bottom. 4. Press START/STOP to turn off the SEAR/SAUTÉ function. Nestle the pork chops into the sauce, overlapping them as necessary. Pour any juice from their bowl on top. 5. Close the lid and move slider to PRESSURE. Make sure the pressure release valve is in the SEAL position. The temperature will default to HIGH, which is the correct setting. Set time to 12 minutes. Select START/STOP to begin cooking. 6. When cooking is complete, turn the pressure relief valve to the VENT position for quick pressure relief. Move slider to the right to unlock the lid, then carefully open it. 7. Transfer the pork chops to serving plates or bowls; ladle the sauce on top.
Per Serving: Calories 199; Fat 10.68g; Sodium 690mg; Carbs 13.24g; Fibre 4.2g; Sugar 3.53g; Protein 12.55g

Bacon Pork Chops

Prep Time: 15 minutes | Cook Time: 25 minutes | Serves: 4

5 strips bacon
4 (2.5-cm thick) bone-in pork chops
240 ml chicken stock
55 g unsalted butter
1 (30g) packet dried ranch seasoning mix
115 g cream cheese, softened
115 g sour cream

1. Select SEAR/SAUTÉ. Select Lo3, and then press START/STOP to begin cooking. 2. When the pot is hot, add bacon and cook until browned and crispy, and then transfer them to paper towels to drain any excess fat. 3. Add the pork chops to the drippings in the pot and brown on both sides. Remove the chops and set aside. 4. Stop the process, and pour the chicken stock into the pot, taking care to scrape up any browned bits from the bottom of the pot. Return the pork chops to the pot and add the butter and ranch seasoning. 5. Close the lid, turn the pressure release valve to SEAL position, and then move the slider to PRESSURE. Select HI and set the cooking time to 20 minutes. Press START/STOP to begin cooking. When finished, release the pressure naturally. 6. Remove the pork chops and place on a serving platter. 7. Add the cream cheese and sour cream to the pot and stir well. Season them and then pour the sauce over the pork chops. 8. Crumble the bacon and sprinkle over the top. Serve.
Per Serving: Calories 818; Fat: 44.52g; Sodium: 1082mg; Carbs: 7.43g; Fibre: 1.5g; Sugar: 2.39g; Protein: 92.84g

Quick Bourbon Barbecue Ribs

Prep Time: 5 minutes | Cook Time: 25 minutes | Serves: 2

1 rack baby back ribs	1 tablespoon liquid smoke
Salt	(optional)
Freshly ground black pepper	60 ml bourbon
15 g barbecue meat rub (optional)	240 g classic barbecue sauce
240 ml water	

1. Remove the membrane from the back of the ribs and cut the rack into four equal pieces. Season generously with salt, pepper, and your favourite barbecue meat rub (if using). 2. Put the ribs in the pot. Add the beef stock and liquid smoke (if using). 3. Close the lid, turn the pressure release valve to SEAL position, and then move the slider to PRESSURE. Select HI and set the cooking time to 25 minutes. Press START/STOP to begin cooking. When finished, release the pressure naturally. 4. Line a baking pan with aluminum foil. 5. Mix the bourbon and barbecue sauce in a small bowl. 6. Transfer the cooked ribs to the prepared baking pan. Brush the bourbon-barbecue sauce all over the ribs, including the bones. 7. Place the baking pan in the pot. Close the lid and move slider to AIR FRY/STOVETOP, then use the dial to select BAKE/ROAST. Adjust the cooking temperature to 220°C and set the cooking time to 12 minutes. Press START/STOP to begin cooking. 8. Flip the food halfway through. 9. Brush the remaining sauce on the ribs before serving.
Per Serving: Calories 1143; Fat: 62.65g; Sodium: 1780mg; Carbs: 63.3g; Fibre: 3.2g; Sugar: 47.53g; Protein: 82.33g

Lamb Stew with Wheat Berries & Pecans

Prep Time: 20 minutes | Cook Time: 60 minutes | Serves: 6

70 g dried wheat berries, preferably soft white wheat berries	1 large yellow onion, chopped
	600 ml chicken stock
55 g butter	60 g chopped pecans
1.3 kg boneless lamb shoulder, any chunks of fat removed, the meat cut into 5 cm pieces	2 teaspoons dried sage
	½ teaspoon red pepper flakes
	½ teaspoon table salt

1. Soak the wheat berries in a big bowl of water for at least 8 hours or up to 12 hours. Drain in a fine-mesh sieve or a small-holed colander set in the sink. 2. Select SEAR/SAUTÉ. Select Lo3, and then press START/STOP to begin cooking. 3. When the pot is hot, melt 2 tablespoons butter; add about half the lamb pieces and brown them for 8 minutes, turning and rearranging occasionally. Transfer these to a nearby bowl, add the remaining 2 tablespoons butter, and brown the remainder of the lamb in the same way before transferring the pieces to the bowl. 4. Add the onion to the pot and cook for 4 minutes until softened; pour in the stock and scrape up any browned bits on the pot's bottom. 5. Stop the process, and stir in the soaked wheat berries, as well as the pecans, sage, red pepper flakes, and salt. Return the lamb pieces and any of the juices in their bowl to the pot. 6. Close the lid, turn the pressure release valve to SEAL position, and then move the slider to PRESSURE. Select HI and set the cooking time to 40 minutes. Press START/STOP to begin cooking. When finished, release the pressure naturally. 7. Stir the dish well before serving.
Per Serving: Calories 622; Fat: 35.42g; Sodium: 792mg; Carbs: 14.1g; Fibre: 3g; Sugar: 1.22g; Protein: 62.36g

South African Lamb Curry

Prep Time: 20 minutes | Cook Time: 60 minutes | Serves: 6

2 tablespoons vegetable, corn, or rapeseed oil	turmeric
	1 teaspoon ground cinnamon
3 medium leeks (about 110 g each), white and pale green parts only, halved lengthwise, well washed, and thinly sliced	Up to ½ teaspoon ground dried cayenne
	½ teaspoon table salt
	1.3 kg boneless leg of lamb, any large chunks of fat removed, the meat cut into 4 cm pieces
1 tablespoon minced peeled fresh ginger	240 ml chicken stock
1½ teaspoons ground coriander	120 ml buttermilk
1½ teaspoons mild paprika	2 tablespoons orange marmalade
1½ teaspoons ground dried	

1. Select SEAR/SAUTÉ. Select Lo3, and then press START/STOP to begin cooking. 2. When the pot is hot, heat the oil for 1 to 2 minutes; add leeks and ginger, and cook them for 3 minutes; stir in the coriander, paprika, turmeric, cinnamon, cayenne, and salt, and cook them for a few seconds until fragrant. 3. Add the lamb and toss until the meat is thoroughly coated in the spices and aromatics. Pour in the stock and stir them well, and then stop the process. 4. Close the lid, turn the pressure release valve to SEAL position, and then move the slider to PRESSURE. Select HI and set the cooking time to 45 minutes. Press START/STOP to begin cooking. When finished, release the pressure naturally. 5. Select SEAR/SAUTÉ and adjust the cooking temperature to Lo3, then stir in the buttermilk and marmalade, and bring to a simmer; cook them for 2 minutes until a little thickened and reduced. 6. Stop the process and set the lid askew over the pot for 5 minutes to blend the flavours. 7. Stir the dish again before serving.
Per Serving: Calories 459; Fat: 20.52g; Sodium: 589mg; Carbs: 9.53g; Fibre: 1.4g; Sugar: 3.26g; Protein: 56.66g

Beef Pot with Potatoes

Prep Time: 20 minutes | Cook Time: 60 minutes | Serves: 2

1 tablespoon oil	2 large carrots, peeled and chopped
675 g lean beef shoulder roast, trimmed	
	300 g fingerling potatoes
Salt	480 ml beef stock
Freshly ground black pepper	1 tablespoon Worcestershire sauce
1 medium onion, chopped	1 tablespoon cornflour
3 garlic cloves, crushed	Fresh thyme, for garnish

1. Season the roast with salt and pepper. 2. Select SEAR/SAUTÉ. Select Lo3, and then press START/STOP to begin cooking. 3. When the pot is hot, heat the oil, and then sear the roast for 3 to 4 minutes on each side. 4. Stop the process, arrange the onion, garlic, carrots, and potatoes around the roast, and then pour in the stock and add the Worcestershire sauce. 5. Close the lid, turn the pressure release valve to SEAL position, and then move the slider to PRESSURE. Select HI and set the cooking time to 60 minutes. Press START/STOP to begin cooking. When finished, release the pressure naturally. 6. Transfer the roast and vegetables to a serving platter. Let rest while you make the gravy. 7. Strain the beef stock into a bowl, discarding the fat solids. 8. Return all but 2 tablespoons of the stock to the pot and select SEAR/SAUTÉ. Whisk the cornflour into the reserved stock in the bowl, then stir the slurry into the pot and bring to a simmer at Lo2 for 5 minutes until thickened, stirring often. 9. Taste and season with more salt, pepper, or Worcestershire sauce if desired. Pour the gravy into a gravy boat. 10. Serve the pot roast and veggies with the gravy and garnish with fresh thyme.
Per Serving: Calories 846; Fat: 27.5g; Sodium: 1426mg; Carbs: 48.64g; Fibre: 6.8g; Sugar: 7.97g; Protein: 96.64g

Spicy Pork Chops with Potatoes

Prep Time: 15 minutes | Cook Time: 10 minutes | Serves: 4

215 g jarred salsa verde	preferably Yukon Gold, quartered
80 ml chicken stock	55 g butter, melted
Four 4 cm-thick, boneless, centre-cut pork loin chops	½ teaspoon mild paprika
	½ teaspoon ground black pepper
Four 150 g yellow potatoes,	

1. Mix the salsa verde and stock in the pot. Nestle the pork chops into the mixture, overlapping them to fit. Make a layer with the potato wedges skin side down on top, then pour the melted butter over them. Sprinkle the potatoes with the paprika and pepper. 2. Close the lid and move slider to PRESSURE. Make sure the pressure release valve is in the SEAL position. The temperature will default to HIGH, which is the correct setting. Set time to 10 minutes. Select START/STOP to begin cooking. 3. When cooking is complete, naturally release the pressure for 5 minutes. Then turn the pressure relief valve to the VENT position for quick pressure relief. Move slider to AIR FRY/STOVETOP to unlock the lid, then carefully open it. 4. Serve the potatoes and pork chops with the sauce ladled around them.
Per Serving: Calories 309; Fat 18.01g; Sodium 798mg; Carbs 15.86g; Fibre 2.3g; Sugar 3.04g; Protein 21.29g

Peppery Beef

Prep Time: 10 minutes | Cook Time: 14 minutes | Serves: 4

675g Tomahawk steaks
2 peppers, sliced
2 tablespoons butter, melted

2 teaspoons steak seasoning
2 tablespoons fish sauce
Sea salt and black pepper, to taste

1. Place the Cook & Crisp Basket in your Pressure Cooker Steam Fryer. 2. Toss all the recipe ingredients in the Cook & Crisp Basket. 3. Put on the Smart Lid on top of the Ninja Foodi Steam Fryer. 4. Move the Lid Slider to the "Air Fry/Stovetop". Select the "Air Fry" mode for cooking. 5. Cook the steak and peppers at 200°C for about 14 minutes, turning it over halfway through the cooking time. 6. Serve.
Per serving: Calories: 299; Fat:15.6g; Carbs: 4.3g; Fibre: 0.7g; Sugars: 2.2g; Proteins: 33.1g

Chipotle & Cheese Meat Loaf

Prep Time: 15 minutes | Cook Time: 36 minutes | Serves: 6

2 tbsp (30 ml) extra-virgin olive oil
1 carrot, diced
1 celery rib, diced
½ medium onion, diced
2 cloves garlic, minced
905 g beef mince
2 large eggs
30 g panko bread crumbs
1 chipotle pepper, chopped, plus 2 tbsp
30 ml adobo sauce, from a can of

chipotle peppers
1 tsp salt
½ tsp freshly ground black pepper
110 g chopped smoked Gouda cheese
237 ml water
Glaze:
180 g ketchup
75 g light brown sugar
2 tbsp (30 ml) adobo sauce, from a can of chipotle peppers

1. Move slider to AIR FRY/STOVETOP. Select SEAR/SAUTÉ and set to 3. Select START/STOP to begin preheating. Allow unit to preheat for 2 minutes. After 2 minutes, heat the olive oil in the pot. Then add the carrot, celery and onion. Cook, stirring occasionally, until the onion starts to soften, about 5 minutes. Add the garlic and cook for about 1 more minute, stirring often. Press START/STOP to turn off the SEAR/SAUTÉ function. 2. Transfer the veggie mixture to a large bowl. Add the beef mince, eggs, bread crumbs, chipotle pepper, salt, black pepper, adobo sauce, and cheese. Using your hands, mix until everything is just incorporated. Gently form the mixture into a meat loaf shape. 3. Pour the water into the pot, then place the bottom layer of the Deluxe Reversible Rack in the lower position in the pot. Fold two large pieces of foil in half lengthwise, then overlap them in the middle to make a plus sign (+). 4. Place the meat loaf in the centre of the overlapped foil. Using the foil as handles, place the meat loaf on the rack, leaving the foil in place and folding it over as needed so as not to obstruct placement of the lid. 5. Prepare the glaze: In a small bowl, whisk together the ketchup, brown sugar and adobo sauce, then brush over the top and sides of the meat loaf. 6. Close the lid and move slider to PRESSURE. Make sure the pressure release valve is in the SEAL position. The temperature will default to HIGH, which is the correct setting. Set time to 30 minutes. Select START/STOP to begin cooking. 7. When the timer beeps, quick release the pressure and carefully open the lid. Allow the meat loaf to rest for about 5 minutes, then remove it from the pot, using the foil handles.
Per Serving: Calories 503; Fat 27.44g; Sodium 1022mg; Carbs 14.62g; Fibre 1.1g; Sugar 8.64g; Protein 47.88g

Smoky Pork Chops with Bacon & Carrots

Prep Time: 15 minutes | Cook Time: 21 minutes | Serves: 4

2 teaspoons mild smoked paprika
1 teaspoon ground black pepper
½ teaspoon table salt
Four 3.5 cm-thick, centre-cut, boneless pork loin chops
2 tablespoons olive oil
100 g slab bacon, chopped
1 small red onion, chopped
2 medium garlic cloves, peeled and minced (2 teaspoons)
1 canned chipotle chile in adobo

sauce, stemmed, seeded (if desired), and chopped
1 tablespoon adobo sauce from the can
1 teaspoon dried oregano
120 ml chicken stock
180 ml porter, preferably a smoky porter
12 baby carrots or 2 medium carrots, cut into 1.5 cm sections

1. Mix the smoked paprika, pepper, and salt in a small bowl. Pat the pork chops dry with paper towels, then pat and rub this spice mixture onto both sides of the meat. Set aside. 2. Move slider to AIR FRY/STOVETOP. Select SEAR/SAUTÉ and set to 3. Select START/STOP to begin preheating. Allow unit to preheat for 2 minutes. After 2 minutes, heat oil in the pot. 3. Set two pork chops in the cooker and brown lightly on both sides, turning a couple of times, about 4 minutes. Transfer them to a nearby bowl and brown the other two pork chops in the same way before transferring them to the bowl. 4. Add the slab bacon and onion. Cook, stirring frequently, until the bacon browns a bit and the onion softens, about 4 minutes. Stir in the chipotle, garlic, adobo sauce, and oregano until aromatic, about 30 seconds. Pour in the stock and scrape up any browned bits on the pot's bottom. 5. Press START/STOP to turn off the SEAR/SAUTÉ function. Stir in the porter, then nestle the pork chops into the sauce, overlapping them as necessary. Pour any juice from their bowl on top, scatter the carrots around the cooker, and close the lid. 6. Close the lid and move slider to PRESSURE. Make sure the pressure release valve is in the SEAL position. The temperature will default to HIGH, which is the correct setting. Set time to 10 minutes. Select START/STOP to begin cooking. 7. When cooking is complete, naturally release the pressure for 5 minutes. Then turn the pressure relief valve to the VENT position for quick pressure relief. Move slider to AIR FRY/STOVETOP to unlock the lid, then carefully open it. 8. Use kitchen tongs to transfer the chops to serving plates; spoon the carrots, onions, bacon, and sauce around them.
Per Serving: Calories 383; Fat 24.68g; Sodium 1032mg; Carbs 12.25g; Fibre 3g; Sugar 5.43g; Protein 29.6g

Beef and Carrot Stew with Bacon

Prep time: 10 minutes | Cook time: 40 minutes | Serves: 6

5 strips bacon, roughly chopped
1.3 kg beef chuck, fat trimmed, cut into 5 cm chunks
Salt and freshly ground black pepper
1 large yellow onion, chopped
120 ml Pinot Noir
3 large carrots, peeled and cut

into 1 cm-thick coins
180 ml store-bought beef stock, or homemade
30 g flour
Optional Add-ins:
5 (8 cm) sprigs fresh thyme, or 1 (8 cm) sprig rosemary
2 tablespoons tomato paste

1. Place the bacon in the pot, move slider to AIR FRY/STOVETOP. Select SEAR/SAUTÉ and set to 3. Select START/STOP to begin cooking, stirring frequently, until the bacon is browned and crisp, 3 to 4 minutes. Press START/STOP. 2. Transfer the bacon to a paper towel–lined plate. Spoon off all but 1½ tablespoons of the drippings in the pot and discard. 3. Season the beef with ¾ teaspoon salt and several grinds of pepper. 4. Select SEAR/SAUTÉ function and set to Hi 5. Add one handful of the meat (6 or 7 pieces) to the pot. Do not overcrowd; there should be space between the pieces of meat so they will brown. Press START/STOP to begin cooking. 5. Cook without stirring until well browned on one side, 3 minutes. Stir and cook for a few minutes more. 6. Add the onion and cook, stirring frequently, until the onion is becoming tender, 3 minutes. 7. Add the wine and simmer for 2 minutes, scraping up the browned bits on the bottom of the pot. Press START/STOP to stop cooking. 8. Add the remaining beef, carrots, bacon, 120 ml of the stock, and the optional add-ins (if using). 9. Close the lid, move slider to PRESSURE, Ensuring the pressure release valve is in the SEAL position. The temperature will default to HIGH, which is the correct setting. Set time to 25 minutes. Select START/STOP to begin cooking. 10. When the cooking time is up, let the pressure come down naturally for 10 minutes and then quick-release the remaining pressure. 11. Discard the herb sprigs, if you used them. 12. Place the flour in a small bowl and gradually whisk in the remaining 60 ml stock. Add the flour mixture to the pot, cook on SEAR/SAUTÉ function and set to 3, and simmer, gently stirring occasionally, until thickened and bubbly, 2 minutes. 13. Season with salt and pepper and serve.
Per Serving: Calories 399; Fat 15.94g; Sodium 423mg; Carbs 12.89g; Fibre 1.8g; Sugar 3.01g; Protein 48.42g

Homemade Beef & Beets Borscht

Prep time: 15 minutes | Cook time: 20 minutes | Serves: 4

1 large bunch red beets with greens	1 yellow onion, chopped
600 g beef chuck roast, trimmed and cut into 1 cm chunks	1 teaspoon caraway seeds
	1 teaspoon dried dill
1 tablespoon extra-virgin olive oil	1 tablespoon balsamic or red wine vinegar
Salt and freshly ground black pepper	Optional Garnish:
600 ml store-bought beef stock, or homemade	180 g sour cream or plain Greek yogurt

1. Wash the beets and the greens well. Peel the beets and cut them into 1 cm pieces; set aside. Finely chop the stems and greens (keep them separate); set aside. 2. Toss half the beef with the oil and season generously with salt and pepper. 3. Move slider to AIR FRY/STOVETOP. Select SEAR/SAUTÉ and set to Hi 5. Select START/STOP to begin preheating. When the pot is hot, add the seasoned beef and cook, stirring occasionally, until well browned, 4 minutes. Press START/STOP. 4. Add the remaining (unbrowned) beef, the stock, onions, beets, beet stems, caraway, and dill to the pot. (You'll add the beet greens at the end of cooking.) 5. Close the lid and move slider to PRESSURE. Ensuring the pressure release valve is in the SEAL position. The temperature will default to HIGH, which is the correct setting. Set time to 15 minutes. Select START/STOP to begin cooking. 6. When cooking is complete, naturally release the pressure for 10 minutes. Then release the pressure quickly by turning the pressure release valve to the VENT position. Move slider to AIR FRY/ STOVETOP to unlock the lid, then carefully open it. 7. Add the vinegar and beet greens to the pot. Cook on SEAR/SAUTÉ function and set to Hi 5. Cook until the soup is simmering and the greens are tender, 1 minute. Press START/STOP. 8. Season with salt and pepper. Garnish with the sour cream, if desired.

Per Serving: Calories 479; Fat 22.3g; Sodium 668mg; Carbs 27.39g; Fibre 2.3g; Sugar 7.9g; Protein 42.3g

Beef Sandwiches with Cheese Sauce

Prep time: 10 minutes | Cook time: 50 minutes | Serves: 4

2 tsp olive oil	30 g plain flour
1 (900 g) chuck roast	480 ml whole milk
Coarse salt	100 g shredded smoked Gouda cheese
Freshly ground black pepper	
1 medium onion, sliced	1 loaf crusty bread, sliced and toasted
240 ml beef stock	

1. Move slider to AIR FRY/STOVETOP. Select SEAR/SAUTÉ and set to 3. Select START/STOP to begin preheating. 2. When the pot is hot, add the oil to the pot. Season your chuck roast well with salt and pepper, then add the roast to the pot and brown it well on all sides. Remove the roast and set aside. 3. Add the onion to the drippings in the pot and scrape up any browned bits on the bottom of the pot. Sauté the onion until it is soft and starting to caramelize, about 10 minutes. Press START/STOP to turn off the SEAR/SAUTÉ function. 4. Add the beef stock, taking care to scrape up any browned bits from the base of the pot. Place the roast directly into the liquid. 5. Close the lid and move slider to PRESSURE. Ensuring the pressure release valve is in the SEAL position. The temperature will default to HIGH, which is the correct setting. Set time to 40 minutes. Select START/STOP to begin cooking. 6. In the meantime, in a small saucepan, whisk together the flour and milk to make a sauce. 7. Cook over medium heat until it starts to thicken, about 3 to 4 minutes. Add the shredded cheese, 1 small handful at a time, gently stirring to incorporate before adding more. Season well with salt and pepper. 8. When the cooking is complete, quick release the pressure and carefully remove the lid. Using two forks to shred the meat with and stir the meat into the liquid in the pot. 9. Divide the meat mixture among the toasted slices of bread. Drizzle with the cheese sauce and serve.

Per Serving: Calories 548; Fat 22.52g; Sodium 1119mg; Carbs 28.29g; Fibre 0.5g; Sugar 17.79g; Protein 55.58g

Beef Lettuce Wraps

Prep time: 10 minutes | Cook time: 20 minutes | Serves: 4

2 tbsp olive or avocado oil	2 tsp sesame oil
900 g top sirloin steak or stew meat	1 tsp ground ginger
	2 tbsp cornflour
120 ml soy sauce, gluten-free tamari or coconut aminos	2 tbsp water
	1 head romaine lettuce
60 ml beef stock	120 g matchstick-sliced carrot
2 tbsp rice vinegar	40 g diced green onion
3 tbsp coconut sugar	10 g chopped fresh coriander (optional)
2 tbsp sriracha or chili garlic sauce	

1. Move slider to AIR FRY/STOVETOP. Select SEAR/SAUTÉ and set to Lo1. Select START/STOP to begin preheating. Heat the oil on the pot and add the meat and brown on all sides. This should take 3 to 4 minutes. Select START/STOP. 2. Combine the soy sauce, coconut sugar, sriracha, beef stock, vinegar, sesame oil and ginger in a medium bowl. Pour the soy sauce mixture over the beef. 3. Close the lid and move slider to PRESSURE. Ensuring the pressure release valve is in the SEAL position. The temperature will default to HIGH, which is the correct setting. Set time to 10 minutes. Select START/STOP to begin cooking. 4. When cooking is complete, naturally release the pressure for 15 minutes. Then release the pressure quickly by turning the pressure release valve to the VENT position. Move slider to AIR FRY/ STOVETOP to unlock the lid, then carefully open it. 5. In a small bowl, stir together the arrowroot starch and water and pour into the pot. Cook on SEAR/SAUTÉ function and set to 3, Select START/STOP to begin cooking. Let the liquid come to a quick boil, then select START/STOP to end the cooking and let the sauce thicken. 6. Assemble the lettuce wraps by adding the beef, carrot, green onion and coriander (if using).

Per Serving: Calories 682; Fat 41.32g; Sodium 671mg; Carbs 24.12g; Fibre 4.3g; Sugar 14.39g; Protein 51.75g

Tofu Pork Soup with Cabbage

Prep time: 20 minutes | Cook time: 35 minutes/6 hours | Serves: 4

190g white miso	Salt and ground white pepper
6 medium garlic cloves, smashed and peeled	½ medium head napa cabbage (455g–675g) halved lengthwise and cut crosswise into 2.5 cm pieces
8cm piece fresh ginger (about 50g), peeled and thinly sliced	
2 tablespoons grapeseed or other neutral oil	350g container firm tofu, drained and cut into 2.5cm cubes
160ml sake	3 tablespoons soy sauce
455g boneless pork shoulder, trimmed and cut across the grain into 1 cm slabs	4 spring onions, thinly sliced on the diagonal
	Toasted sesame oil, to serve

1. Add the miso, garlic, ginger and oil to the cooking pot, and sauté them at MD on SEAR/SAUTÉ mode for 3 to 4 minutes until the miso sticks to the bottom of the pot and browns evenly. 2. Stop the process, and add the sake and 960ml of water to the cooking pot, scraping up the browned bits; add the pork and 1 teaspoon white pepper; stir, then distribute in an even layer. 3. Install the pressure lid and turn the pressure release valve to the SEAL position. 4. Select PRESSURE COOK, set the cooking temperature to HI and adjust the cooking time to 27 minutes. 5. When cooked, let the unit naturally release pressure. 6. If you want to cook them slowly, cook them at HI on SLOW COOK mode for 5 to 6 hours. 7. Skim off and discard the fat from the surface. 8. Select SEAR/SAUTÉ again and bring to a simmer at LO. 9. Add the cabbage and tofu, then cook for 2 to 4 minutes until the leaves are wilted and the stems are crisp-tender, stirring constantly. 10. Stop the process, and stir in the soy sauce, then taste and season with salt and pepper. 11. Serve sprinkled with the spring onions and drizzled with sesame oil.

Per Serving: Calories 481; Fat 23.1g; Sodium 2771mg; Carbs 26.49g; Fibre 4.6g; Sugar 10.22g; Protein 36.02g

Pulled Pork and Pineapple Sandwiches

Prep time: 10 minutes | Cook time: 55 minutes | Serves: 8

2 tbsp olive oil	2 tsp dried thyme
1 tsp ground cinnamon	½ tsp cayenne pepper
2 tsp allspice	1 (1.6 kg) pork shoulder
1 tsp coarse salt	240 ml water or chicken stock
1 tsp freshly ground black pepper	Crusty rolls
¼ tsp freshly ground nutmeg	Sliced pineapple

1. Combine the olive oil, cinnamon, salt, black pepper, allspice, nutmeg, thyme and cayenne in a small bowl. Rub the mixture all over the pork roast. 2. Move slider to AIR FRY/STOVETOP. Select SEAR/SAUTÉ and set to 3. Select START/STOP to begin preheating. 3. Add the roast to the preheated pot and brown it well on all sides, adding a little oil to the pot, if necessary. 4. Remove the roast and set aside. Add the water or stock to the pot, taking care to scrape up any browned bits from the bottom of the pot. Return the roast to the pot. Press START/STOP to turn off the SEAR/SAUTÉ function. 5. Close the lid and move slider to PRESSURE. Ensuring the pressure release valve is in the SEAL position. The temperature will default to HIGH, which is the correct setting. Set time to 50 minutes. Select START/STOP to begin cooking. 6. When the time is up, quick release the pressure and carefully remove the lid. Shred the meat with two forks and stir in with the liquid in the pot. 7. Divide the meat mixture among the rolls and top each with a slice of pineapple.

Per Serving: Calories 704; Fat 45.87g; Sodium 573mg; Carbs 4.6g; Fibre 0.5g; Sugar 1.2g; Protein 63.96g

Corn Pork Stew

Prep time: 30 minutes | Cook time: 35 minutes/5 hours | Serves: 4-6

2 ears fresh corn, husks and silk removed	900g boneless pork shoulder, trimmed and cut into 2.5cm chunks
3 tablespoons extra-virgin olive oil	200g peeled and seeded butternut squash, cut into 2.5cm chunks
2 medium yellow onions, halved and thinly sliced	150g grape or cherry tomatoes, halved
4 medium garlic cloves, finely chopped	Salt
1 tablespoon sweet paprika	10g lightly packed fresh coriander, chopped
1 tablespoon cumin seeds	Lemon wedges, to serve
¼ teaspoon cayenne pepper	

1. One at a time, stand each ear of corn in a bowl and use a chef's knife to cut off the kernels. 2. Use the back of the knife to scrape from top to bottom all around each cob, allowing the liquid to fall into the bowl. 3. Add the kernels to the bowl, then cut each cob in half and reserve separately. 4. Heat the oil in the cooking pot at MD on SEAR/SAUTÉ mode until simmering; add the onions and sauté them for 5 to 7 minutes until just browned; stir in the garlic, paprika, cumin and cayenne and sauté them for 30 seconds until fragrant; stir in the pork, squash, corn kernels and liquid, tomatoes, 480ml water and 1 teaspoon salt, then distribute in an even layer. 5. Stop the process, and add the corn cobs to the pot. 6. Install the pressure lid and turn the pressure release valve to the SEAL position. 7. Select PRESSURE COOK, set the cooking temperature to HI and adjust the cooking time to 25 minutes. 8. When cooked, let the unit naturally release pressure. 9. If you want to cook them slowly, cook them at HI on SLOW COOK mode for 4 to 5 hours. 10. Remove and discard the corn cobs. Skim off and discard the fat from the surface. Taste and season the dish with salt and pepper. 11. Serve sprinkled with the coriander and with lemon wedges on the side.

Per Serving: Calories 291; Fat 9.23g; Sodium 180mg; Carbs 16.12g; Fibre 2.5g; Sugar 2.45g; Protein 36.54g

Delicious Dan Dan Noodles

Prep time: 50 minutes | Cook time: 40 minutes | Serves: 4

250g dried Asian wheat noodles, cooked, drained and rinsed	4 baby bok choy, roughly chopped
2 tablespoons plus 2 teaspoons toasted sesame oil	Salt
	2 tablespoons unseasoned rice vinegar
35g sesame seeds	60ml oyster sauce
4 medium shallots, halved and thinly sliced	3 tablespoons hoisin sauce
300g pork mince	1 tablespoon chili-garlic sauce, plus more as needed
4 medium garlic cloves, finely chopped	1 tablespoon finely grated fresh ginger
180ml low-sodium beef stock or water	Chili oil, to serve (optional)

1. Drizzle the rinsed noodles with the 2 teaspoons of sesame oil, then toss until evenly coated; transfer to a serving bowl and set aside. 2. In a medium bowl, combine the bok choy and 1 teaspoon salt. 3. Massage the salt into the bok choy, then stir in the vinegar; set aside. 4. Cook the sesame seeds in the cooking pot at HI on SEAR/SAUTÉ mode for 5 minutes until golden brown and fragrant. 5. Pause the process, and pour the seeds into a small bowl. 6. Still in the cooking pot, add the 2 tablespoons oil and shallots, and sauté them for 3 to 5 minutes until the shallots are golden brown; add the pork and sauté for 3 to 5 minutes; stir in the garlic and sauté for 30 seconds until fragrant. 7. Stop the process, and stir in the stock, oyster sauce, hoisin, 1 tablespoon of chili-garlic sauce and the sesame seeds, scraping the bottom of the pot; distribute the mixture in an even layer. 8. Install the pressure lid and turn the pressure release valve to the SEAL position. Select PRESSURE COOK, set the cooking temperature to HI and adjust the cooking time to 12 minutes. 9. When cooked, let the unit naturally release pressure. 10. Skim off and discard the fat from the surface. 11. Select SEAR/SAUTÉ again, and bring the mixture to a boil at HI; cook them for 5 minutes until the mixture begins to boil. Stir in the ginger and cook for 30 seconds until fragrant. 12. Carefully remove the insert from the housing. 13. Add the bok choy mixture and stir to combine. Let stand for 5 minutes. Taste and season with additional chili-garlic sauce, if desired. 14. Pour the sauce onto the noodles and drizzle with chili oil, if using.

Per Serving: Calories 474; Fat 27.32g; Sodium 1165mg; Carbs 28.42g; Fibre 4.7g; Sugar 6.79g; Protein 29.26g

Pork Ragu with Green Olives

Prep time: 30 minutes | Cook time: 40 minutes/6 hours | Serves: 4-6

2 tablespoons extra-virgin olive oil	¼ teaspoon ground allspice
200g cremini mushrooms, trimmed and roughly chopped	350g can crushed tomatoes
3 bay leaves	3 medium carrots, halved and cut into 1cm pieces
Salt and ground black pepper	2 medium celery stalks, sliced 1cm thick
180ml dry red wine	90g chopped pitted green olives
4 medium garlic cloves, smashed and peeled	900g boneless pork shoulder, trimmed and cut into 2.5cm chunks
1 teaspoon ground cinnamon	

1. Heat the oil in the cooking pot at HI on SEAR/SAUTÉ mode until simmering; add the mushrooms, bay and 1 teaspoon salt, and sauté them for 7 minutes until the liquid released by the mushrooms has evaporated; stir in the wine, garlic, cinnamon and allspice, scraping up any browned bits, and bring the mixture to a simmer, and then cook for 5 to 7 minutes until the wine has reduced to a syrup. 2. Stop the process, and stir in the tomatoes, carrots, celery, half of the olives and ½ teaspoon pepper. 3. Add the pork and stir to combine, then distribute in an even layer. 4. Install the pressure lid and turn the pressure release valve to the SEAL position. 5. Select PRESSURE COOK, set the cooking temperature to HI and adjust the cooking time to 25 minutes. 6. When cooked, let the unit naturally release pressure. 7. If you want to cook them slowly, cook them at HI on SLOW COOK mode for 5 to 6 hours. 8. Remove and discard the bay. Skim off and discard the fat from the surface. Stir in the remaining olives, slightly breaking up the meat and carrots to lightly thicken the sauce. Taste and season the dish with salt and pepper.

Per Serving: Calories 360; Fat 7.87g; Sodium 238mg; Carbs 36.05g; Fibre 7.1g; Sugar 4.52g; Protein 38.92g

Portuguese Pork

Prep time: 30 minutes | Cook time: 40 minutes/6 hours |
Serves: 6

900g boneless pork shoulder, trimmed and cut into 4cm chunks
150g roasted red peppers, patted dry and thinly sliced
120ml dry white wine
6 medium garlic cloves, finely chopped
4 teaspoons sweet paprika
3 bay leaves

2 tablespoons extra-virgin olive oil, plus more to serve
Salt and ground black pepper
900g hard-shell clams (about 4 cm diameter), such as littleneck, scrubbed
60g lightly packed fresh coriander, roughly chopped
Lemon wedges, to serve

1. Add the pork, roasted peppers, wine, garlic, paprika, bay, and oil, 1 teaspoon each salt and pepper, and 60ml water to the cooking pot. Stir them well and then distribute in an even layer. 2. Install the pressure lid and turn the pressure release valve to the SEAL position. 3. Select PRESSURE COOK, set the cooking temperature to HI and adjust the cooking time to 25 minutes. 4. When cooked, let the unit naturally release pressure. 5. If you want to cook them slowly, cook them at HI on SLOW COOK mode for 5 to 6 hours; the pork is done when a skewer inserted into a chunk meets no resistance. 6. Select SEAR/SAUTÉ again and bring the pork mixture to a simmer at HI; add the clams and stir, breaking the pork into slightly smaller pieces; cook them for 2 to 5 minutes until the clams just begin to open. 7. Stop the process, and re-cover without locking the lid in place and let stand for 5 to 7 minutes until the clams are fully opened. 8. Remove and discard any that do not open. Stir in the coriander, then taste and season with salt and pepper. Serve drizzled with additional oil and with lemon wedges on the side.
Per Serving: Calories 361; Fat 8.21g; Sodium 283mg; Carbs 35.14g; Fibre 2.6g; Sugar 27.43g; Protein 38.43g

Delectable Filipino Pork Adobo

Prep time: 25 minutes | Cook time: 45 minutes/5 hours |
Serves: 4-6

2 tablespoons grapeseed or other neutral oil
2 bunches spring onions, white and light green parts cut into 2.5 cm pieces, green parts thinly sliced, reserved separately
8 medium garlic cloves, smashed and peeled
3 bay leaves

120ml low-sodium soy sauce
60ml white vinegar
2 tablespoons honey
2 Serrano chilies, stemmed and halved
Ground black pepper
1.3kg boneless pork shoulder, trimmed and cut into 5cm chunks
1 tablespoon cornflour

1. Heat the oil in the cooking pot at HI on SEAR/SAUTÉ mode until simmering; add the scallion whites, garlic and bay, then cook for 4 minutes without stirring until golden brown on the bottom; Stir and continue to cook for 2 minutes until deeply browned, stirring only once or twice. 2. Stop the process, and stir in the soy, vinegar, honey, Serrano chilies and 1 teaspoon of pepper, scraping up any browned bits. 3. Add the pork; stir to combine, then distribute in an even layer. 4. Install the pressure lid and turn the pressure release valve to the SEAL position. 5. Select PRESSURE COOK, set the cooking temperature to HI and adjust the cooking time to 30 minutes. 6. When cooked, let the unit naturally release pressure. 7. If you want to cook them slowly, cook them at HI on SLOW COOK mode for 4 to 5 hours; the pork is done when a skewer inserted into a piece meets no resistance. 8. Skim off and discard the fat from the surface. Remove and discard the chilies and bay. 9. In a small bowl, whisk the cornflour with 3 tablespoons of the cooking liquid, then stir into the pot. 10. Select SEAR/SAUTÉ again and bring to a simmer at MD, stirring constantly, and cook for 1 minute until lightly thickened. 11. Taste and season the dish with salt and pepper. 12. Serve sprinkled generously with the scallion greens.
Per Serving: Calories 379; Fat 12.38g; Sodium 890mg; Carbs 10.56g; Fibre 0.6g; Sugar 6.13g; Protein 53.51g

Agrodolce Pork Loin with Grapes

Prep time: 35 minutes | Cook time: 55 minutes | Serves: 4-6

900g–1.1kg boneless pork loin
Salt and ground black pepper
1 teaspoon grapeseed or other neutral oil
3 medium shallots, chopped
2 tablespoons honey
240ml balsamic vinegar

3 tablespoons salted butter, cut into 1cm pieces
30g lightly packed fresh flat-leaf parsley, chopped
75g seedless red grapes, halved
40g hazelnuts, toasted and finely chopped

1. Season the pork on all sides with salt and pepper. 2. Heat the oil in the cooking pot at HI on SEAR/SAUTÉ mode until simmering; add the pork fat side down and cook for 10 minutes until golden brown; transfer the pork to a plate. 3. Add shallots to the pot and sauté for 4 minutes until browned and slightly softened; add the honey and sauté for 1 to 2 minutes until slightly darker. 4. Stir in the vinegar, bring to a simmer and cook for 2 minutes until slightly reduced, stirring occasionally. 5. Add any accumulated juices to the cooking pot, place the reversible rack in the pot in the lower position and drop the lower rack through the reversible rack handles. 6. Arrange the pork onto the rack with fat-side up. Install the pressure lid and turn the pressure release valve to the SEAL position. 7. Select PRESSURE COOK, set the cooking temperature to LO and adjust the cooking time to 25 minutes. 8. When cooked, let the unit naturally release pressure. 9. The centre of the pork loin should register 135°F. 10. Carefully grab the handles of the rack and lift it out with the pork loin. Set on a large plate or cutting board. 11. Select SEAR/SAUTÉ again, and bring the liquid to a simmer at HI; whisk in the butter one piece at a time until fully incorporated. 12. After all the butter has been added, cook for 10 to 12 minutes until the sauce is glossy and a spoon drawn through it leaves a trail. 13. In a small bowl, stir together the parsley, grapes, hazelnuts and ¼ teaspoon each salt and pepper; set aside. 14. When the sauce is done, stop the process. Taste and season the dish with salt and pepper. 15. Transfer the pork from the rack directly to the cutting board. 16. Thinly slice the pork and transfer to a platter, then spoon the sauce on and around the meat. 17. Serve with the parsley-grape mixture.
Per Serving: Calories 264; Fat 12.27g; Sodium 85mg; Carbs 18.71g; Fibre 1.5g; Sugar 15.24g; Protein 18.97g

Cheese Meatballs with Spaghetti

Prep Time: 15 minutes | Cook Time: 15 minutes | Serves: 2

115 g beef mince
115 g pork mince
2 slices white bread
25 g grated Parmesan cheese
1 large egg
1 garlic clove, minced
½ teaspoon dried oregano
½ tablespoon dried parsley

Pinch salt
Pinch freshly ground black pepper
Oil, for shaping the meatballs
720 g easy marinara sauce, divided
150 g spaghetti
240 ml beef stock

1. In a medium bowl, put the minced beef and pork. Dampen the bread with water, gently squeeze the excess water out, then crumble over the meat. Whisk in the egg, cheese, garlic, parsley, oregano, salt, and pepper. Coat your hands with a bit of the oil, mix the meat together well by hand, and roll into tablespoon-size balls, setting them aside on a plate as you work. Refrigerate for 20 minutes. 2. Add half of the marinara sauce to the pot. Place the meatballs on top in an even layer. Cover the meatballs with another thin layer of sauce. Break the spaghetti in half and lay on top of the meatballs. Pour the remaining sauce on top, then add the beef stock. 3. Close the lid and move slider to PRESSURE. Make sure the pressure release valve is in the SEAL position. The temperature will default to HIGH, which is the correct setting. Set time to 15 minutes. Select START/STOP to begin cooking. 4. When cooking is complete, turn the pressure relief valve to the VENT position for quick pressure relief. Move slider to the right to unlock the lid, then carefully open it. 5. Stir the contents of the pot, breaking apart any noodles stuck together. Divide the spaghetti and meatballs between two bowls or plates and serve with grated Parmesan and garlic bread.
Per Serving: Calories 800; Fat 35.83g; Sodium 1032mg; Carbs 70.15g; Fibre 13.5g; Sugar 24.02g; Protein 49.25g

Apple Cider-Braised Kielbasa Sausage with Carrots & Potatoes

Prep Time: 15 minutes | Cook Time: 25 minutes | Serves: 2

1 teaspoon oil
225 g uncooked thick-cut bacon, chopped
225 g fully cooked kielbasa sausage, cut into 5 cm pieces
1 onion, chopped
2 garlic cloves, minced
1 bay leaf
½ teaspoon dried tarragon
Salt
Freshly ground black pepper
2 medium potatoes, quartered and thickly sliced
2 carrots, peeled and chopped
240 ml apple cider
1 teaspoon ham bouillon powder
10 g chopped fresh parsley

1. Move slider to AIR FRY/STOVETOP. Select SEAR/SAUTÉ and set to 3. Select START/STOP to begin preheating. Allow unit to preheat for 2 minutes. After 2 minutes, add the oil. Add the bacon and kielbasa and sauté until crisp and brown, 3 to 5 minutes. Transfer to a plate and set aside. 2. Add the onion to the rendered bacon fat in the pot and sauté until softened, 3 to 4 minutes. Add the garlic, bay leaf, and tarragon and sauté for 1 minute. Season with salt and pepper. 3. Add the potatoes and carrots, then return the bacon and sausage to the pot. Stir in the apple cider and ham bouillon powder. 4. Close the lid and move slider to PRESSURE. Make sure the pressure release valve is in the SEAL position. The temperature will default to HIGH, which is the correct setting. Set time to 12 minutes. Select START/STOP to begin cooking. When the timer beeps, quick release the pressure to naturally release for 5 minutes. Open the lid. 5. Discard the bay leaf. Taste and season with more salt and pepper if needed. Divide between serving bowls and garnish with the parsley.
Per Serving: Calories 949; Fat 46.9g; Sodium 1526mg; Carbs 88.77g; Fibre 12.3g; Sugar 15.27g; Protein 46.59g

Pork Stroganoff with Noodles

Prep Time: 15 minutes | Cook Time: 20 minutes | Serves: 6

900 g pork loin, cut into 1 cm strips
1 tbsp olive oil
½ tsp salt
½ tsp ground black pepper
1 onion, chopped
3 carrots, chopped
2 stalks of celery, chopped
480 ml chicken stock
1 tbsp flour
1 tbsp Dijon mustard
120 g sour cream
1 package egg noodles, cooked

1. Move slider to AIR FRY/STOVETOP. Select SEAR/SAUTÉ and set to 3. Select START/STOP to begin preheating. Allow unit to preheat for 2 minutes. After 2 minutes, heat the oil in the pot. 2. Season the meat with salt and pepper and put into the pot. 3. Cook until all the meat is browned. You may do it in two batches. 4. Remove the pork from the pot. Add the onion and sauté for 3 minutes. 5. Pour in 240 ml of stock and deglaze the pot by scraping the bottom to remove all of the brown bits. 6. Add the carrots and celery. 7. In a bowl, combine 240 ml of stock, flour and Dijon mustard. 8. Pour the mixture in the pot. Stir well and bring to a boil. 9. Press START/STOP to turn off the SEAR/SAUTÉ function. 10. Return the meat to the pot. Close the lid. Move slider to PRESSURE. Make sure the pressure release valve is in the SEAL position. The temperature will default to HIGH, which is the correct setting. Set time to 7 minutes. Select START/STOP to begin cooking. 11. When the timer beeps, use a natural release for 10 minutes, then release any remaining pressure manually. Open the lid. 12. Move slider to AIR FRY/STOVETOP. Select SEAR/SAUTÉ and set to Lo1. Select START/STOP to begin cooking. Add the sour cream and mix well. Simmer for 1 minute. Press the START/STOP button to stop the SEAR/SAUTÉ function. 13. Serve the meat with the sauce and cooked noodles.
Per Serving: Calories 409; Fat 21.58g; Sodium 657mg; Carbs 10.4g; Fibre 1.6g; Sugar 2.95g; Protein 41.18g

Korean Beef Rolls

Prep time: 10 minutes | Cook time: 40 minutes | Serves: 8

80 ml beef stock
120 ml soy sauce
75 g light brown sugar
4 cloves garlic, minced
2 tbsp sesame oil
2 tbsp rice vinegar
2 tbsp grated fresh ginger
2 tbsp Korean chili sauce
(gochujang)
1.3 kg chuck roast, cut into bite-sized pieces
8 rolls

Toppings: mayonnaise, sliced jalapeño pepper, cucumber, fresh coriander
1. Add the stock, soy sauce, brown sugar, garlic, sesame oil, vinegar, ginger and chili sauce to a bowl and mix well. Pour the mixture into the pot and add the beef. 2. Close the lid and move slider to PRESSURE. Ensuring the pressure release valve is in the SEAL position. The temperature will default to HIGH, which is the correct setting. Set time to 40 minutes. Select START/STOP to begin cooking. 3. When the timer sounds, quick release the pressure and carefully remove the lid. Divide the beef mixture among the rolls and add toppings as desired.
Per Serving: Calories 403; Fat 14.39g; Sodium 1082mg; Carbs 28.47g; Fibre 1.5g; Sugar 6.98g; Protein 37.49g

Balsamic Beef Roast with Potatoes & Carrots

Prep Time: 15 minutes | Cook Time: 55 minutes | Serves: 6

1.8 kg chuck beef roast, cut into 4 pieces, fat trimmed
2 tsp (12 g) sea salt, plus more to taste
1 tsp paprika
1 tsp dried rosemary
1 tsp dried basil
1 tsp dried thyme
1 tsp onion powder
1 tsp garlic powder
3 tbsp (45 ml) olive or avocado oil
1 small yellow onion, diced
237 ml cabernet sauvignon wine
355 ml beef stock
60 ml balsamic vinegar
2 tbsp (30 ml) gluten-free tamari or coconut aminos
4 large carrots, peeled and cut into 5- to 7.5-cm pieces
340 g sliced bella mushrooms or button mushrooms
680 g baby potatoes
3 tbsp (24 g) tapioca starch

1. Pat the beef dry. In a medium bowl, combine together the salt, paprika, basil, thyme, rosemary, onion powder and garlic powder. Generously rub the mixture on all sides of the beef pieces. 2. Move slider to AIR FRY/STOVETOP. Select SEAR/SAUTÉ and set to 3. Select START/STOP to begin cooking. Add oil to the pot, heat the oil for 1 minute and then toss in the onion. Cook for 2 minutes, then add the meat, a few pieces at a time. Cook for about 2 minutes per side, and repeat until all of the pieces have been seared. Press START/STOP to turn off the SEAR/SAUTÉ function. Remove the beef from the pot and set aside. 3. Deglaze the pot by pouring in the wine and beef stock. Scrape the bottom for any leftover browned bits. Pour in the vinegar and gluten-free tamari. Place the beef on top of the liquid mixture, then top with the carrots, mushrooms and potatoes. 4. Close the lid and move slider to PRESSURE. Make sure the pressure release valve is in the SEAL position. The temperature will default to HIGH, which is the correct setting. Set time to 40 minutes. Select START/STOP to begin cooking. 5. When cooking is complete, naturally release the pressure for 10 minutes. Then turn the pressure relief valve to the VENT position for quick pressure relief. Move slider to AIR FRY/ STOVETOP to unlock the lid, then carefully open it. 6. Gently remove the vegetables and then the beef. Set both aside separately, tented with foil to keep warm. 7. Transfer about 60 ml of the cooking liquid into a small bowl, whisk in the tapioca starch, then return the liquid to the pot and stir. Cook on SEAR/SAUTÉ function and set the heat to 4, and allow the sauce to thicken, 5 to 7 minutes. 8. While the sauce is cooking, shred or cut the beef. Place back in the pot. Spoon the beef and sauce over the vegetables and serve warm.
Per Serving: Calories 822; Fat 34.32g; Sodium 1183mg; Carbs 36.39g; Fibre 5.1g; Sugar 7.1g; Protein 86.81g

Chapter 5 Seafood Mains Recipes

Grilled Salmon with Capers

Prep Time: 10 minutes | Cook Time: 8 minutes | Serves: 2

1 teaspoon capers, chopped
2 sprigs dill, chopped
1 lemon zest
Dressing:
5 capers, chopped
1 sprig dill, chopped
2 tablespoons plain yogurt

1 tablespoon olive oil
4 slices lemon
275g salmon fillet

Pinch of lemon zest
Salt and black pepper to taste

1. Place the Cook & Crisp Basket in your Pressure Cooker Steam Fryer. 2. Mix dill, capers, lemon zest, olive oil and salt in a suitable bowl. Cover the salmon with this mixture. Put on the Smart Lid on top of the Ninja Foodi Steam Fryer. 3. Move the Lid Slider to the "Air Fry/Stovetop". Select the "Air Fry" mode for cooking. 4. Adjust the cooking temperature to 200°C. Cook salmon for around 8 minutes. Mix the dressing ingredients in another bowl. 5. When salmon is cooked, place on serving plate and drizzle dressing over it. Place lemon slices at the side of the plate and serve.
Per serving: Calories 669; Fat: 53.8g; Sodium 905mg; Carbs: 41.7g; Fibre: 8.6g; Sugars 12.3g; Protein 14g

Cod with Grapes

Prep Time: 10 minutes | Cook Time: 15 minutes | Serves: 2

2 fillets black cod (200g)
90g kale, minced
2 teaspoons white balsamic vinegar
55g pecans
90g grapes, halved

1 small bulb fennel, cut into 2.5 cm-thick slices
4 tablespoons extra-virgin olive oil
Salt and black pepper to taste

1. Place the Cook & Crisp Basket in your Pressure Cooker Steam Fryer. 2. Use black pepper and salt to season your fish fillets. Drizzle with 1 teaspoon of olive oil. Place the fish in the Cook & Crisp Basket with the skin side down. 3. Put on the Smart Lid on top of the Ninja Foodi Steam Fryer. Move the Lid Slider to the "Air Fry/Stovetop". Select the "Air Fry" mode for cooking. Adjust the cooking temperature to 200°C. Cook for around 10 minutes. 4. Take the fish out and cover loosely with aluminum foil. Mix fennel, pecans, and grapes. Pour 2 tablespoons of olive oil and season with black pepper and salt. 5. Add to the Ninja Foodi Pressure Steam Fryer basket. Put on the Smart Lid on top of the Ninja Foodi Steam Fryer. 6. Move the Lid Slider to the "Air Fry/Stovetop". Select the "Air Fry" mode for cooking. Cook for an additional 5 minutes. 7. In a suitable bowl mix minced kale and cooked grapes, fennel and pecans. Cover ingredients with balsamic vinegar and remaining 1 tablespoon of olive oil. 8. Toss gently. Serve fish with sauce and enjoy!
Per serving: Calories 194; Fat: 2.6g; Sodium 1257mg; Carbs: 35.4g; Fibre: 3.7g; Sugars 3.1g; Protein 9.4g

Asian Style Sea Bass

Prep Time: 10 minutes | Cook Time: 20 minutes | Serves: 2

1 medium sea bass or halibut
2 garlic cloves, minced
1 tablespoon olive oil
3 slices of ginger, julienned
2 tablespoons cooking wine

1 tomato, cut into quarters
1 lime, cut
1 green onion, chopped
1 chili, diced

1. Place the Cook & Crisp Basket in your Pressure Cooker Steam Fryer. 2. Prepare ginger, garlic oil mixture: sauté ginger and garlic with oil until golden brown in a suitable saucepan over medium-heat on top of the stove. Prepare fish: clean, rinse, and pat dry. Cut in half to fit into basket. 3. Place the fish inside of "cook & crisp basket" then drizzle it with cooking wine. Layer tomato and lime slices on top of fish. Cover with garlic ginger oil mixture. Top with green onion and slices of chili. Cover with aluminum foil. 4. Put on the Smart Lid on top of the Ninja Foodi Steam Fryer. Move the Lid Slider to the "Air Fry/Stovetop". Select the "Air Fry" mode for cooking. Adjust the cooking temperature to 180°C. 5. Cook for around 20 minutes.
Per serving: Calories 105; Fat: 2.4g; Sodium 812mg; Carbs: 12.2g; Fibre: 2.4g; Sugars 2.4g; Protein 9.5g

Fish Fingers

Prep Time: 10 minutes | Cook Time: 10 minutes | Serves: 2

250g codfish, sliced into strips
2 teaspoons mixed dried herbs
2 eggs
¼ teaspoon baking soda
1 teaspoon rice flour
2 teaspoons cornflour
2 tablespoons almond flour
½ lemon, juiced

1 teaspoon ginger garlic
½ teaspoon turmeric powder
½ teaspoon red chili flakes
2 teaspoons garlic powder
2 tablespoons olive oil
100g breadcrumbs
Tartar sauce or ketchup

1. Place the Cook & Crisp Basket in your Pressure Cooker Steam Fryer. 2. Place fish fingers in a suitable bowl. Add a teaspoon of mixed herbs, 1 teaspoon of garlic powder, red chili flakes, turmeric powder, ginger garlic, lemon juice, salt and black pepper. Stir well and set aside for around 10 minutes. 3. In another bowl, mix almond flour, rice flour, corn flour and baking soda. Break eggs into this bowl. Stir well then add fish. Set aside for around 10 minutes. 4. Mix breadcrumbs and remaining 1 teaspoon of mixed herbs and 1 teaspoon of garlic powder. Cover fish with breadcrumb mixture. 5. Lay aluminum foil in the Cook & Crisp Basket. Lay the fish fingers in the basket and cover with olive oil. Put on the Smart Lid on top of the Ninja Foodi Steam Fryer. 6. Move the Lid Slider to the "Air Fry/Stovetop". Select the "Air Fry" mode for cooking. Adjust the cooking temperature to 180°C. 7. Cook for around 10 minutes and serve with tartar sauce or ketchup.
Per serving: Calories 541; Fat: 12.4g; Sodium 250mg; Carbs: 85.4g; Fibre: 21.3g; Sugars 6.1g; Protein 26.5g

Mustard Coconut Prawns

Prep Time: 10 minutes | Cook Time: 20 minutes | Serves: 2

50g breadcrumbs
Salt and black pepper to taste
45g shredded coconut, unsweetened
½ teaspoon cayenne pepper
200g coconut milk

8 large prawns
1 tablespoon sugar-free syrup
¼ teaspoon hot sauce
160g orange jam, sugar-free
1 teaspoon mustard

1. Place the Cook & Crisp Basket in your Pressure Cooker Steam Fryer. 2. Place breadcrumbs, coconut, salt, pepper, and cayenne pepper in a suitable bowl and mix. 3. Dip the prawns in coconut milk first, then in breadcrumb mixture. 4. Line baking sheet and arrange prawns on it. Place in the Cook & Crisp Basket. Put on the Smart Lid on top of the Ninja Foodi Steam Fryer. Move the Lid Slider to the "Air Fry/Stovetop". Select the "Air Fry" mode for cooking. 5. Adjust the cooking temperature to 175°C. Cook for around 20 minutes. 6. Mix the orange jam, mustard, syrup, and hot sauce. Add the prawns to a serving platter and drizzle with sauce and serve.
Per serving: Calories 459; Fat: 3.6g; Sodium 1614mg; Carbs: 82g; Fibre: 11.5g; Sugars 8.3g; Protein 25.9g

Crispy Fish Sticks

Prep Time: 10 minutes | Cook Time: 13 minutes | Serves: 4

3 eggs
200g breadcrumbs
455g. codfish

90g almond flour
3 tablespoons skim milk
Salt and black pepper to taste

1. Place the Cook & Crisp Basket in your Pressure Cooker Steam Fryer. 2. Mix milk and egg in a suitable mixing bowl. In another bowl, add breadcrumbs, and in a third bowl mix flour. Slice the fish into strips and season with black pepper and salt. 3. Dip each piece into flour, then into egg mixture and then into breadcrumbs. 4. Put on the Smart Lid on top of the Ninja Foodi Steam Fryer. Move the Lid Slider to the "Air Fry/Stovetop". Select the "Air Fry" mode for cooking. Adjust the cooking temperature to 170°C. Cook for around 13 minutes. 5. Turn once during cooking.
Per serving: Calories 357; Fat: 16.1g; Sodium 80mg; Carbs: 26g; Fibre: 7.3g; Sugars 9.2g; Protein 29.4g

Salmon Potato Patties

Prep Time: 10 minutes | Cook Time: 10 minutes | Serves: 2

3 large russet potatoes, boiled, mashed
1 salmon fillet
1 egg
Breadcrumbs

2 tablespoons olive oil
Parsley, fresh, chopped
Handful of parboiled vegetables
½ teaspoon dill
Black pepper and salt to taste

1. Place the Cook & Crisp Basket in your Pressure Cooker Steam Fryer. 2. Peel, chop, and mash cooked potatoes. Put potatoes in the Cook & Crisp Basket. 3. Put on the Smart Lid on top of the Ninja Foodi Steam Fryer. Move the Lid Slider to the "Air Fry/Stovetop". Select the "Air Fry" mode for cooking. Air Fry salmon for 5 minutes. 4. Use a fork to flake salmon then set aside. Add vegetables, parsley, flaked salmon, dill, salt, and pepper to mashed potatoes. 5. Add egg and mix. Shape the mixture into six patties. Cover with breadcrumbs. Cook at 180°C for around 10 minutes.
Per serving: Calories 403; Fat: 23.8g; Sodium 782mg; Carbs: 4.4g; Fibre: 1.9g; Sugars 0.7g; Protein 48.9g

Breaded Salmon

Prep Time: 10 minutes | Cook Time: 20 minutes | Serves: 4

200g breadcrumbs
4 salmon fillets

2 eggs, beaten
100g Swiss cheese, shredded

1. Place the Cook & Crisp Basket in your Pressure Cooker Steam Fryer. 2. Dip each salmon filet into eggs. Top with Swiss cheese. Dip into breadcrumbs, coating entire fish. 3. Put into the Cook & Crisp Basket. Put on the Smart Lid on top of the Ninja Foodi Steam Fryer. Move the Lid Slider to the "Air Fry/Stovetop". Select the "Air Fry" mode for cooking. Adjust the cooking temperature to 200°C. 4. Cook for around 20 minutes.
Per serving: Calories 347; Fat: 17.7g; Sodium 1655mg; Carbs: 6.8g; Fibre: 1.2g; Sugars 2.8g; Protein 33.3g

Maple-Mustard Salmon with Asparagus & Cherry Tomatoes

Prep Time: 10 minutes | Cook Time: 3 minutes | Serves: 4

1 tablespoon pure maple syrup
1 tablespoon Dijon mustard
⅛ teaspoon salt

4 (150 g) salmon fillets
455 g asparagus, trimmed
150 g cherry tomatoes, halved

1. In a small bowl, mix together the mustard, maple syrup, and salt. Spread the sauce onto the salmon fillets. 2. Pour 240 ml of water into the pot and place the bottom layer of the Deluxe Reversible Rack in the lower position in the pot. Place the salmon fillets on the rack. 3. Close the lid and move slider to PRESSURE. Make sure the pressure release valve is in the SEAL position. The temperature will default to HIGH, which is the correct setting. Set time to 2 minutes. Select START/STOP to begin cooking. 4. When cooking is complete, turn the pressure relief valve to the VENT position for quick pressure relief. Move slider to the right to unlock the lid, then carefully open it. 5. Add the asparagus. Lock the lid in place. Still cook on high pressure for 1 minute. When the cook time is complete, quick release the pressure. 6. Carefully open the lid. Remove the asparagus from the pot and mix it with the tomatoes. Serve alongside the salmon.
Per Serving: Calories 276; Fat 7.81g; Sodium 255mg; Carbs 13.43g; Fibre 3.2g; Sugar 9.83g; Protein 37.98g

Mussels with Potatoes & Olives

Prep Time: 15 minutes | Cook Time: 12 minutes | Serves: 6

900 g baby Yukon Gold potatoes, cut in half
120 ml water
2 tablespoons olive oil, divided
1 medium yellow onion, peeled and diced
1 tablespoon chopped fresh oregano

½ teaspoon paprika
4 cloves garlic, peeled and minced
¼ teaspoon salt
¼ teaspoon ground black pepper
1 (375 g) can diced tomatoes
360 ml water
900 g mussels, scrubbed and

beards removed
55 g sliced green olives

2 tablespoons chopped fresh parsley

1. Place the potatoes, water, and 1 tablespoon oil in the pot. Close the lid and move slider to PRESSURE. Make sure the pressure release valve is in the SEAL position. The temperature will default to HIGH, which is the correct setting. Set time to 2 minutes. Select START/STOP to begin cooking. 2. Drain the potatoes. Set aside. Wash and dry the pot. 3. Move slider to AIR FRY/STOVETOP. Select SEAR/SAUTÉ and set to 3. Select START/STOP to begin preheating. Allow unit to preheat for 2 minutes. After 2 minutes, heat remaining 1 tablespoon oil. Add onion and cook until tender, about 4 minutes. Add the oregano, garlic, paprika, salt, and pepper, and cook until very fragrant, about 30 seconds. Add tomatoes and water, and stir well. Press START/STOP to turn off the SEAR/SAUTÉ function. 4. Stir in mussels, olives, and potatoes. Cook on high pressure for 5 minutes. When the timer beeps, turn the pressure relief valve to the VENT position for quick pressure relief. Move slider to the right to unlock the lid, then carefully open it. 5. Discard any mussels that haven't opened. Garnish with parsley and serve immediately.
Per Serving: Calories 312; Fat 8.34g; Sodium 632mg; Carbs 37.69g; Fibre 5.5g; Sugar 4.04g; Protein 22.12g

Lemon Prawns with Asparagus

Prep Time: 10 minutes | Cook Time: 1 minute | Serves: 4

240 ml water
1 bunch asparagus, trimmed
½ teaspoon salt, divided
455 g prawns, peeled and

deveined
1½ tablespoons lemon juice
2 tablespoons olive oil

1. Pour water into the pot. Then place the bottom layer of the Deluxe Reversible Rack in the lower position in the pot. 2. Spread asparagus on the bottom of the rack. Sprinkle with ¼ teaspoon salt. Add prawns. Drizzle with lemon juice and sprinkle with remaining ¼ teaspoon salt. Drizzle olive oil over prawns. 3. Close the lid and move slider to PRESSURE. Make sure the pressure release valve is in the SEAL position. The temperature will default to HIGH, which is the correct setting. Set time to 1 minute. Select START/STOP to begin cooking. 4. When cooking is complete, turn the pressure relief valve to the VENT position for quick pressure relief. Move slider to the right to unlock the lid, then carefully open it. 5. Transfer prawns and asparagus to a platter and serve.
Per Serving: Calories 178; Fat 8.33g; Sodium 1279mg; Carbs 1.17g; Fibre 0.4g; Sugar 0.52g; Protein 23.62g

Lemon Crab with Orzo

Prep Time: 15 minutes | Cook Time: 16 minutes | Serves: 4

2 tablespoons light olive oil
1 medium shallot, peeled and minced
1 clove garlic, peeled and minced
10 g chopped fresh flat-leaf parsley
2 tablespoons chopped fresh basil

¼ teaspoon salt
¼ teaspoon ground black pepper
480 ml water
200 g orzo
200 g jumbo lump crabmeat
1 tablespoon lemon juice
25 g grated Parmesan cheese

1. Move slider to AIR FRY/STOVETOP. Select SEAR/SAUTÉ and set to 3. Select START/STOP to begin cooking. Heat the oil for 1 minute or 2, add shallot and garlic. Cook until garlic is very fragrant, about 1 minute. Add parsley, basil, salt, and pepper. Stir well. Add water and pasta. Press START/STOP to turn off the SEAR/SAUTÉ function. 2. Close the lid and move slider to PRESSURE. Make sure the pressure release valve is in the SEAL position. The temperature will default to HIGH, which is the correct setting. Set time to 4 minutes. Select START/STOP to begin cooking. 3. When cooking is complete, turn the pressure relief valve to the VENT position for quick pressure relief. Move slider to the right to unlock the lid, then carefully open it. 4. Add crab and lemon juice. Stir gently to combine, then let stand, uncovered, on the Keep Warm setting for 10 minutes to heat crab. Top with cheese and serve immediately.
Per Serving: Calories 210; Fat 12.78g; Sodium 818mg; Carbs 20.65g; Fibre 3.5g; Sugar 0.97g; Protein 5.91g

Delicious Tomato-Stewed Calamari

Prep Time: 15 minutes | Cook Time: 15 minutes | Serves: 6

2 tablespoons olive oil	1 (700 g) can diced tomatoes
1 small carrot, peeled and grated	120 ml white wine
1 stalk celery, finely diced	80 ml water
1 small white onion, peeled and diced	1 teaspoon dried parsley
3 cloves garlic, peeled and minced	1 teaspoon dried basil
	½ teaspoon salt
1.3 kg calamari	½ teaspoon ground black pepper

1. Move slider to AIR FRY/STOVETOP. Select SEAR/SAUTÉ and set to 3. Select START/STOP to begin preheating. Allow unit to preheat for 2 minutes. After 2 minutes, heat the oil. Add carrot and celery, and cook until just tender, about 2 minutes. 2. Add onion and cook until tender, about 3 minutes. Stir in garlic and cook until fragrant, about 30 seconds. Press START/STOP to turn off the SEAR/SAUTÉ function. 3. Add calamari, tomatoes, water, wine, basil, parsley, salt, and pepper to the pot. Close the lid and move slider to PRESSURE. Make sure the pressure release valve is in the SEAL position. The temperature will default to HIGH, which is the correct setting. Set time to 10 minutes. Select START/STOP to begin cooking. 4. When cooking is complete, turn the pressure relief valve to the VENT position for quick pressure relief. Move slider to the right to unlock the lid, then carefully open it. Serve immediately.
Per Serving: Calories 422; Fat 10.11g; Sodium 1175mg; Carbs 19.55g; Fibre 3.3g; Sugar 4.92g; Protein 60.26g

Garlicky Octopus and Potatoes

Prep Time: 15 minutes | Cook Time: 16 minutes | Serves: 8

900 g potatoes (about 6 medium)	2 teaspoons whole peppercorns
3 teaspoons salt, divided	120 ml olive oil
1 (900 g) frozen octopus, thawed, cleaned, and rinsed	60 ml white wine vinegar
3 cloves garlic, peeled, divided	½ teaspoon ground black pepper
1 bay leaf	20 g chopped fresh parsley

1. Place potatoes and 2 teaspoons salt in the pot. Pour into enough water to just cover the potatoes halfway. Close the lid and move slider to PRESSURE. Make sure the pressure release valve is in the SEAL position. The temperature will default to HIGH, which is the correct setting. Set time to 6 minutes. Select START/STOP to begin cooking. 2. When cooking is complete, quick release the pressure by turning the pressure release valve to the VENT position. Move slider to the right to unlock the lid, then carefully open it. 3. Remove potatoes with tongs (reserve the cooking water), and peel them as soon as you can handle them. Dice the potatoes into bite-sized pieces. Set aside. 4. Add octopus to potato cooking water in the pot and add more water to cover if needed. Add 1 garlic clove, bay leaf, and peppercorns. Close the lid and still cook on high pressure for 10 minutes. When the timer beeps, quick-release the pressure until the float valve drops and open lid. Remove and discard bay leaf. 5. Check octopus for tenderness by seeing if a fork will sink easily into the thickest part of the flesh. If not, close the top and bring it to pressure for another minute or two and check again. 6. Remove octopus and drain. Chop head and tentacles into small, bite-sized chunks. 7. Crush remaining 2 garlic cloves and place in a small jar or plastic container. Add olive oil, vinegar, remaining 1 teaspoon salt, and pepper. Close the lid and shake well. 8. In a large serving bowl, mix the potatoes with octopus, cover with vinaigrette, and sprinkle with parsley.
Per Serving: Calories 306; Fat 14.87g; Sodium 1143mg; Carbs 23.37g; Fibre 2.7g; Sugar 1.17g; Protein 19.48g

Tasty Lobster Tails with Herbs

Prep Time: 10 minutes | Cook Time: 5 minutes | Serves: 4

60 ml extra-virgin olive oil	1 teaspoon chopped fresh dill
¼ teaspoon salt	240 ml low-sodium chicken stock
¼ teaspoon ground black pepper	2 tablespoons Old Bay seafood seasoning
1 clove garlic, peeled and minced	
1 tablespoon grated lemon zest	900 g fresh cold-water lobster
1 teaspoon chopped fresh tarragon	tails

1. In a small saucepan over low heat, add the oil, salt, pepper, garlic, and lemon zest and cook until oil is warm. Stir in tarragon and dill, and immediately turn off heat. Cover, set aside, and keep warm. 2. Add stock and seafood seasoning to the pot and stir well. Then place the bottom layer of the Deluxe Reversible Rack in the lower position in the pot. 3. Place lobster tails shell side down on the rack. Close the lid and move slider to PRESSURE. Make sure the pressure release valve is in the SEAL position. The temperature will default to HIGH, which is the correct setting. Set time to 3 minutes. Select START/STOP to begin cooking. 4. When cooking is complete, turn the pressure relief valve to the VENT position for quick pressure relief. Move slider to the right to unlock the lid, then carefully open it. 5. Transfer the lobster tails to a platter. Carefully cut bottom of each shell with kitchen shears and pull tail meat out in one piece. Slice into 1.5 cm-thick pieces. Serve immediately with herbed olive oil.
Per Serving: Calories 70; Fat 6.34g; Sodium 285mg; Carbs 2.54g; Fibre 0.4g; Sugar 0.33g; Protein 1.56g

Rice Pilaf with Corn and Prawns

Prep time: 20 minutes | Cook time: 20 minutes | Serves: 4

4 tablespoons salted butter	360 ml low-sodium chicken stock or water
2 large shallots, halved and thinly sliced	455 g extra-large or large prawns, peeled (tails removed), deveined and chopped into 2 cm pieces
¾ teaspoon red pepper flakes	
2 teaspoons grated lemon zest, plus 2 teaspoons lemon juice	60 g lightly packed baby rocket, roughly chopped
Salt	75 g roasted red peppers, patted dry and diced
300 g long-grain white rice, rinsed and drained	
120 g fresh or frozen corn kernels	

1. Move slider to AIR FRY/STOVETOP. Select SEAR/SAUTÉ and set to Lo1. Select START/STOP to begin preheating. Add the butter and let melt. 2. Add the shallots, lemon zest, pepper flakes and 1 teaspoon salt, then cook, stirring occasionally, until the shallots are softened, about 3 minutes. 3. add the rice and cook, stirring, until the grains turn translucent, about 2 minutes. add the corn and stock; stir to combine, then distribute in an even layer, press START/STOP. 4. Close the lid and move slider to PRESSURE. Ensuring the pressure release valve is in the SEAL position. The temperature will default to LOW, which is the correct setting. Set time to 13 minutes. Select START/STOP to begin cooking. 5. When cooking is complete, release the pressure quickly by turning the pressure release valve to the VENT position. Move slider to the right to unlock the lid, then carefully open it. 6. Scatter the prawns in an even layer on the rice, then drape a kitchen towel across the pot and re-cover without locking the lid in place. Let stand for 10 minutes. 7. Stir the prawns into the rice mixture, then re-cover with the towel and lid for another 5 minutes. 8. Fluff the mixture, stirring in the rocket, roasted peppers and lemon juice. 9. Taste and season with salt.
Per Serving: Calories 526; Fat 21.36g; Sodium 864mg; Carbs 76.08g; Fibre 6.1g; Sugar 3.22g; Protein 9.77g

Salmon with Broccoli

Prep time: 20 minutes | Cook time: 5 minutes | Serves: 2

200g salmon fillet	Salt and ground black pepper to taste
240ml water	
200g broccoli	

1. Cut the broccoli into florets. 2. Season the salmon fillets and broccoli with salt and pepper. 3. Add the water to the cooking pot, place the reversible rack in the pot in the lower position and drop the lower rack through the reversible rack handles. 4. Arrange the fillets and florets onto the rack. 5. Install the pressure lid and turn the pressure release valve to the SEAL position. 6. Select STEAM and set the cooking time to 5 minutes. 7. When cooked, let the unit naturally release pressure. 8. Serve and enjoy.
Per Serving: Calories 207; Fat 8.73g; Sodium 532mg; Carbs 5.36g; Fibre 3.4g; Sugar 1.58g; Protein 27.44g

Jollof Rice with Prawns & Peas

Prep time: 30 minutes | Cook time: 30 minutes | Serves: 4

2 tablespoons extra-virgin olive oil	2 tablespoons curry powder
1 large yellow onion, chopped	360 g can diced tomatoes
2 medium carrots, peeled, halved lengthwise and thinly sliced	300 g basmati rice, rinsed and drained
1 medium red pepper, stemmed, seeded and chopped	480 ml low-sodium chicken stock
Salt and ground black pepper	1 teaspoon dried thyme
2 medium garlic cloves, smashed and peeled	300 g extra-large prawns, peeled (tails removed), deveined, halved crosswise and patted dry
	120 g frozen green peas

1. Move slider to AIR FRY/STOVETOP. Select SEAR/SAUTÉ and set to Hi 5. Select START/STOP to begin preheating. Add the oil and heat until shimmering. 2. Add the onion, carrots, pepper and 1 teaspoon salt, then cook, stirring, until the onion is softened and golden brown at the edges, 5 to 7 minutes. 3. Stir in the garlic and curry powder, then cook until fragrant, about 30 seconds. 4. Add the tomatoes with their juices, the rice, stock and thyme; stir to combine then distribute in an even layer, press START/STOP. 5. Close the lid and move slider to PRESSURE. Ensuring the pressure release valve is in the SEAL position. The temperature will default to LOW, which is the correct setting. Set time to 10 minutes. Select START/STOP to begin cooking. 6. In the meantime, season the prawns with salt and black pepper; set aside. 7. When pressure-cooking is complete, quick-release the steam by moving the pressure valve to Vent. Press START/STOP, then carefully open the pot. 8. Scatter the prawns and peas evenly on the rice, then re-cover without locking the lid in place. 9. Let stand until the prawns are opaque throughout, about 10 minutes. 10. Fluff the rice, stirring in the prawns and peas. Taste and season with salt and pepper.
Per Serving: Calories 382; Fat 25.34g; Sodium 885mg; Carbs 43.9g; Fibre 18.4g; Sugar 7.8g; Protein 12.91g

Garlicky Salmon

Prep time: 10 minutes | Cook time: 12 minutes | Serves: 2-4

½ tsp salt	1 tbsp olive oil
¼ tsp garlic powder	1 tbsp unsalted butter
¼ tsp onion powder	Juice of ½ lemon
¼ tsp dried chives	1 tbsp white wine
¼ tsp freshly ground black pepper	1½ tsp chopped fresh dill
2 (300 g) salmon fillets	1½ tsp chopped fresh parsley

1. In a small bowl, combine the salt, onion powder, garlic powder, chives and pepper. Season each salmon fillet liberally with the mixture. 2. Move slider to AIR FRY/STOVETOP. Select SEAR/SAUTÉ and set to Lo1. Select START/STOP to begin preheating. 3. Add the oil and butter to the preheated pot. Add the salmon fillets, skin side down. Sauté for 7 to 9 minutes, or until the skin is nice and crispy. Press START/STOP. 4. Carefully remove the salmon with a fish spatula. Some parts of the skin might stick; work carefully so as to not break the fish. Transfer the fish to a large plate. 5. Deglaze the pot with the lemon juice and white wine. Scrape up any browned bits from the bottom of the pot. 6. Then place the bottom layer of the Deluxe Reversible Rack in the lower position in the pot. 7. Place the fillets on the rack. Close the lid and move slider to PRESSURE. Ensuring the pressure release valve is in the SEAL position. The temperature will default to HIGH, which is the correct setting. Set time to 3 minutes. Select START/STOP to begin cooking. 8. When the cooking is complete, quick release the pressure. 9. Remove the lid and carefully transfer each fillet to a serving plate. 10. Spoon some of the sauce from the pot over each fish, then top with fresh dill and parsley.
Per Serving: Calories 244; Fat 15.39g; Sodium 882mg; Carbs 1.72g; Fibre 0.4g; Sugar 0.28g; Protein 23.88g

Lime Prawns & Corn Salad

Prep time: 10 minutes | Cook time: 2 minutes | Serves: 4

Juice and zest of 1 lime	2 cloves garlic, minced
1 tsp soy sauce or coconut aminos	1 jalapeño pepper, seeded and minced
1 tbsp chili powder	
½ tsp ground cumin	1 head romaine lettuce, chopped
1 tsp smoked paprika	40 g shredded purple cabbage
¼ tsp freshly ground black pepper, plus more to taste	135 g Pico de Gallo
½ tsp salt, plus more to taste	Dressing:
2 tbsp hot sauce, such as Valentina	2 tbsp light sour cream
455 g frozen and thawed deveined prawns	1 tbsp fresh lime juice
2 ears corn, husked	1 tsp sauce from the pot
	Salt
	Freshly ground black pepper

1. Add the lime juice and zest, soy sauce, chili powder, garlic, jalapeño, cumin, paprika, salt, black pepper and hot sauce to the pot, stir to mix well. Add the prawns and mix until evenly coated. 2. Then place the bottom layer of the Deluxe Reversible Rack in the lower position in the pot. 3. Place the ears of corn on the rack. Close the lid and move slider to PRESSURE. Ensuring the pressure release valve is in the SEAL position. The temperature will default to HIGH, which is the correct setting. Set time to 2 minutes. Select START/STOP to begin cooking. 4. When the time is up, quick release the pressure. Use tongs to remove the ears of corn and transfer them to a cutting board. Stand an ear on one end. Use a knife to slice along each cob to remove the kernels from the cob. 5. To assemble the salad, place the lettuce and then cabbage on the bottom of a large bowl. Top with the Pico de Gallo, corn kernels and prawns. 6. To prepare the dressing, in a separate bowl, whisk together the sour cream, lime juice, cooking liquid from the pot and salt and pepper to taste. 7. Dress the salad with the dressing. Add more salt and pepper to taste, if desired.
Per Serving: Calories 287; Fat 7.37g; Sodium 863mg; Carbs 53.34g; Fibre 7.1g; Sugar 31.34g; Protein 9.22g

Salmon in Chicken Stock with Rice

Prep time: 10 minutes | Cook time: 5 minutes | Serves: 2

2 wild salmon fillets, frozen	30g vegetable soup mix, dried
100g jasmine rice	A pinch of saffron
240ml chicken stock	Salt and ground black pepper to taste
1 tablespoon butter	

1. In the cooking pot, combine the rice, stock, butter, soup mix, and saffron. 2. Add the water to the cooking pot, place the reversible rack in the pot in the lower position and drop the lower rack through the reversible rack handles. 3. Sprinkle the salmon with salt and pepper, and arrange the molds onto the rack. 4. Install the pressure lid and turn the pressure release valve to the VENT position. 5. Select STEAM and adjust the cooking time to 5 minutes. 6. When cooked, let the unit naturally release pressure. 7. Serve and enjoy.
Per Serving: Calories 751; Fat 35.9g; Sodium 811mg; Carbs 19.72g; Fibre 6.7g; Sugar 3.25g; Protein 91.17g

Salmon with Broccoli & Potatoes

Prep time: 25 minutes | Cook time: 5 minutes | Serves: 2-4

2 salmon fillets	240ml water
Salt and ground black pepper to taste	455g new potatoes
	90g broccoli, chopped
Fresh herbs, optional	½ tablespoon butter

1. In a bowl, season the potatoes with salt, pepper and fresh herbs. 2. Add the water to the cooking pot, place the reversible rack in the pot in the lower position and drop the lower rack through the reversible rack handles. 3. Arrange the potatoes onto the rack. 4. Install the pressure lid and turn the pressure release valve to the SEAL position. 5. Select PRESSURE COOK, set the cooking temperature to HI and adjust the cooking time to 2 minutes. 6. When cooked, let the unit naturally release pressure. 7. In a bowl, season the broccoli and salmon with salt and pepper. 8. Place the broccoli and salmon on the steam rack along with the potatoes. 9. Resume cooking the food on PRESSURE COOK mode at HI for 2 minutes more. 10. Let the unit naturally release pressure. 11. Transfer the potatoes to a separate bowl and add the butter. Gently stir to coat the potatoes with the butter. 12. Serve the cooked fish with potatoes and broccoli.
Per Serving: Calories 309; Fat 8.61g; Sodium 143mg; Carbs 21.16g; Fibre 2.9g; Sugar 1.5g; Protein 35.44g

Prawns & Asparagus with Risotto

Prep time: 5 minutes | Cook time: 25 minutes | Serves: 8

3 tablespoon unsalted butter
1 small onion, finely diced
6 garlic cloves, minced
300g uncooked arborio rice
240ml white wine
960ml reduced-sodium chicken stock
50g shredded Parmesan cheese, divided

2 tablespoon olive oil
3 garlic cloves, minced
900g uncooked prawns peeled and deveined
1 tablespoon unsalted butter
120g Italian salad dressing
455g fresh asparagus, trimmed
Salt and pepper to taste

1. Melt the butter in the cooking pot at MD on SEAR/SAUTÉ mode; add the onion and sauté for 4 to 5 minutes; add garlic and sauté for 1 minute; add rice and sauté for 2 minutes; stir in 120ml wine and stir until absorbed. 2. Stop the process, and add remaining wine, stock and 25g cheese. 3. Install the pressure lid and turn the pressure release valve to the SEAL position. 4. Select PRESSURE COOK, set the cooking temperature to HI and adjust the cooking time to 8 minutes. 5. When cooked, let the unit naturally release pressure. 6. Heat oil in a large frying pan over medium-high heat. 7. Add garlic; cook 1 minute. Add prawns; cook and stir for 5 minutes until the prawns begin to turn pink. 8. Add butter and dressing; stir until butter melts. Reduce heat. Add asparagus; cook them for 3 to 5 minutes until tender. 9. Serve the dish over risotto; season the dish with salt and pepper and sprinkle with the remaining cheese.
Per Serving: Calories 531; Fat 27.16g; Sodium 1748mg; Carbs 20.8g; Fibre 6.7g; Sugar 3.88g; Protein 56.26g

Tuna Casserole

Prep time: 25 minutes | Cook time: 15 minutes | Serves: 10

55g butter, cubed
225g sliced fresh mushrooms
1 medium onion, chopped
1 medium sweet pepper, chopped
1 teaspoon salt, divided
1 teaspoon pepper, divided
2 garlic cloves, minced
30g plain flour
480ml reduced-sodium chicken stock

480g cream
200g uncooked egg noodles
3 cans (125g each) light tuna in water
2 tablespoon lemon juice
200g shredded Monterey Jack cheese
200g frozen peas, thawed
75g crushed potato chips

1. Melt the butter in the cooking pot at MD on SEAR/SAUTÉ mode; add mushrooms, onion, sweet pepper, ½ teaspoon salt and ½ teaspoon pepper for 6 to 8 minutes until the vegetables are tender; add garlic and cook for 1 minute. 2. Stir in flour until blended. Gradually whisk in stock. Bring to a boil, stirring constantly; cook and stir for 1-2 minutes until thickened. 3. Stop the cooker, and stir in the cream and noodles. 4. Install the pressure lid and turn the pressure release valve to the SEAL position. 5. Select PRESSURE COOK, set the cooking temperature to HI and adjust the cooking time to 3 minutes. 6. In a small bowl, combine tuna, lemon juice and the remaining salt and pepper. 7. When cooked, let the unit naturally release pressure. 8. Stir the cheese, tuna mixture and peas into noodle mixture, and then cook the food at LO on SEAR/SAUTÉ mode. 9. Sprinkle the dish with potato chips and enjoy.
Per Serving: Calories 800; Fat 22.72g; Sodium 1847mg; Carbs 33.85g; Fibre 3.2g; Sugar 4.68g; Protein 115.66g

Prawns Mac & Cheese

Prep time: 15 minutes | Cook time: 10 minutes | Serves: 6

480ml low fat milk
240g cream
1 tablespoon unsalted butter
1 teaspoon ground mustard
½ teaspoon onion powder
¼ teaspoon white pepper
¼ teaspoon ground nutmeg
150g uncooked elbow macaroni
200g shredded cheddar cheese
100g shredded Gouda or Swiss

cheese
340g frozen cooked salad prawns, thawed
120g crumbled blue cheese
2 tablespoon Louisiana-style hot sauce
2 tablespoon minced fresh chives
2 tablespoon minced fresh parsley
Additional Louisiana-style hot sauce, optional

1. Combine the milk, cream, butter, mustard, onion powder, white pepper, nutmeg, and macaroni in the cooking pot. 2. Install the pressure lid and turn the pressure release valve to the SEAL position. 3. Select PRESSURE COOK, set the cooking temperature to HI and adjust the cooking time to 3 minutes. 4. When cooked, let the unit naturally release pressure.
5. Add the shredded cheeses, prawns, blue cheese and hot sauce to the pot, and cook them at MD on SEAR/SAUTÉ mode for 5 to 6 minutes. 6. Stir in the chives, parsley and more hot sauce (optional) before serving.
Per Serving: Calories 595; Fat 32.56g; Sodium 442mg; Carbs 47.85g; Fibre 2.3g; Sugar 23.85g; Protein 28.89g

Simple Salmon Fillets

Prep time: 20 minutes | Cook time: 10 minutes | Serves: 2

2 salmon fillets
240ml water

Salt and ground black pepper to taste

1. Season the salmon with salt and pepper. 2. Add the water to the cooking pot, place the reversible rack in the pot in the lower position and drop the lower rack through the reversible rack handles. 3. Arrange the salmon fillets onto the rack. 4. Install the pressure lid and turn the pressure release valve to the VENT position. 5. Select STEAM and set the cooking time to 10 minutes. 6. When cooked, let the unit naturally release pressure. 7. Serve the dish with lemon wedges.
Per Serving: Calories 484; Fat 14.97g; Sodium 202mg; Carbs 2.13g; Fibre 0.3g; Sugar 1.15g; Protein 80.2g

Dijon Salmon Fillets

Prep time: 10 minutes | Cook time: 5 minutes | Serves: 2

2 fish fillets or steaks, such as salmon, cod, or halibut (2.5cm thick)
240ml water

Salt and ground black pepper to taste
2 teaspoon Dijon mustard

1. Add the water to the cooking pot, place the reversible rack in the pot in the lower position and drop the lower rack through the reversible rack handles. 2. Sprinkle the fish with salt and pepper and arrange onto the rack with skin-side down, and then spread the Dijon mustard on top of each fillets. 3. Install the pressure lid and turn the pressure release valve to the SEAL position. 4. Select PRESSURE COOK, set the cooking temperature to HI and adjust the cooking time to 5 minutes. 5. When cooked, let the unit naturally release pressure. Pour the water into the cooking pot and insert a steam rack. 6. Serve warm.
Per Serving: Calories 223; Fat 11.4g; Sodium 543mg; Carbs 17.86g; Fibre 1g; Sugar 1.19g; Protein 13.98g

Pecan-Coated Salmon

Prep time: 15 minutes | Cook time: 10 minutes | Serves: 2-4

2 salmon fillets
120ml olive oil
½ teaspoon salt
30g flour

1 egg, beaten
30g pecans, finely chopped
240ml water

1. Season the fillets with salt. 2. Dip the fillets in the flour, then in whisked egg, then in pecans. 3. Heat the oil in the cooking pot at MD on SEAR/SAUTÉ mode; brown the fillets on both sides. 4. Remove the salmon from the pot, and place the reversible rack in the pot in the lower position and drop the lower rack through the reversible rack handles. 5. Pour in the water and place the fillets on the rack. Install the pressure lid and turn the pressure release valve to the SEAL position. 6. Select PRESSURE COOK, set the cooking temperature to HI and adjust the cooking time to 4 minutes. 7. When cooked, let the unit naturally release pressure. 8. Serve and enjoy.
Per Serving: Calories 544; Fat 40.94g; Sodium 437mg; Carbs 7.08g; Fibre 0.86g; Sugar 0.43g; Protein 36.21g

Onion Prawns Gumbo

Prep Time: 25 minutes | Cook Time: 16 minutes | Serves: 8

60 ml vegetable oil
30 g plain flour
4 stalks celery, chopped
1 large yellow onion, peeled and diced
1 large green pepper, seeded and diced
2 cloves garlic, peeled and minced
1 (400 g) can diced tomatoes
¼ teaspoon dried thyme

¼ teaspoon cayenne pepper
2 bay leaves
1 tablespoon fileé powder
2 teaspoons Worcestershire sauce
960 ml seafood stock
455 g smoked sausage, sliced
455 g medium prawns, peeled and deveined
¼ teaspoon salt
¼ teaspoon ground black pepper
400 g cooked long-grain rice

1. Add the oil to the pot. Select SEAR/SAUTÉ. Select Lo3, and then press START/STOP to begin cooking. 2. When the oil is hot, add flour and cook for 15 minutes until flour is medium brown in color; add celery, onion, green pepper, garlic, and tomatoes, and cook them for 8 minutes until they are tender; stir in the thyme, cayenne, bay leaves, fileé, Worcestershire sauce, and stock, making sure nothing is stuck to the bottom of the pot. 3. Stop the process and add the sausage to the pot. 4. Close the lid, turn the pressure release valve to SEAL position, and then move the slider to PRESSURE. Select HI and set the cooking time to 8 minutes. Press START/STOP to begin cooking. When finished, release the pressure quickly. 5. Stir in prawns, salt, and black pepper, and then cook them at Lo3 on SEAR/SAUTÉ mode for 8 minutes or until prawns are cooked through. Discard bay leaves. 6. Serve hot over rice.
Per Serving: Calories 393; Fat: 19.86g; Sodium: 1421mg; Carbs: 30.81g; Fibre: 5.2g; Sugar: 4.22g; Protein: 26.34g

Chipotle Salmon

Prep Time: 20 minutes | Cook Time: 5 minutes | Serves: 3-4

240 ml water
¾ tsp. sea salt, divided
½ tsp. chipotle chili powder
1 tsp. ground cumin
3 to 4 (140-g) salmon fillets with skin, about 2.5 cm thick
Juice of 2 limes

1 tbsp. white vinegar
120 ml avocado oil or olive oil
1 chipotle pepper in adobo sauce
1 tbsp. adobo sauce
10 g chopped fresh coriander
Cooked rice or cauliflower rice, for serving

1. Pour the water into the pot and insert the rack. 2. In a small bowl, combine ¼ teaspoon of the salt and the chipotle chili powder and cumin. 3. Season the salmon with the spice mixture, rubbing it onto the fillets. Place the salmon on the rack with skin side down. 4. Close the lid, turn the pressure release valve to SEAL position, and then move the slider to PRESSURE. Select HI and set the cooking time to 4 minutes. Press START/STOP to begin cooking. When finished, release the pressure quickly. 5. In a blender or food processor, combine the lime juice, vinegar, oil, chipotle pepper, adobo sauce, coriander and remaining ½ teaspoon of salt and blend until smooth. Set aside. 6. Serve the salmon over a bed of rice or cauliflower rice and pour the vinaigrette on top.
Per Serving: Calories 330; Fat: 29.9g; Sodium: 493mg; Carbs: 3.7g; Fibre: 0.5g; Sugar: 1.18g; Protein: 13.45g

Red Curry Prawns

Prep Time: 20 minutes | Cook Time: 15 minutes | Serves: 6

1 (400-ml) can plus 60 ml coconut milk, divided
1 tsp. ground cumin
1 tsp. paprika
2 tsp. curry powder
3 tbsp fresh lime juice
1½ tsp sea salt, divided, plus more to taste
1 tbsp grated fresh ginger, divided
3 cloves garlic, minced, divided

905 g large prawns, peeled and deveined
2 tbsp coconut oil or olive oil
1 small white onion, diced
1 (800-g) can diced tomatoes
3 tbsp Thai red curry paste
15 g chopped fresh coriander, for garnish (optional)
745 g cooked rice or 440 g cauliflower rice, for serving

1. In a large bowl, combine 60 ml coconut milk and the cumin, paprika, curry powder, lime juice, ½ teaspoon of the salt, 1 teaspoon

of the ginger and ⅓ of the garlic, and then add the prawns. Toss to coat and let sit while you prepare the sauce. 2. Select SEAR/SAUTÉ. Select Lo3, and then press START/STOP to begin cooking. 3. Once hot, coat the bottom of the pot with the coconut oil; add onion, remaining ginger and remaining garlic, and sauté them for a few minutes. 4. Stop the process, and add tomatoes, curry paste, the remaining 13.125 g of coconut milk and the remaining teaspoon of salt to the pot. 5. Close the lid, turn the pressure release valve to SEAL position, and then move the slider to PRESSURE. Select HI and set the cooking time to 7 minutes. Press START/STOP to begin cooking. When finished, release the pressure quickly. 6. Toss in the prawns, plus its marinade, and then simmer them at Lo2 on SEAR/SAUTÉ mode for 2 to 5 minutes. 7. Garnish the dish with chopped fresh coriander (optional) and salt to taste, and serve over rice or cauliflower rice.
Per Serving: Calories 255; Fat: 9.73g; Sodium: 1644mg; Carbs: 17.84g; Fibre: 7.1g; Sugar: 9.57g; Protein: 26.32g

Coconut Prawns

Prep Time: 10 minutes | Cook Time: 10 minutes | Serves: 4

240 ml full-fat coconut milk
2 tablespoons freshly squeezed lime juice
1 tablespoon Sriracha
1 red pepper, seeded and chopped
½ teaspoon fine sea salt
Freshly ground black pepper
1 small head cauliflower, cut into

florets
455 g fresh or frozen raw prawns, peeled and deveined
200 g sugar snap peas
20 g lightly packed chopped fresh coriander
Lime wedges, for serving

1. Combine the coconut milk, lime juice, Sriracha, pepper, salt, and several grinds of pepper in the pot. 2. Place the rack in the pot and arrange the cauliflower on it. 3. Close the lid, turn the pressure release valve to SEAL position, and then move the slider to PRESSURE. Select HI and set the cooking time to 1 minute. Press START/STOP to begin cooking. When finished, release the pressure quickly. 4. Lift the rack of cauliflower out of the pot. 5. Add the prawns and snap peas to the pot, stir them well, and then simmer them at Lo2 on SEAR/SAUTÉ mode for 3 minutes until they are cooked through with a pink exterior (5 to 6 minutes for frozen). 6. Transfer the cooked cauliflower to a large bowl and use a potato masher to break up the florets into ricelike pieces. 7. Add the coriander to the pot, then ladle the prawns and vegetables over the cauliflower "rice." 8. Serve with lime wedges on the side.
Per Serving: Calories 337; Fat: 18.95g; Sodium: 397mg; Carbs: 38.84g; Fibre: 4.4g; Sugar: 29.78g; Protein: 8.06g

Prawns Pasta

Prep time: 20 minutes | Cook time: 20 minutes | Serves: 6

2 tablespoon rapeseed oil
4 boneless skinless chicken thighs (about 455g), cut into 5 x 2.5cm strips
1 can (700g) crushed tomatoes
360ml water
2 celery ribs, chopped
1 medium green pepper, cut into 2.5cm pieces
1 medium onion, coarsely chopped

2 garlic cloves, minced
1 tablespoon sugar
½ teaspoon salt
½ teaspoon Italian seasoning
⅛ to ¼ teaspoon cayenne pepper
1 bay leaf
120g uncooked orzo or other small pasta
455g. peeled and deveined cooked prawns

1. Heat 1 tablespoon of oil in the cooking pot at MD:HI for 30 seconds on SEAR/SAUTÉ mode; when hot, brown the chicken in batches, adding oil as needed. 2. Stop the cooker, and stir in the remaining ingredients except the orzo and prawns. 3. Install the pressure lid and turn the pressure release valve to the SEAL position. 4. Select PRESSURE COOK, set the cooking temperature to HI and adjust the cooking time to 8 minutes. 5. When cooked, let the unit naturally release pressure. 6. Discard bay leaf. 7. Select SEAR/SAUTÉ, stir in orzo and cook at HI until al dente. 8. Stir in prawns and cook for 2 minutes until the prawns are heated through.
Per Serving: Calories 068; Fat 45.81g; Sodium 2483mg; Carbs 42.42g; Fibre 5.8g; Sugar 7.09g; Protein 94.12g

Chapter 6 Snack and Appetizers

Olive-Stuffed Jalapeños

Prep Time: 10 minutes | Cook Time: 8 minutes | Serves: 5

60g plain cream cheese
25g finely grated Cheddar cheese
2 tablespoons chopped black

olives
5 medium jalapeño peppers, cut
lengthwise, seeded

1. Place the Cook & Crisp Basket in your Pressure Cooker Steam Fryer. 2. In a suitable bowl, cream cheese, Cheddar cheese, and black olives. 3. Press cream cheese mixture into each jalapeño half. 4. Lay stuffed peppers in ungreased "cook & crisp basket". 5. Put on the Smart Lid on top of the Ninja Foodi Steam Fryer. 6. Move the Lid Slider to the "Air Fry/Stovetop". Select the "Air Fry" mode for cooking. 7. Adjust the cooking temperature to 175°C for 8 minutes. 8. Once done, transfer stuffed peppers to a suitable serving plate and serve warm.
Per serving: Calories 319; Fat: 15.6g; Sodium 99mg; Carbs: 4.8g; Fibre: 0.7g; Sugars 2.9g; Protein 38.5g

Cheese Quesadillas

Prep Time: 10 minutes | Cook Time: 24 minutes | Serves: 4

8 tablespoons Mexican blend
shredded cheese

8 (15 cm) soft corn tortillas
2 teaspoons olive oil

1. Place the Cook & Crisp Basket in your Pressure Cooker Steam Fryer. 2. Evenly sprinkle cheese over four tortillas. Top each with a remaining tortilla and brush the tops with oil. 3. Place one quesadilla in ungreased "cook & crisp basket". 4. Put on the Smart Lid on top of the Ninja Foodi Steam Fryer. 5. Move the Lid Slider to the "Air Fry/Stovetop". Select the "Air Fry" mode for cooking. 6. Adjust the cooking temperature to 175°C for 6 minutes. 7. Remove and repeat with remaining quesadillas. 8. Transfer quesadillas to a suitable serving tray and serve warm.
Per serving: Calories 349; Fat: 15.1g; Sodium 157mg; Carbs: 25.6g; Fibre: 2.6g; Sugars 22.5g; Protein 29.7g

Deviled Eggs

Prep Time: 5 minutes | Cook Time: 15 minutes | Serves: 4

4 large eggs
240g ice cubes
240ml water
2 tablespoons mayonnaise
1 tablespoon Thousand Island
dressing
⅛ teaspoon salt

⅛ teaspoon black pepper
2 tablespoons finely chopped
corned beef
1 teaspoon caraway seeds
2 tablespoons finely chopped
Swiss cheese

1. Place the Cook & Crisp Basket in your Pressure Cooker Steam Fryer. 2. Place eggs in silicone cupcake liners to avoid eggs from moving around or cracking during cooking process. Add silicone cups to "cook & crisp basket". 3. Put on the Smart Lid on top of the Ninja Foodi Steam Fryer. 4. Move the Lid Slider to the "Air Fry/Stovetop". Select the "Air Fry" mode for cooking. Cook at 120°C for 15 minutes. 5. Add ice and water to a suitable bowl. Transfer cooked eggs to water bath immediately to stop cooking process. After 5 minutes, carefully peel eggs. 6. Cut eggs in half lengthwise. Spoon yolks into a suitable bowl. Arrange white halves on a suitable plate. 7. Using a fork, blend egg yolks with mayonnaise, dressing, salt, pepper, corned beef, and caraway seeds. Fold in cheese. Spoon mixture into egg white halves. Serve.
Per serving: Calories 182; Fat: 14.1g; Sodium 18mg; Carbs: 8.9g; Fibre: 4.1g; Sugars 4g; Protein 7.2g

Hot Wings

Prep Time: 15 minutes | Cook Time: 44 minutes | Serves: 6

900g chicken wings, split at the
joint
1 tablespoon water
1 tablespoon butter, room

temperature
120ml buffalo wing sauce
Cooking oil

1. Place the Cook & Crisp Basket in your Pressure Cooker Steam Fryer. 2. Place water in bottom of the Cook & Crisp Basket to ensure minimum smoke from fat: drippings. 3. Place half of chicken wings in "cook & crisp basket" greased with cooking oil. Put on the Smart Lid on top of the Ninja Foodi Steam Fryer. Move the Lid Slider to the "Air Fry/Stovetop". Select the "Air Fry" mode for cooking. 4. Adjust the cooking temperature to 120°C. 5. Cook 6 minutes. Flip wings, then cook an additional 6 minutes. 6. While wings are cooking, mix butter and wing sauce in a suitable bowl. 7. Increase temperature on air fryer to 200°C. Flip wings and cook for 5 minutes. 8. Once done, transfer to bowl with sauce and toss. Set aside. 9. Repeat process with remaining wings. Serve warm.
Per serving: Calories 271; Fat: 19.2g; Sodium 124mg; Carbs: 7.2g; Fibre: 2.9g; Sugars 0.5g; Protein 18.6g

Mustard Wings

Prep Time: 15 minutes | Cook Time: 44 minutes | Serves: 6

90g chicken wings, split at the
joint
1 tablespoon butter, melted
1 tablespoon water
1 tablespoon Dijon mustard

2 tablespoons yellow mustard
85g honey
1 teaspoon apple cider vinegar
⅛ teaspoon salt
Cooking oil

1. Place the Cook & Crisp Basket in your Pressure Cooker Steam Fryer. 2. Place water in bottom of the Cook & Crisp Basket to ensure minimum smoke from fat: drippings. 3. Place half of wings in "cook & crisp basket" greased with cooking oil. Put on the Smart Lid on top of the Ninja Foodi Steam Fryer. Move the Lid Slider to the "Air Fry/Stovetop". Select the "Air Fry" mode for cooking. Adjust the cooking temperature to 120°C. 4. Cook for 6 minutes. Flip wings, then cook an additional 6 minutes. 5. While wings are cooking, mix butter, Dijon mustard, yellow mustard, honey, cider vinegar, and salt in a suitable bowl. 6. Raise temperature to 200°C. Flip wings and cook for 5 minutes. Flip wings once more. Cook for an additional 5 minutes. 7. Transfer cooked wings to bowl with sauce and toss. Repeat process with remaining wings. Serve warm.
Per serving: Calories 309; Fat: 5.1g; Sodium 245mg; Carbs: 43g; Fibre: 9.6g; Sugars 14.2g; Protein 25.8g

Parmesan Pizza Bread

Prep Time: 15 minutes | Cook Time: 25 minutes | Serves: 4

310 g plain flour
4 teaspoons baking powder
½ teaspoon salt
230 g butter, chilled and divided
240 ml whole milk
2 tablespoons Italian seasoning

1 teaspoon chili powder
½ teaspoon garlic powder
100 g grated Parmesan cheese
360 ml water
120 g pizza sauce

1. Spray a baking pan with cooking spray and set aside. 2. Whisk the flour, baking powder, and salt in a medium bowl. 3. Cut 115 g butter into small cubes and place them into dry ingredients. Use a fork to mix in the butter until dry ingredients are crumbly and about the size of peas. 4. Slowly pour in milk, mixing until a dough forms. 5. Use clean hands to knead the dough about 10 minutes until smooth. 6. Pour dough onto a lightly floured surface and pat into a 23 cm round. Cut dough up into 2.5 cm pieces and set aside. 7. In a zip-top bag, combine Italian seasoning, chili powder, garlic powder, and Parmesan. Close bag and shake to mix. 8. Place cut pieces of dough into bag of spices. Gently knead bag until each piece of dough is coated in spice mixture. 9. Remove dough pieces and arrange evenly in the greased baking pan. 10. Select SEAR/SAUTÉ. Select Hi5, and then press START/STOP to begin cooking. 11. When the pot is hot, add the remaining butter and whisk for 1 minute until melted. 12. Stop the process, and pour the butter over the top of pizza bread pieces in the baking pan. 13. Clean the pot and return it to the unit. 14. Pour water into the pot and place in the rack. 15. Cover the pan with a paper towel and foil. Crimp edges to discourage water from getting inside pan. Create a foil sling and carefully lower the pan into the pot. 16. Close the lid, turn the pressure release valve to SEAL position, and then move the slider to PRESSURE. Select HI and set the cooking time to 21 minutes. Press START/STOP to begin cooking. When finished, release the pressure naturally. 17. Remove foil and paper towel from the top of pan and let cool on a rack for 5 minutes. 18. Serve the dish with pizza sauce for dipping.
Per Serving: Calories 890; Fat: 56.11g; Sodium: 1578mg; Carbs: 79.18g; Fibre: 3.7g; Sugar: 9.81g; Protein: 18.51g

Courgette Fries

Prep Time: 10 minutes | Cook Time: 20 minutes | Serves: 2

1 large courgette, cut into ½ cm fries	120ml buttermilk
1 teaspoon salt	75g gluten-free bread crumbs
	2 teaspoons dried thyme

1. Place the Cook & Crisp Basket in your Pressure Cooker Steam Fryer. 2. Scatter courgette fries evenly over a paper towel. Sprinkle with salt. Let sit 10 minutes, then pat with paper towels. 3. Pour buttermilk into a shallow dish. Place bread crumbs in a second shallow dish. Dip courgette in buttermilk, then dredge in bread crumbs. 4. Place half of courgette fries in ungreased "cook & crisp basket". Put on the Smart Lid on top of the Ninja Foodi Steam Fryer. Move the Lid Slider to the "Air Fry/Stovetop". Select the "Air Fry" mode for cooking. 5. Adjust the cooking temperature to 190°C. 6. Cook for 5 minutes. Flip fries, then cook an additional 5 minutes. 7. Transfer fries to a suitable serving dish. Repeat cooking steps with remaining fries. Season with thyme and serve warm.
Per serving: Calories 393; Fat: 11.7g; Sodium 591mg; Carbs: 16.4g; Fibre: 4.3g; Sugars 6.6g; Protein 56.4g

Honey Barbecue Beef Meatballs

Prep Time: 10 minutes | Cook Time: 10 minutes | Serves: 6

455 g beef mince	⅛ teaspoon black pepper
1 large egg	2 tablespoons olive oil
50 g bread crumbs	240 ml water
1 teaspoon minced onion	240 g barbecue sauce
¼ teaspoon garlic powder	70 g honey
¼ teaspoon salt	2 tablespoons brown sugar

1. Combine beef mince, egg, bread crumbs, onion, garlic powder, salt, and pepper in a medium bowl for 3 minutes or until fully combined. 2. Roll beef mixture into golf ball–sized meatballs. 3. Select SEAR/SAUTÉ. Select Hi5, and then press START/STOP to begin cooking. 4. When the pot is hot, heat the oil; brown the meatballs for 1 minute on each side until golden brown on the outside. Transfer the meatballs to a bowl and set aside. Stop the process. 5. Pour water into the pot and deglaze the pot. 6. Whisk together barbecue sauce, honey, and brown sugar in a small bowl. Place the meatballs in the pot and pour the sauce over them, turn the meatballs to coat them well. 7. Close the lid, turn the pressure release valve to SEAL position, and then move the slider to PRESSURE. Select HI and set the cooking time to 4 minutes. Press START/STOP to begin cooking. When finished, release the pressure naturally. 8. Serve the meatballs on toothpicks.
Per Serving: Calories 415; Fat: 14.09g; Sodium: 655mg; Carbs: 51.22g; Fibre: 1.1g; Sugar: 44.61g; Protein: 21.78g

Teriyaki Beef Meatballs

Prep Time: 10 minutes | Cook Time: 10 minutes | Serves: 6

455 g beef mince	30 g shredded carrots
1 large egg	1 clove garlic, minced
50 g bread crumbs	2 tablespoons olive oil
30 g diced green onions	360 g teriyaki sauce

1. Combine the beef mince, egg, bread crumbs, green onions, carrots, and garlic in a medium bowl for 3 minutes until fully combined. 2. Roll beef mixture into golf ball–sized meatballs. 3. Select SEAR/SAUTÉ. Select Hi5, and then press START/STOP to begin cooking. 4. When the pot is hot, heat the oil, and brown the meatballs for 1 minute on each side until golden brown on the outside. Transfer the meatballs to a bowl and set aside. 5. Pour teriyaki sauce into the pot and deglaze the pot, and stop the process. 6. Place meatballs in the pot and turn to coat in sauce. 7. Close the lid, turn the pressure release valve to SEAL position, and then move the slider to PRESSURE. Select HI and set the cooking time to 4 minutes. Press START/STOP to begin cooking. When finished, release the pressure naturally. 8. Serve the meatballs on toothpicks.
Per Serving: Calories 286; Fat: 13.78g; Sodium: 1346mg; Carbs: 13.54g; Fibre: 0.3g; Sugar: 10.67g; Protein: 25.21g

Breaded Chicken Meatballs

Prep Time: 10 minutes | Cook Time: 20 minutes | Serves: 6

455 g chicken mince	2 cloves garlic, minced
1 large egg	55 g blue cheese crumbles
50 g bread crumbs	2 tablespoons olive oil
125 g shredded carrots	120 ml water
15 g minced green onions	240 g buffalo sauce
25 g minced celery	

1. Combine the chicken, egg, bread crumbs, carrots, green onions, celery, garlic, and blue cheese in a medium bowl for 3 minutes until fully combined, about 3 minutes. 2. Roll chicken mixture into golf ball–sized meatballs. 3. Select SEAR/SAUTÉ. Select Hi5, and then press START/STOP to begin cooking. 4. When the pot is hot, heat the oil, and brown the meatballs for 1 minute on each side until golden brown on the outside. Transfer the meatballs to a bowl and set aside. 5. Pour water into the pot and deglaze the pot. Stop the process. 6. Place meatballs in the pot and pour buffalo sauce on top. Turn meatballs to coat in sauce. 7. Close the lid, turn the pressure release valve to SEAL position, and then move the slider to PRESSURE. Select HI and set the cooking time to 15 minutes. Press START/STOP to begin cooking. When finished, release the pressure naturally. 8. Serve the meatballs on toothpicks with drizzled sauce from pot.
Per Serving: Calories 278; Fat: 19.63g; Sodium: 510mg; Carbs: 6.93g; Fibre: 1.5g; Sugar: 2.95g; Protein: 18.33g

Buffalo Chicken Wings

Prep Time: 10 minutes | Cook Time: 15 minutes | Serves: 4

900 g frozen chicken wings	360 ml water
½ tablespoon Cajun seasoning	240 g buffalo wing sauce

1. Toss the chicken wings with Cajun seasoning in a large bowl so they are evenly coated. 2. Pour water in the pot and place in the rack. 3. Place wings in a spring-form pan. Create a foil sling and lower pan into the pot. 4. Close the lid, turn the pressure release valve to SEAL position, and then move the slider to PRESSURE. Select HI and set the cooking time to 15 minutes. Press START/STOP to begin cooking. When finished, release the pressure naturally. 5. Remove the wings and brush with buffalo sauce. Serve hot.
Per Serving: Calories 311; Fat: 9.63g; Sodium: 311mg; Carbs: 1.29g; Fibre: 0.2g; Sugar: 0.13g; Protein: 51.1g

Chili Tomato Nachos

Prep Time: 15 minutes | Cook Time: 45 minutes | Serves: 8

1 tablespoon olive oil	1 can diced tomatoes, including juice
1 small red onion, peeled and diced	1 (100 g) can chopped green chilis, including juice
1 medium green pepper, seeded and diced	100 g cream cheese
225 g beef mince	50 g shredded Cheddar cheese
115 g ground pork	2 Roma tomatoes, seeded and diced
1 tablespoon chili powder	4 spring onions, sliced
1 teaspoon garlic powder	1 bag corn tortilla chips
1 teaspoon ground cumin	
1 teaspoon salt	

1. Select SEAR/SAUTÉ. Select Hi5, and then press START/STOP to begin cooking. 2. When the pot is hot, heat the oil for 30 seconds; add onion and pepper, and cook them for 5 minutes until onions are translucent; add beef and pork, and cook them for 5 minutes, chopping them during cooking. 3. Stop the process, and stir in the chili powder, garlic powder, cumin, salt, tomatoes with juice, and chilis with juice. 4. Close the lid, turn the pressure release valve to SEAL position, and then move the slider to PRESSURE. Select HI and set the cooking time to 35 minutes. Press START/STOP to begin cooking. When finished, release the pressure naturally. 5. Stir in cream cheese until melted and evenly distributed. 6. Transfer the chili mixture to a serving dish. Garnish with cheese, Roma tomatoes, and spring onion s. 7. Serve the dish warm with chips.
Per Serving: Calories 360; Fat: 22.05g; Sodium: 658mg; Carbs: 24.88g; Fibre: 3.9g; Sugar: 3.84g; Protein: 17.17g

Curried Chicken Meatball Lettuce Wraps

Prep Time: 15 minutes | Cook Time: 15 minutes | Serves: 6

1 large egg, lightly beaten	Sauce:
1 small onion, finely chopped	240 g plain yogurt
20 g Rice Krispies	10 g minced fresh coriander
30 g golden raisins	Wraps:
10 g minced fresh coriander	24 small Bibb or Boston lettuce
2 tsp. curry powder	leaves
½ tsp. salt	1 medium carrot, shredded
455 g lean chicken mince	60 g golden raisins
2 tbsp. olive oil	60 g chopped salted peanuts

1. In a big bowl, combine the first 7 ingredients. Add chicken; mix lightly but thoroughly. Shape the mixture into 24 balls with wet hands. 2. Move slider to AIR FRY/STOVETOP. Select SEAR/SAUTÉ and set to 3. Select START/STOP to begin preheating. Allow unit to preheat for 2 minutes. After 2 minutes, heat the oil and brown meatballs in batches; remove and keep warm. Add 240 ml water to the pot. Cook 1 minute, stirring to loosen browned bits from pan. Press START/STOP to turn off the SEAR/SAUTÉ function. 3. Then place the Cook & Crisp Basket in the lower position in the pot. 4. Place meatballs on the basket, overlapping if needed. 5. Close the lid and move slider to PRESSURE. Make sure the pressure release valve is in the SEAL position. The temperature will default to HIGH, which is the correct setting. Set time to 7 minutes. Select START/STOP to begin cooking. 6. When cooking is complete, turn the pressure relief valve to the VENT position for quick pressure relief. Move slider to the right to unlock the lid, then carefully open it. 7. In a small bowl, mix the sauce ingredients. To serve, place 2 tsp. sauce and 1 meatball in each lettuce leaf; top with remaining ingredients. If desired, serve with additional minced fresh coriander.
Per Serving: Calories 442; Fat 26.21g; Sodium 386mg; Carbs 35.36g; Fibre 7.9g; Sugar 19.1g; Protein 25.55g

Deviled Eggs

Prep Time: 15 minutes | Cook Time: 5 minutes | Serves: 4

360 ml water	1 teaspoon white vinegar
6 large eggs	⅛ teaspoon salt
15 g mayonnaise	⅛ teaspoon black pepper
20 g mustard	¼ teaspoon paprika

1. Pour water into the pot. Place a rack in the pot and arrange eggs on top of rack. 2. Close the lid, turn the pressure release valve to SEAL position, and then move the slider to PRESSURE. Select HI and set the cooking time to 5 minutes. Press START/STOP to begin cooking. When finished, release the pressure naturally. 3. Carefully place eggs into a bowl of ice water. Leave eggs in ice bath 5 minutes. Remove eggs and peel. 4. Slice eggs in half and carefully scoop out yolk with a spoon. Place all yolks in a small bowl. 5. Add mayonnaise, mustard, vinegar, salt, and pepper to bowl of yolks. Mix them until fully combined. 6. Scoop heaping spoonfuls of egg yolk mixture into centre of halved hard-boiled eggs. 7. Sprinkle paprika on top of each deviled egg. 8. Chill eggs up to 24 hours until ready to be served.
Per Serving: Calories 151; Fat: 10.76g; Sodium: 348mg; Carbs: 1.47g; Fibre: 0.5g; Sugar: 0.47g; Protein: 11.35g

Baked Baby Potatoes

Prep Time: 15 minutes | Cook Time: 20 minutes | Serves: 10

4 slices bacon, halved	25 g grated Cheddar cheese
900 g baby yellow potatoes	2 tablespoons whole milk
(approximately 10), scrubbed	½ teaspoon salt
240 ml water	½ teaspoon ground black pepper
2 tablespoons unsalted butter	2 tablespoons chopped fresh
60 g sour cream	chives

1. Use a fork to pierce each potato four times. Set aside. 2. Select SEAR/SAUTÉ. Select Hi5, and then press START/STOP to begin cooking. 3. When the pot is hot, cook the bacon for 4 minutes until crisp; transfer the bacon to a plate and set aside, leaving rendered fat in the pot; add potatoes to the pot and sauté them for 3 minutes to absorb some of the bacon flavour. 4. Stop the process and pour the water in the pot. 5. Close the lid, turn the pressure release valve to SEAL position, and then move the slider to PRESSURE. 6. Select HI and set the cooking time to 7 minutes. Press START/STOP to begin cooking. 7. When finished, release the pressure quickly. 8. Transfer the potatoes to a plate. Let them cool for 5 minutes until you can handle them. 9. Cut potatoes in half lengthwise. Scoop out approximately half of the potato, creating a boat. Add scooped-out potato to a medium bowl. Place potato halves on a baking sheet lined with parchment paper. 10. In medium bowl with scooped-out potatoes, add butter, sour cream, Cheddar cheese, milk, salt, and pepper. Combine them until ingredients are well distributed. Spoon the mixture into potato halves. 11. Place the potato halves to the cleaned pot. Close the lid and move slider to AIR FRY/STOVETOP, then use the dial to select BAKE/ROAST. Adjust the cooking temperature to 180°C and set the cooking time to 5 minutes. Press START/STOP to begin cooking. 12. Crumble the bacon. 13. Transfer the potato halves to a serving dish; garnish the dish with bacon and chives. 14. Serve and enjoy.
Per Serving: Calories 226; Fat: 12.66g; Sodium: 484mg; Carbs: 23.47g; Fibre: 2g; Sugar: 0.57g; Protein: 4.7g

Aubergine Caponata

Prep Time: 15 minutes | Cook Time: 3 minutes | Serves: 8

2 medium aubergines, cut into 1	2 tbsp. red wine vinegar
cm. pieces	4 tsp. capers, undrained
1 can diced tomatoes, undrained	5 bay leaves
1 medium onion, chopped	1½ tsp. salt
120 ml dry red wine	¼ tsp. coarsely ground pepper
12 garlic cloves, sliced	French bread baguette slices,
3 tbsp. extra virgin olive oil	toasted

Optional toppings: Fresh basil leaves, toasted pine nuts and additional olive oil
1. Place the first 11 ingredients in the pot, do not stir. Close the lid and move slider to PRESSURE. Make sure the pressure release valve is in the SEAL position. The temperature will default to HIGH, which is the correct setting. Set time to 3 minutes. Select START/STOP to begin cooking. 2. When cooking is complete, turn the pressure relief valve to the VENT position for quick pressure relief. Move slider to the right to unlock the lid, then carefully open it. 3. Cool slightly; discard bay leaves. Serve with toasted baguette slices. If desired, serve with toppings.
Per Serving: Calories 89; Fat 2.88g; Sodium 570mg; Carbs 14.6g; Fibre 5.8g; Sugar 7.14g; Protein 2.67g

Delicious Ranch Deviled Eggs

Prep Time: 10 minutes | Cook Time: 5 minutes | Serves: 4

360 ml water	¼ teaspoon dill weed
6 large eggs	⅛ teaspoon salt
30 g mayonnaise	⅛ teaspoon garlic powder
30 g full-fat sour cream	⅛ teaspoon onion powder
1 teaspoon white vinegar	⅛ teaspoon dried basil
¼ teaspoon dried parsley	

1. Pour water into the pot. 2. Then place the bottom layer of the Deluxe Reversible Rack in the lower position in the pot. Arrange eggs on top of the rack. 3. Close the lid and move slider to PRESSURE. Make sure the pressure release valve is in the SEAL position. The temperature will default to HIGH, which is the correct setting. Set time to 5 minutes. Select START/STOP to begin cooking. 4. When cooking is complete, naturally release the pressure for 10 minutes. Then turn the pressure relief valve to the VENT position for quick pressure relief. Move slider to AIR FRY/ STOVETOP to unlock the lid, then carefully open it. 5. Carefully place eggs into a bowl of ice water. Leave eggs in ice bath 5 minutes. Remove eggs and peel. 6. Slice eggs in half and carefully scoop out yolk with a spoon. Place all yolks in a small bowl. 7. Add mayonnaise, sour cream, vinegar, dill weed, parsley, salt, onion powder, garlic powder, and basil to bowl of yolks. Mix until fully combined. 8. Scoop heaping spoonfuls of egg yolk mixture into centre of halved hard-boiled eggs. 9. Chill eggs up to 24 hours until ready to be served.
Per Serving: Calories 114; Fat 9.25g; Sodium 163mg; Carbs 2.52g; Fibre 0.1g; Sugar 0.25g; Protein 4.79g

Chili Pork Picadillo Lettuce Wraps

Prep Time: 30 minutes | Cook Time: 30 minutes | Serves: 4

3 garlic cloves, minced
1 tbsp. chili powder
1 tsp. salt
½ tsp. pumpkin pie spice
½ tsp. ground cumin
½ tsp. pepper
2 pork tenderloins
1 large onion, chopped
1 small sweet red pepper, chopped
1 can diced tomatoes and green

chilies, undrained
1 small Granny Smith apple, peeled and chopped
240 ml water
60 g golden raisins
55 g chopped pimiento-stuffed olives
24 Bibb or Boston lettuce leaves
30 g slivered almonds, toasted

1. Mix garlic and seasonings in a small bowl. Rub this mixture over the pork and transfer the pork to the pot. Add the onion, apple, tomatoes, sweet pepper and water. 2. Close the lid and move slider to PRESSURE. Make sure the pressure release valve is in the SEAL position. The temperature will default to HIGH, which is the correct setting. Set time to 25 minutes. Select START/STOP to begin cooking. 3. When cooking is complete, naturally release the pressure for 10 minutes. Then turn the pressure release valve to the VENT position for quick pressure relief. Move slider to AIR FRY/ STOVETOP to unlock the lid, then carefully open it. 4. Remove the pork and let cool slightly. Shred meat into bite-size pieces; return to the pot. 5. Move slider to AIR FRY/STOVETOP. Select SEAR/SAUTÉ and set to Lo1. Select START/STOP to begin cooking. Stir in raisins and olives; heat through about 5 minutes. 6. Serve in lettuce leaves; sprinkle with slivered almonds.
Per Serving: Calories 515; Fat 11.23g; Sodium 1218mg; Carbs 39.62g; Fibre 7.9g; Sugar 21.61g; Protein 66.53g

Cheddar Cream Bacon Beer Dip

Prep Time: 15 minutes | Cook Time: 10 minutes | Serves: 6

450 g cream cheese, softened
60 g sour cream
1½ tbsp. Dijon mustard
1 tsp. garlic powder
240 ml beer or nonalcoholic beer
455 g bacon strips, cooked and

crumbled
200 g shredded cheddar cheese
60 g heavy whipping cream
1 green onion, thinly sliced
Soft pretzel bites

1. Combine the cream cheese, sour cream, mustard and garlic powder in the pot, stir until smooth. Stir in beer, crumbled bacon, reserving 2 tbsp. 2. Close the lid and move slider to PRESSURE. Make sure the pressure release valve is in the SEAL position. The temperature will default to HIGH, which is the correct setting. Set time to 5 minutes. Select START/STOP to begin cooking. 3. When cooking is complete, turn the pressure relief valve to the VENT position for quick pressure relief. Move slider to the right to unlock the lid, then carefully open it. 4. Move slider to AIR FRY/STOVETOP. Select SEAR/SAUTÉ and set to 3. Select START/STOP to begin cooking. Stir in the cheese and heavy cream. Cook and stir until mixture has thickened, 3 to 4 minutes. 5. Transfer to a serving dish. Sprinkle with onion and reserved bacon. Serve with pretzel bites.
Per Serving: Calories 755; Fat 62.98g; Sodium 1580mg; Carbs 24.5g; Fibre 2.5g; Sugar 3.42g; Protein 25.61g

Orange, Apple and Pear Compote

Prep Time: 20 minutes | Cook Time: 10 minutes | Serves: 8

5 medium apples, peeled and chopped
3 medium pears, chopped
1 medium orange, thinly sliced
60 g dried cranberries
105 g packed brown sugar
100 g maple syrup

80 ml butter, cubed
2 tbsp. lemon juice
2 tsp. ground cinnamon
1 tsp. ground ginger
5 tbsp. orange juice, divided
4 tsp. cornflour

1. Combine the first 10 ingredients in the pot. Stir in 2 tbsp. orange juice. 2. Close the lid and move slider to PRESSURE. Make sure the pressure release valve is in the SEAL position. The temperature will default to HIGH, which is the correct setting. Set time to 6 minutes. Select START/STOP to begin cooking. 3. When cooking is complete,

naturally release the pressure for 10 minutes. Then turn the pressure relief valve to the VENT position for quick pressure relief. Move slider to AIR FRY/ STOVETOP to unlock the lid, then carefully open it. 4. Move slider to AIR FRY/STOVETOP. Select SEAR/SAUTÉ and set to 4. Select START/STOP to begin cooking. Bring the liquid to a boil. 5. Stir the cornflour and remaining orange juice in a small bowl, mix until smooth; gradually stir into fruit mixture. 6. Cook and stir until sauce is thickened, 1 to 2 minutes.
Per Serving: Calories 302; Fat 8.01g; Sodium 69mg; Carbs 61.08g; Fibre 6.1g; Sugar 46.38g; Protein 1.03g

Cheese Artichoke Dip

Prep Time: 5 minutes | Cook Time: 7 minutes | Serves: 6

1 can quartered artichoke hearts, drained
1 can mild diced green chilies
240 g mayonnaise

1 teaspoon paprika
½ teaspoon garlic powder
220 g shredded mozzarella cheese
100 g grated Parmesan cheese

1. Add the artichoke hearts, green chilies, paprika, mayonnaise, and garlic powder to the pot. 2. Close the lid and move slider to PRESSURE. Make sure the pressure release valve is in the SEAL position. The temperature will default to HIGH, which is the correct setting. Set time to 7 minutes. Select START/STOP to begin cooking. 3 When the timer beeps, quick release pressure and then unlock the lid. 4. Mix in cheeses and serve hot.
Per Serving: Calories 271; Fat 17.5g; Sodium 996mg; Carbs 9.03g; Fibre 3.1g; Sugar 1.22g; Protein 20.18g

Classic Muddy Buddies

Prep Time: 15 minutes | Cook Time: 15 minutes | Serves: 6

480 ml water
105 g semisweet chocolate chips
105 g smooth peanut butter
55 g butter

½ teaspoon vanilla extract
160 g square rice cereal
100 g icingsugar

1. Pour water into the pot and press SEAR/SAUTÉ, set the heat to Hi5 and bring the water to a boil. 2. Place a large metal bowl on the top of the pot, so it is sitting partially inside pot. 3. Place chocolate chips, peanut butter, butter, and vanilla in the bowl, stir constantly until fully melted and smooth, about 15 minutes. 4. Pour in cereal and stir until fully coated. 5. Sprinkle icing sugar on top and mix until evenly coated. Press START/STOP to turn off the SEAR/SAUTÉ function. 6. Spread muddy buddies onto parchment-lined baking pan and let cool. 7. Store in an air-tight container at room temperature. Muddy Buddies can be stored up to three days.
Per Serving: Calories 437; Fat 27.39g; Sodium 198mg; Carbs 39.87g; Fibre 5.1g; Sugar 18.78g; Protein 10.04g

Hot Nacho Cheese Dip

Prep Time: 15 minutes | Cook Time: 15 minutes | Serves: 8

2 tablespoons unsalted butter
2 tablespoons plain flour
240 ml whole milk
1 teaspoon hot sauce

410 g shredded sharp Cheddar cheese
1 (250 g) can diced tomatoes with green chilies

1. Move slider to AIR FRY/STOVETOP. Select SEAR/SAUTÉ and set to 3. Select START/STOP to begin preheating. Allow unit to preheat for 1 minute. After 1 minute, melt the butter. 2. Whisk in flour and stir constantly 3 minutes until flour is combined with butter and golden brown. 3. Slowly whisk in milk. Continue mixing 3 minutes until sauce is no longer lumpy. Mix in hot sauce. 4. Add in cheese 100 g at a time and stir 5 minutes until fully melted. 5. Fold in diced tomatoes. Let cook for 3 minutes, stirring occasionally, until hot. 6. Press START/STOP to turn off the SEAR/SAUTÉ function and serve hot.
Per Serving: Calories 287; Fat 22.02g; Sodium 534mg; Carbs 7.59g; Fibre 0.1g; Sugar 4.11g; Protein 15.08g

Cereal Party Mix

Prep Time: 15 minutes | Cook Time: 2½ hours | Serves: 12

105 g square corn cereal
105 g square rice cereal
45 g square wheat cereal
55 g bagel chips
55 g small pretzels

55 g fish-shaped cheese crackers
60 ml Worcestershire sauce
6 tablespoons butter, melted
3 teaspoons garlic salt
¾ teaspoon onion powder

1. Spray inside of the pot with cooking spray. 2. Add the corn cereal, wheat cereal, rice cereal, pretzels, bagel chips, and cheese crackers to the pot and stir to combine. 3. In a small bowl, mix together the Worcestershire sauce, garlic salt, butter, and onion powder. Pour over cereal and stir. 4. Place two paper towels overlapping on top of the pot and top with a glass lid. 5. Move slider to the AIR FRY/ STOVETOP. Select Slow Cook button and set the temperature to HIGH. Cook for 2½ hours. Stir every 30 minutes. 6. When cooking is complete, pour the party mix onto a parchment-lined baking pan to cool. 7. Serve at room temperature and store any unused portion in an air-tight container. Party Mix can be stored up to three days.

Per Serving: Calories 311; Fat 6.87g; Sodium 210mg; Carbs 54.26g; Fibre 2.5g; Sugar 1.95g; Protein 7.28g

Chapter 7 Dessert Recipes

Zesty Raspberry Muffins

Prep Time: 10 minutes | Cook Time: 35 minutes | Serves: 10

1 egg
250g frozen raspberries, coated with some flour
185g flour
100g sugar
80ml vegetable oil

2 teaspoon baking powder
Yogurt, as needed
1 teaspoon lemon zest
2 tablespoon lemon juice
Pinch of sea salt

1. Place the Cook & Crisp Basket in your Pressure Cooker Steam Fryer. 2. Place all of the dry recipe ingredients in a bowl and mix well. 3. Beat the egg and pour it into a cup. Mix it with the oil and lemon juice. Add in the yogurt, to taste. 4. Mix the dry and wet recipe ingredients. 5. Add in the lemon zest and raspberries. 6. Coat the insides of 10 muffin tins with a little butter. 7. Spoon an equal amount of the mixture into each muffin tin. 8. Transfer to the Cook & Crisp Basket. Put on the Smart Lid on top of the Ninja Foodi Steam Fryer. Move the Lid Slider to the "Air Fry/Stovetop". Select the "Air Fry" mode for cooking. Adjust the cooking temperature to 175°C. 9. Cook for around 10 minutes, in batches if necessary.
Per serving: Calories 257; Fat: 16.5g; Sodium 1031mg; Carbs: 23.6g; Fibre: 3.4g; Sugars 6.1g; Protein 4.7g

Vanilla Pecan Pie

Prep Time: 10 minutes | Cook Time: 1 hour 10 minutes | Serves: 4

1x 20 cm pie dough
½ teaspoon cinnamon
¾ teaspoon vanilla extract
2 eggs
235g maple syrup
⅛ teaspoon nutmeg

2 tablespoon butter
1 tablespoon butter, melted
2 tablespoon sugar
55g chopped pecans
Oil

1. Place the Cook & Crisp Basket in your Pressure Cooker Steam Fryer. 2. In a suitable bowl, coat the pecans in the melted butter. 3. Transfer the pecans to the Cook & Crisp Basket. Put on the Smart Lid on top of the Ninja Foodi Steam Fryer. Move the Lid Slider to the "Air Fry/Stovetop". Select the "Air Fry" mode for cooking. Cook at 185°C for 10 minutes. Then grease the Cook & Crisp Basket with oil. Put the pie dough in it and add the pecans on top. 4. In a suitable bowl, mix the rest of the ingredients. Pour this over the pecans. 5. Put on the Smart Lid on top of the Ninja Foodi Steam Fryer. Move the Lid Slider to the "Air Fry/Stovetop". Select the "Air Fry" mode for cooking. Adjust the cooking temperature to 370°F/190°C. 6. Air Fry for around 25 minutes.
Per serving: Calories 194; Fat: 13g; Sodium 208mg; Carbs: 30.6g; Fibre: 5.6g; Sugars 20.7g; Protein 9.1g

Honey Chocolate Cookies

Prep Time: 10 minutes | Cook Time: 30 minutes | Serves: 8

75g sugar
100g butter
1 tablespoon honey

150g flour
1½ tablespoon milk
50g chocolate chips

1. Place the Cook & Crisp Basket in your Pressure Cooker Steam Fryer. 2. Mix the sugar and butter using an electric mixer, until a fluffy texture is achieved. 3. Stir in the remaining ingredients, minus the chocolate chips. 4. Gradually fold in the chocolate chips. 5. Spoon equal portions of the mixture onto a lined baking sheet and flatten out each one with a spoon. Ensure the cookies are not touching. 6. Place in the Cook & Crisp Basket. Put on the Smart Lid on top of the Ninja Foodi Steam Fryer. Move the Lid Slider to the "Air Fry/Stovetop". Select the "Air Fry" mode for cooking. Adjust the cooking temperature to 175°C. 7. Cook for around 18 minutes.
Per serving: Calories 148; Fat: 0.7g; Sodium 3mg; Carbs: 57.4g; Fibre: 5.1g; Sugars 40.4g; Protein 2g

Easy Butter Cake

Prep Time: 10 minutes | Cook Time: 25 minutes | Serves: 2

1 egg   60g flour

7 tablespoon butter, at room temperature
6 tablespoon milk
6 tablespoon sugar

Pinch of sea salt
Cooking spray
Dusting of sugar to serve

1. Place the Cook & Crisp Basket in your Pressure Cooker Steam Fryer. 2. Spritz the inside of a suitable ring cake tin with cooking spray. 3. In a suitable bowl, mix the butter and sugar using a whisk. 4. Stir in the egg and continue to mix everything until the mixture is smooth and fluffy. 5. Pour the flour through a sieve into the bowl. 6. Pour in the milk, before adding a pinch of salt, and mix once again to incorporate everything well. 7. Pour the prepared batter into the tin and use the back of a spoon to made sure the surface is even. 8. Place in the Cook & Crisp Basket. Put on the Smart Lid on top of the Ninja Foodi Steam Fryer. Move the Lid Slider to the "Air Fry/Stovetop". Select the "Air Fry" mode for cooking. Adjust the cooking temperature to 180°C. 9. Cook for around 15 minutes. 10. Before removing it from Pressure Cooker Steam Fryer, ensure the cake is cooked through by inserting a toothpick into the centre and checking that it comes out clean. 11. Allow the cake to cool and serve with dusting of sugar.
Per serving: Calories 281; Fat: 6.7g; Sodium 187mg; Carbs: 52.7g; Fibre: 6.6g; Sugars 29g; Protein 5.1g

Chocolate Mug Cake

Prep Time: 10 minutes | Cook Time: 15 minutes | Serves: 1

1 tablespoon cocoa powder
3 tablespoon coconut oil
30g flour

3 tablespoons whole milk
5 tablespoon sugar

1. Place the Cook & Crisp Basket in your Pressure Cooker Steam Fryer. 2. In a suitable bowl, stir all of the recipe ingredients to mix them completely. 3. Take a short, stout mug and pour the mixture into it. 4. Put the mug in your Ninja Foodi Pressure Steam Fryer. Put on the Smart Lid on top of the Ninja Foodi Steam Fryer. Move the Lid Slider to the "Air Fry/Stovetop". Select the "Air Fry" mode for cooking. Cook for around 10 minutes at 200°C.
Per serving: Calories 361; Fat: 31.3g; Sodium 385mg; Carbs: 13.8g; Fibre: 7.3g; Sugars 2.5g; Protein 9.7g

Dough Dippers with Chocolate Sauce

Prep Time: 10 minutes | Cook Time: 45 minutes | Serves: 5

150g sugar
455g friendly bread dough
240g heavy cream
150g high quality semi-sweet

chocolate chips
115g butter, melted
2 tablespoon extract

1. Place the Cook & Crisp Basket in your Pressure Cooker Steam Fryer. 2. Coat the inside of the basket with a little melted butter. 3. Halve and roll up the prepared dough to create two 38 cm logs. Slice each log into 20 disks. 4. Halve each disk and twist it 3 or 4 times. 5. Lay out a cookie sheet and lay the twisted dough pieces on top. Brush the pieces with some more melted butter and sprinkle on the sugar. 6. Place the sheet in the Cook & Crisp Basket. Put on the Smart Lid on top of the Ninja Foodi Steam Fryer. Move the Lid Slider to the "Air Fry/Stovetop". Select the "Air Fry" mode for cooking. 7. Adjust the cooking temperature to 175°C. 8. Air Fry for around 5 minutes. Flip the prepared dough twists over, and brush the other side with more butter. Cook for an additional 3 minutes. It may be necessary to complete this step in batches. 9. In the meantime, make the chocolate sauce. Firstly, put the heavy cream into a suitable saucepan over medium heat and allow it to simmer. 10. Put the chocolate chips into a large bowl and add the simmering cream on top. Mix the chocolate chips everything until a smooth consistency is achieved. Stir in 2 tablespoons of extract. 11. Transfer the fried cookies in a shallow dish, pour over the rest of the melted butter and sprinkle on the sugar. 12. Drizzle on the chocolate sauce before serving.
Per serving: Calories 469; Fat: 36.5g; Sodium 46mg; Carbs: 31.4g; Fibre: 4.5g; Sugars 17.9g; Protein 9.1g

Butter Peach Crumble

Prep Time: 10 minutes | Cook Time: 35 minutes | Serves: 6

675g peaches, peeled and chopped	1 tablespoon water
2 tablespoon lemon juice	100g sugar
125g flour	5 tablespoons cold butter
	Pinch of sea salt

1. Place the Cook & Crisp Basket in your Pressure Cooker Steam Fryer. 2. Mash the peaches a little with a fork to achieve a lumpy consistency. 3. Add in two tablespoons of sugar and the lemon juice. 4. In a bowl, mix the flour, salt, and sugar. Throw in a tablespoon of water before adding in the cold butter, mixing until crumbly. 5. Grease the Cook & Crisp Basket and arrange the berries at the bottom. Top with the crumbs. 6. Put on the Smart Lid on top of the Ninja Foodi Steam Fryer. Move the Lid Slider to the "Air Fry/Stovetop". Select the "Air Fry" mode for cooking. Air Fry for around 20 minutes at 200°C.
Per serving: Calories 363; Fat: 10.7g; Sodium 253mg; Carbs: 63.7g; Fibre: 3.8g; Sugars 22.9g; Protein 4.9g

Pumpkin Pudding

Prep Time: 10 minutes | Cook Time: 25 minutes | Serves: 4

865g pumpkin puree	1 teaspoon nutmeg
3 tablespoon honey	240g full-fat cream
1 tablespoon ginger	2 eggs
1 tablespoon cinnamon	200g sugar
1 teaspoon clove	

1. Place the Cook & Crisp Basket in your Pressure Cooker Steam Fryer. 2. In a suitable bowl, stir all of the recipe ingredients to mix. 3. Grease inside of the Cook & Crisp Basket. 4. Pour the mixture into the Cook & Crisp Basket. 5. Put on the Smart Lid on top of the Ninja Foodi Steam Fryer. 6. Move the Lid Slider to the "Air Fry/Stovetop". Select the "Air Fry" mode for cooking. 7. Adjust the cooking temperature to 200°C. 8. Cook for around 15 minutes. Serve with whipped cream if desired.
Per serving: Calories 360; Fat: 7.8g; Sodium 280mg; Carbs: 74.4g; Fibre: 8g; Sugars 47.4g; Protein 2.7g

Walnut Bread

Prep Time: 10 minutes | Cook Time: 40 minutes | Serves: 1 loaf

175g flour	2 medium eggs
¼ teaspoon baking powder	100g bananas, peeled
125g butter	200g chopped walnuts
125g sugar	

1. Place the Cook & Crisp Basket in your Pressure Cooker Steam Fryer. 2. Grease the Cook & Crisp Basket with butter. 3. Mix the flour and the baking powder in a suitable bowl. 4. In a separate bowl, beat the sugar and butter until fluffy and pale. Gradually add in the flour and egg. Stir. 5. Throw in the walnuts and mix again. 6. Mash the bananas using a fork and transfer to the bowl. Mix once more, until everything is incorporated. 7. Pour the mixture into the Cook & Crisp Basket. Put on the Smart Lid on top of the Ninja Foodi Steam Fryer. Move the Lid Slider to the "Air Fry/Stovetop". Select the "Air Fry" mode for cooking. 8. Adjust the cooking temperature to 175°C. 9. Cook for around 10 minutes.
Per serving: Calories 488; Fat: 34.3g; Sodium 130mg; Carbs: 42.4g; Fibre: 1.7g; Sugars 21.5g; Protein 4.8g

Air-Fried Peach Slices

Prep Time: 10 minutes | Cook Time: 40 minutes | Serves: 4

615g peaches, sliced	2 tablespoons unsalted butter
2–3 tablespoon sugar	¼ teaspoon vanilla extract
2 tablespoon flour	1 teaspoon cinnamon
25g oats	

1. Place the Cook & Crisp Basket in your Pressure Cooker Steam Fryer. 2. In a large bowl, mix the peach slices, sugar, vanilla extract, and cinnamon. Pour the prepared mixture into the Cook & Crisp Basket. 3. Put on the Smart Lid on top of the Ninja Foodi Steam Fryer.

4. Move the Lid Slider to the "Air Fry/Stovetop". Select the "Air Fry" mode for cooking. 5. Cook for around 20 minutes on 145°C. 6. In the meantime, mix the oats, flour, and unsalted butter in a separate bowl. 7. Once the peach slices cooked, pour the butter mixture on top of them. 8. Cook for around 10 minutes at 155°C. 9.Remove from the Pressure Cooker Steam Fryer and allow to crisp up for around 5–10 minutes. Serve with ice cream if desired.
Per serving: Calories 130; Fat: 3.9g; Sodium 3mg; Carbs: 21.6g; Fibre: 1.6g; Sugars 9.8g; Protein 3.6g

Cream Chocolate Cheesecake

Prep Time: 10 minutes | Cook Time: 30 minutes | Serves: 6

Crust:	100 g sugar
20 vanilla wafers	25 g unsweetened cocoa
2 tablespoons creamy peanut butter	2 large eggs, room temperature
3 tablespoons melted butter	1 teaspoon vanilla extract
Cheesecake Filling:	480 ml water
300 g cream cheese, cubed and room temperature	30 g mini semisweet chocolate chips
2 tablespoons sour cream, room temperature	30 g chopped peanuts
	2 tablespoons chocolate syrup
	240 g whipped cream

1. Grease a baking pan and set aside. 2. Add vanilla wafers to a food processor and pulse to combine. Add in peanut butter and melted butter. Pulse them to blend. 3. Transfer crumb mixture to the pan and press down along the bottom and about ⅓ of the way up the sides of the pan. Place a square of aluminum foil along the outside bottom of the pan and crimp up around the edges. 4. Cream together cream cheese, sour cream, sugar, and cocoa in a food processor until smooth. Slowly add eggs and vanilla extract. Pulse them for another 10 seconds. Scrape the bowl and pulse until batter is smooth. 5. Transfer the batter into the pan. 6. Pour water into the pot and place in the rack. Set the pan on the rack. 7. Close the lid, turn the pressure release valve to SEAL position, and then move the slider to PRESSURE. Select HI and set the cooking time to 30 minutes. Press START/STOP to begin cooking. When finished, release the pressure quickly. 8. Lift pan out of pot. Garnish immediately with chocolate chips and chopped peanuts. Let cool at room temperature for 10 minutes. 9. The cheesecake will be a little jiggly in the centre. Refrigerate the cake for a minimum of 2 hours to allow it to set. 10. Release side pan and serve with drizzled chocolate syrup and whipped cream.
Per Serving: Calories 634; Fat: 39.65g; Sodium: 471mg; Carbs: 37.38g; Fibre: 2.4g; Sugar: 30.06g; Protein: 10.79g

Homemade Fruitcake

Prep Time: 15 minutes | Cook Time: 20 minutes | Serves: 8

1 (200 g) can crushed pineapple, including juice	55 g melted butter, cooled
65 g raisins	2 teaspoons vanilla extract
65 g dried unsweetened cherries	2 tablespoons fresh orange juice
65 g pitted and diced dates	4 large eggs
120 g pecan halves	125 g plain flour
60 g chopped walnuts	2 teaspoons baking powder
60 g unsweetened coconut flakes	¼ teaspoon salt
100 g sugar	¼ teaspoon ground nutmeg
	240 ml water

1. Combine all ingredients except water in a medium bowl. Grease a cake pan, and press mixture into the pan. 2. Pour 240 ml water into the pot and place in the rack. Lower the pan onto rack. 3. Close the lid, turn the pressure release valve to SEAL position, and then move the slider to PRESSURE. Select HI and set the cooking time to 20 minutes. Press START/STOP to begin cooking. When finished, release the pressure naturally. 4. Transfer the pan to a cooling rack. Refrigerate the cake covered overnight. 5. Flip onto a cutting board, slice, and serve.
Per Serving: Calories 735; Fat: 22.25g; Sodium: 179mg; Carbs: 128.68g; Fibre: 4.9g; Sugar: 110.46g; Protein: 10.06g

Red Wine–Poached Pears

Prep Time: 15 minutes | Cook Time: 15 minutes | Serves: 4

4 ripe but still firm pears	50 g sugar
2 tablespoons fresh lemon juice	1 cinnamon stick
960 ml dry red wine	½ teaspoon ground cloves
120 ml freshly squeezed orange juice	½ teaspoon ground ginger
2 teaspoons grated orange zest	1 sprig fresh mint

1. Rinse and peel the pears leaving the stem. 2. Using a corer or melon baller, remove the cores from underneath without going through the top so you can maintain the stem. Brush the pears inside and out with the lemon juice. 3. Combine the wine, orange juice, orange zest, sugar, cinnamon stick, cloves, and ginger in the pot. 4. Bring the mixture to a slow boil at Lo4 on SEAR/SAUTÉ mode for 3 to 5 minutes; stir to blend and dissolve the sugar. 5. Carefully place the pears in liquid, and cook them at Lo2 for 5 minutes. Stop the process. 6. Close the lid, turn the pressure release valve to SEAL position, and then move the slider to PRESSURE. Select LO and set the cooking time to 3 minutes. Press START/STOP to begin cooking. When finished, release the pressure quickly. 7. Transfer the pears to a serving platter. Garnish the dish with mint sprig. Enjoy.

Per Serving: Calories 235; Fat: 1.57g; Sodium: 22mg; Carbs: 46.92g; Fibre: 5.9g; Sugar: 33.46g; Protein: 1.19g

Bread Pudding

Prep Time: 10 minutes | Cook Time: 20 minutes | Serves: 6

280 g cubed cinnamon-raisin bread, dried out overnight	2 tablespoons pure maple syrup
1 apple, peeled, cored, and diced small	¼ teaspoon ground cinnamon
	Pinch of ground nutmeg
30 g raisins	Pinch of sea salt
480 ml whole milk	3 tablespoons butter, cut into 3 pats
3 large eggs	
½ teaspoon vanilla extract	360 ml water

1. Grease a glass dish. Add bread, apple, and raisins. Set aside. 2. In a small bowl, whisk together milk, eggs, vanilla, maple syrup, cinnamon, nutmeg, and salt. Pour over bread in glass dish and place pats of butter on top. 3. Pour water into the pot and place rack in the pot. Place glass dish on top of rack. 4. Close the lid, turn the pressure release valve to SEAL position, and then move the slider to PRESSURE. Select HI and set the cooking time to 20 minutes. Press START/STOP to begin cooking. When finished, release the pressure naturally. 5. Remove glass bowl from the pot. Transfer to a rack until cooled. Serve.

Per Serving: Calories 225; Fat: 11.24g; Sodium: 167mg; Carbs: 26.88g; Fibre: 1.3g; Sugar: 18.03g; Protein: 5.11g

Easy Customizable Cheesecake

Prep Time: 25 minutes | Cook Time: 45 minutes | Serves: 6-8

4 tablespoons salted butter, melted (plus more for greasing the pan)	1 tablespoon plain flour
	1 (85 g) package Vanilla Jell-O Instant Pudding (it must be instant)
50 g digestive biscuit crumbs	
2 (200 g) bricks of cream cheese, at room temperature (a must)	1½ teaspoons vanilla extract
	½ teaspoon almond extract
150 g granulated sugar	2 large eggs, at room temperature
120 g sour cream, at room temperature (also a must)	Any cookies, candy, fruit, or topping you wish (optional)

1. Generously grease a springform pan all over with butter, then line the bottom with a parchment paper round and grease the top of the parchment paper as well. 2. Mix the biscuit crumbs and melted butter in a bowl. Add the crust mixture to the bottom of the greased pan and, using the bottom of a drinking glass, flatten the crust so it's even on the bottom and slightly climbs the sides of the pan. Pop in the freezer for at least 15 minutes to set. 3. Using a stand mixer with the paddle attached to beat the cream cheese on low speed until smooth and creamy. Then, while the mixer is still running, add in this order: the sugar, sour cream, flour, pudding mix, flavour extracts, and eggs (one at a time). Keep mixing on low speed for 1 minute until super thick and creamy and no lumps remain. 4. Take out the pan from the freezer. Spoon them in the batter, leaving about 1 cm of room from the brim of the pan. Smooth the top with a spatula and cover with aluminum foil. 5. Pour 480 ml of water in the pot and place in the rack. Place the pan on the rack. 6. Close the lid, turn the pressure release valve to SEAL position, and then move the slider to PRESSURE. Select HI and set the cooking time to 45 minutes. Press START/STOP to begin cooking. When finished, release the pressure naturally. 7. Carefully remove the pan from the pot, remove the foil, and let sit on the rack on the counter to cool for 30 minutes. 8. Then, place in the fridge, still in the springform pan, and let sit for at least 5 hours. 9. When ready to serve, use a sharp knife to separate the edges from the sides of the pan, and slowly open the latch of the springform pan. 10. Top the cheesecake however you wish and serve!

Per Serving: Calories 453; Fat: 24.12g; Sodium: 922mg; Carbs: 54.03g; Fibre: 0.1g; Sugar: 50.99g; Protein: 5.72g

Fudge Cookie Dough Tart

Prep Time: 10 minutes | Cook Time: 25 minutes | Serves: 4-6

200 g granulated sugar	125 g plain flour
5 tablespoons unsalted butter	1 teaspoon baking powder
2 tablespoons smooth peanut butter	½ teaspoon salt
	55 g peanut butter chips
1 tablespoon vegetable oil	25 g chocolate chips
35 g unsweetened cocoa powder	125 g store-bought chocolate chip cookie dough, rolled into teaspoon-size balls
2 tablespoons water	
2 teaspoons vanilla extract	
2 large eggs	

1. Place the sugar, butter, and peanut butter in a microwave-safe bowl and microwave for 90 seconds. 2. Add the vegetable oil and whisk until combined. Whisk in the cocoa powder, water, and vanilla extract. 3. Whisk in the eggs, followed by the flour, baking powder, and salt. Stir in the two kinds of chips and set aside. 4. Generously spray the sides and bottom of a springform pan with nonstick cooking spray. Line the bottom with parchment paper, and spray that too. 5. Pour the batter into the pan and use a spatula to level the top. Arrange the cookie-dough balls and lightly push them into the batter so they're still visible on the surface. 6. Pour 480 ml of water in the pot and place in the rack. Place the pan on the rack. 7. Close the lid, turn the pressure release valve to SEAL position, and then move the slider to PRESSURE. Select HI and set the cooking time to 25 minutes. Press START/STOP to begin cooking. When finished, release the pressure naturally. 8. Carefully remove the pan and rack from the pot and let cool for 1 hour, resting the pan on the rack on the counter. 9. When ready to serve, carefully use a knife to cut the edges of the tart away from the pan before slowly unlatching and opening the springform pan. 10. If you're not serving right away, keep in the refrigerator until ready to serve.

Per Serving: Calories 557; Fat: 27.26g; Sodium: 528mg; Carbs: 68.35g; Fibre: 4g; Sugar: 23.03g; Protein: 13.81g

Rose Water Poached Peaches

Prep Time: 10 minutes | Cook Time: 1 minute | Serves: 6

240 ml water	1 teaspoon vanilla bean paste
240 ml rose water	6 large yellow peaches, pitted and quartered
60 g wildflower honey	
8 green cardamom pods, lightly crushed	60 g chopped unsalted roasted pistachio meats

1. Add water, rose water, cardamom, honey, and vanilla to the pot. Whisk well, then add peaches. Close the lid and move slider to PRESSURE. Make sure the pressure release valve is in the SEAL position. The temperature will default to HIGH, which is the correct setting. Set time to 1 minute. Select START/STOP to begin cooking. 2. When the timer beeps, turn the pressure relief valve to the VENT position for quick pressure relief. Move slider to the right to unlock the lid, then carefully open it. 3. Allow peaches to rest for 10 minutes. Carefully remove peaches from poaching liquid with a slotted spoon. 4. Slip skins from peach slices. Arrange slices on a plate and garnish with pistachios. Serve warm or at room temperature.

Per Serving: Calories 192; Fat 5.13g; Sodium 1146mg; Carbs 36.88g; Fibre 5g; Sugar 30.5g; Protein 4.73g

Apple Brown Betty

Prep Time: 15 minutes | Cook Time: 10 minutes | Serves: 8

200 g dried bread crumbs
100 g sugar
1 teaspoon ground cinnamon
3 tablespoons lemon juice
1 tablespoon grated lemon zest

240 ml olive oil, divided
8 medium apples, peeled, cored, and diced
480 ml water

1. In a medium bowl, mix together the crumbs, sugar, cinnamon, lemon zest, lemon juice, and 120 ml oil. Set aside. 2. In a greased oven-safe dish that will fit in your pressure cooker pot loosely, add a thin layer of crumbs, then one diced apple. Continue filling the container with alternating layers of crumbs and apples until all ingredients are finished. Pour remaining 120 ml oil on top. 3. Add water to the pot and place the Deluxe Reversible Rack inside. Make a foil sling by folding a long piece of foil in half lengthwise and lower the uncovered container on the rack using the sling. 4. Close the lid and move slider to PRESSURE. Make sure the pressure release valve is in the SEAL position. The temperature will default to HIGH, which is the correct setting. Set time to 10 minutes. Select START/STOP to begin cooking. 5. When cooking is complete, naturally release the pressure for 20 minutes. Then turn the pressure relief valve to the VENT position for quick pressure relief. Move slider to AIR FRY/STOVETOP to unlock the lid, then carefully open it. 6. Using the sling, remove the baking dish from the pot and let rest for 5 minutes before serving.
Per Serving: Calories 383; Fat 27.62g; Sodium 47mg; Carbs 36.48g; Fibre 4.8g; Sugar 25.72g; Protein 1.29g

Red Wine–Poached Figs with Toasted Almond & Ricotta

Prep Time: 10 minutes | Cook Time: 1 minute | Serves: 4

480 ml water
480 ml red wine
60 g honey
1 cinnamon stick
1 star anise
1 teaspoon vanilla bean paste

12 dried mission figs
240 g ricotta cheese
1 tablespoon icing sugar
¼ teaspoon almond extract
120 g toasted sliced almonds

1. Add the water, wine, cinnamon, honey, star anise, and vanilla to the pot and whisk well. Add figs. Close the lid and move slider to PRESSURE. Make sure the pressure release valve is in the SEAL position. The temperature will default to HIGH, which is the correct setting. Set time to 1 minute. Select START/STOP to begin cooking. 2. When cooking is complete, turn the pressure relief valve to the VENT position for quick pressure relief. Move slider to the right to unlock the lid, then carefully open it. 3. With a slotted spoon, transfer figs to a plate and set aside to cool for 5 minutes. 4. In a small bowl, mix together ricotta, sugar, and almond extract. Serve the figs with a dollop of sweetened ricotta and a sprinkling of almonds.
Per Serving: Calories 259; Fat 8.57g; Sodium 68mg; Carbs 40.43g; Fibre 3.1g; Sugar 33.48g; Protein 8.76g

Honey Apple and Brown Rice Pudding

Prep Time: 15 minutes | Cook Time: 20 minutes | Serves: 6

480 ml almond milk
200 g long-grain brown rice
60 g golden raisins
1 Granny Smith apple, peeled,

cored, and chopped
60 g honey
1 teaspoon vanilla extract
½ teaspoon ground cinnamon

1. Combine all ingredients in the pot. Stir to mix well. Close the lid and move slider to PRESSURE. Make sure the pressure release valve is in the SEAL position. The temperature will default to HIGH, which is the correct setting. Set time to 20 minutes. Select START/STOP to begin cooking. 2. When cooking is complete, naturally release the pressure for 15 minutes. Then turn the pressure relief valve to the VENT position for quick pressure relief. Move slider to AIR FRY/STOVETOP to unlock the lid, then carefully open it. 3. Serve warm or at room temperature.
Per Serving: Calories 267; Fat 3.68g; Sodium 40mg; Carbs 54.33g; Fibre 2.6g; Sugar 26.88g; Protein 5.65g

Banana Cake

Prep Time: 10 minutes | Cook Time: 55 minutes | Serves: 6

400g bananas, mashed
200g flour
150g sugar
125g walnuts, chopped

125g butter
2 eggs
¼ teaspoon baking soda
Oil

1. Place the Cook & Crisp Basket in your Pressure Cooker Steam Fryer. 2. Coat the Cook & Crisp Basket with a little oil. 3. In a suitable bowl mix the sugar, butter, egg, flour and soda using a whisk. Throw in the bananas and walnuts. 4. Transfer the mixture to the Cook & Crisp Basket. Put on the Smart Lid on top of the Ninja Foodi Steam Fryer. Move the Lid Slider to the "Air Fry/Stovetop". Select the "Air Fry" mode for cooking. Adjust the cooking temperature to 180°C. 5. Cook for around 10 minutes. 6. Reduce its heat to 165°C. Cook for another 15 minutes. Serve hot.
Per serving: Calories 363; Fat: 10.7g; Sodium 253mg; Carbs: 63.7g; Fibre: 3.8g; Sugars 22.9g; Protein 4.9g

Lemon Cake

Prep Time: 10 minutes | Cook Time: 60 minutes | Serves: 6

125g ricotta cheese
100g sugar
3 eggs
3 tablespoon flour

1 lemon, juiced and zested
2 teaspoon vanilla extract
[optional]

1. Place the Cook & Crisp Basket in your Pressure Cooker Steam Fryer. 2. Mix all of the recipe ingredients until a creamy consistency is achieved. 3. Place the mixture in a cake tin. 4. Transfer the tin to the Cook & Crisp Basket. Put on the Smart Lid on top of the Ninja Foodi Steam Fryer. Move the Lid Slider to the "Air Fry/Stovetop". Select the "Air Fry" mode for cooking. Adjust the cooking temperature to 160°C. 5. Cook for the cakes for around 25 minutes. 6. Remove the cake from the fryer, allow to cool, and serve.
Per serving: Calories 420; Fat: 17.1g; Sodium 282mg; Carbs: 65.7g; Fibre: 4.5g; Sugars 35.1g; Protein 7g

Lemon Cake

Prep Time: 15 minutes | Cook Time: 35 minutes | Serves: 8

240 ml water
6 tablespoons olive oil
75 g sugar
2 large eggs
1 tablespoon grated lemon zest
1 teaspoon vanilla extract

160 g plain flour
1½ teaspoons baking powder
½ teaspoon salt
120 ml whole milk, at room temperature

1. Spray a heatproof glass bowl with nonstick cooking spray. Add water to the pot and place the Deluxe Reversible Rack inside. Fold a long piece of aluminum foil in half lengthwise. Lay foil over the rack to form a sling. 2. In a big bowl, cream together olive oil and sugar until completely combined. Add the eggs, one at a time, and blend well. Add lemon zest and vanilla and stir to incorporate. 3. In a medium bowl, mix together the flour, baking powder, and salt. Add dry ingredients alternately with milk to creamed olive oil and sugar, starting and ending with the flour. Do not overmix. 4. Pour batter carefully into the prepared bowl. Cover bowl with aluminum foil, crimping the edges tightly. 5. Place bowl on the rack so it rests on the sling. Close the lid and move slider to PRESSURE. Make sure the pressure release valve is in the SEAL position. The temperature will default to HIGH, which is the correct setting. Set time to 35 minutes. Select START/STOP to begin cooking. 6. When cooking is complete, naturally release the pressure for 10 minutes. Then turn the pressure relief valve to the VENT position for quick pressure relief. Move slider to AIR FRY/ STOVETOP to unlock the lid, then carefully open it. 7. Carefully use sling to remove the bowl from the pot. Uncover the bowl and set aside to cool for 10 minutes, then turn out onto a serving platter and serve warm.
Per Serving: Calories 211; Fat 11.93g; Sodium 156mg; Carbs 22.74g; Fibre 0.6g; Sugar 6.19g; Protein 3.28g

Poached Pears with Yogurt & Pistachio

Prep Time: 15 minutes | Cook Time: 3 minutes | Serves: 8

480 ml water
420 ml apple cider
60 ml lemon juice
1 cinnamon stick
1 teaspoon vanilla bean paste

4 large Bartlett pears, peeled
240 g low-fat plain Greek yogurt
60 g unsalted roasted pistachio meats

1. Add water, apple cider, cinnamon, vanilla, lemon juice, and pears to the pot. Close the lid and move slider to PRESSURE. Make sure the pressure release valve is in the SEAL position. The temperature will default to HIGH, which is the correct setting. Set time to 3 minutes. Select START/STOP to begin cooking. 2. When the timer beeps, turn the pressure relief valve to the VENT position for quick pressure relief. Move slider to the right to unlock the lid, then carefully open it. With a slotted spoon remove pears to a plate and allow to cool to room temperature. 3. To serve, carefully slice pears in half with a sharp paring knife and scoop out core with a melon baller. Lay pear halves on dessert plates or in shallow bowls. Top with yogurt and garnish with pistachios. Serve immediately.
Per Serving: Calories 164; Fat 4.2g; Sodium 28mg; Carbs 28.79g; Fibre 4.6g; Sugar 19.45g; Protein 3.81g

Banana Chocolate Bundt Cake

Prep Time: 20 minutes | Cook Time: 55 minutes | Serves: 8

120 ml room temperature coconut oil
35 g monk fruit sweetener
2 large eggs, room temperature
3 medium bananas, mashed

200 g oat flour
1½ teaspoons baking soda
½ teaspoon salt
50 g stevia-sweetened chocolate chips

1. In a large bowl of a stand mixer with a paddle attachment, add the oil, sweetener, and eggs and beat together on medium speed until well combined. 2. Add the mashed banana and beat until combined. 3. Add the flour, baking soda, and salt and beat again until combined. 4. Remove the paddle attachment and stir in the chocolate chips. 5. Spray a Bundt cake pan that fits the pot with cooking oil. Transfer the batter into the pan. Place a paper towel over the top of the pan and then cover with aluminum foil. 6. Add 360 ml water to the pot and then place the Deluxe Reversible Rack inside. Place the Bundt cake pan on the rack. 7. Close the lid and move slider to PRESSURE. Make sure the pressure release valve is in the SEAL position. The temperature will default to HIGH, which is the correct setting. Set time to 55 minutes. Select START/STOP to begin cooking. 8. When cooking is complete, naturally release the pressure for 10 minutes. Then turn the pressure relief valve to the VENT position for quick pressure relief. Move slider to AIR FRY/ STOVETOP to unlock the lid, then carefully open it. 9. Allow to cool completely before removing from pan and slicing to serve.
Per Serving: Calories 363; Fat 17.91g; Sodium 420mg; Carbs 45.24g; Fibre 3.3g; Sugar 15.84g; Protein 6.85g

Maple Dates Dip

Prep Time: 5 minutes | Cook Time: 1 minute | Serves: 10

210 g pitted dates
115 g tahini

55 g maple syrup
60 ml water, plus more if needed

1. Add the dates, maple syrup tahini, and 60 ml water to the pot and stir to combine. 2. Close the lid and move slider to PRESSURE. Make sure the pressure release valve is in the SEAL position. The temperature will default to HIGH, which is the correct setting. Set time to 1 minute. Select START/STOP to begin cooking. 3. When the timer beeps, turn the pressure relief valve to the VENT position for quick pressure relief. Move slider to the right to unlock the lid, then carefully open it. 4. Allow the mixture to cool slightly, and then transfer to a blender. 5. Blend the mixture on high until super smooth, adding additional water as needed, 1 tablespoon at a time, if the mixture is too thick.
Per Serving: Calories 175; Fat 6.57g; Sodium 15mg; Carbs 29.88g; Fibre 3.5g; Sugar 23.45g; Protein 2.76g

Vanilla Cheesecake

Prep time: 20 minutes | Cook time: 65 minutes | Serves: 6

240 g water
40 g digestive biscuit crumbs
1 tbsp. plus 140 g sugar, divided
¼ tsp. ground cinnamon
2½ tbsp. butter, melted
2 pkg. (200 g each) cream cheese, softened
2 to 3 tsp. vanilla extract

2 large eggs, lightly beaten
Topping (optional):
100 g. white baking chocolate, chopped
3 tbsp. heavy whipping cream
Sliced fresh strawberries or raspberries, optional

1. Grease a 15 cm springform pan; pour water into the pot of your Ninja XL Pressure Cooker. Mix cracker crumbs, 1 tbsp. sugar and cinnamon; stir in butter. Press onto bottom and about 2.5 cmup sides of the prepared pan. 2. In a separate bowl, beat cream cheese and remaining sugar until smooth. Beat in vanilla. Add the eggs and beat on low speed just until combined. Pour over crust. 3. Cover cheesecake tightly with foil. Then place the bottom layer of the Deluxe Reversible Rack in the lower position in the pot. Place springform pan on the rack in the pot. 4. Close the lid and move slider to PRESSURE. Ensuring the pressure release valve is in the SEAL position. The temperature will default to LOW, which is the correct setting. Set time to 1 hour and 5 minutes. Select START/STOP to begin cooking. 5. When cooking is complete, release the pressure quickly by moving the pressure release valve to the VENT position. Move slider to the right to unlock the lid, then carefully open it. 6. Carefully remove springform pan from pressure cooker; remove foil. Cool cheesecake on a wire rack for 1 hour. 7. To release the cheesecake from the pan, use a knife to loosen the sides. 8. Then, refrigerate the cheesecake overnight and cover it once it has completely cooled. 9. To make the topping, melt chocolate and cream in a microwave, stir until it becomes smooth, and let it cool for a bit. Remove the rim from the springform pan and pour the chocolate mixture over the cheesecake. You can sprinkle berries on top if you wish to serve.
Per Serving: Calories 374; Fat 29.38g; Sodium 399mg; Carbs 21.37g; Fibre 0.1g; Sugar 19.78g; Protein 6.76g

Delicious Maple Crème Brule

Prep time: 20 minutes | Cook time: 15 minutes | Serves: 3

320 g heavy whipping cream
3 large egg yolks
105 g packed brown sugar
¼ tsp. ground cinnamon
½ tsp. maple flavouring

240 ml water
Topping:
1½ tsp. sugar
1½ tsp. brown sugar

1. Move slider to AIR FRY/STOVETOP. Select SEAR/SAUTÉ and set to Lo1. Select START/STOP to begin preheating. 2. Add cream. Heat until bubbles form around sides of cooker. Mix together egg yolks, brown sugar and cinnamon in a small bowl. Press START/STOP to turn off the SEAR/SAUTÉ function. 3. Stir a small amount of hot cream into egg mixture. Return all to the pressure cooker, stirring frequently. Stir in maple flavouring. 4. Transfer cream mixture to three greased. ramekins or custard cups. Wipe pressure cooker clean. Pour in water, then place the bottom layer of the Deluxe Reversible Rack in the lower position in the pot. 5. Place ramekins on the rack, loosely cover with foil to prevent moisture from getting into ramekins. 6. Close the lid and move slider to PRESSURE. Ensuring the pressure release valve is in the SEAL position. The temperature will default to HIGH, which is the correct setting. Set time to 10 minutes. Select START/STOP to begin cooking. 7. When cooking is complete, naturally release the pressure for 10 minutes. Then release the pressure quickly by turning the pressure release valve to the VENT position. Move slider to AIR FRY/ STOVETOP to unlock the lid, then carefully open it. 8. A knife inserted in the centre should come out clean, though centre will still be soft. Using tongs, remove ramekins. Cool for 10 minutes; refrigerate, covered, for at least 4 hours. 9. For the topping, combine sugars and sprinkle over ramekins. Hold a kitchen torch about 2 in. above custard surface; rotate slowly until sugar is evenly caramelized. Serve right away.
Per Serving: Calories 395; Fat 24.2g; Sodium 41mg; Carbs 42.51g; Fibre 0.1g; Sugar 41.29g; Protein 3.84g

Homemade Molten Mocha Cake

Prep time: 10 minutes | Cook time: 25 minutes | Serves: 6

240 ml water	50 g baking cocoa
4 large eggs	1 tbsp. instant coffee granules
300 g sugar	¼ tsp. Salt
115 g butter, melted	Fresh raspberries or sliced fresh
1 tbsp. vanilla extract	strawberries and vanilla ice
125 g plain flour	cream, optional

1. Pour water into the pot. Mix together the eggs, butter, sugar and vanilla in a large bowl and toss well. In a separate bowl, whisk flour, coffee granules, cocoa and salt; gradually beat into egg mixture. 2. Transfer the mixture to a greased baking dish that can fit the pot. Cover loosely with foil to prevent moisture from getting into dish. 3. Then place the bottom layer of the Deluxe Reversible Rack in the lower position in the pot. 4. Place the pan on the rack. Close the lid and move slider to PRESSURE. Ensuring the pressure release valve is in the SEAL position. The temperature will default to HIGH, which is the correct setting. Set time to 25 minutes. Select START/STOP to begin cooking. 5. When cooking is complete, naturally release the pressure for 10 minutes. Then release the pressure quickly by turning the pressure release valve to the VENT position. Move slider to AIR FRY/ STOVETOP to unlock the lid, then carefully open it. 6. A toothpick should come out with moist crumbs. If desired, serve warm cake with berries and ice cream.
Per Serving: Calories 373; Fat 19.5g; Sodium 228mg; Carbs 47.19g; Fibre 2.9g; Sugar 25.93g; Protein 5.51g

Oats Lemon Bars

Prep Time: 15 minutes | Cook Time: 12 minutes | Serves: 6

60 g gluten-free rolled oats	¼ teaspoon salt, divided
75 g almond flour	2 large eggs, beaten
60 ml melted coconut oil	Zest and juice of 2 lemons
2 tablespoons honey, plus 50 g	1 teaspoon cornflour
1 teaspoon vanilla extract	

1. Line a square cake pan that fits the pot with aluminum foil. 2. In a medium bowl, mix together the oats, almond flour, coconut oil, the vanilla, 2 tablespoons of honey, and ⅛ teaspoon of salt to form a stiff dough. Press the dough into the bottom of the prepared pan. 3. In a separate bowl, whisk together the eggs, lemon zest and juice, honey, cornflour, and the remaining ⅛ teaspoon of salt. Pour the mixture over the crust. Cover the pan with foil. 4. Pour 240 ml of water into the pot and place the bottom layer of the Deluxe Reversible Rack in the lower position in the pot. Place the pan on top of the rack and close the lid. 5. Move slider to PRESSURE. Make sure the pressure release valve is in the SEAL position. The temperature will default to HIGH, which is the correct setting. Set time to 12 minutes. Select START/STOP to begin cooking. 6. When the cook time is complete, let the pressure release naturally for 15 minutes, then quick release any remaining pressure. 7. Carefully open the lid and lift out the pan. Chill the lemon bars in the refrigerator for at least 2 hours before slicing them into six portions and serving.
Per Serving: Calories 477; Fat 11.53g; Sodium 105mg; Carbs 102.73g; Fibre 2.1g; Sugar 93.5g; Protein 3.36g

Cinnamon Fruit Compote

Prep Time: 15 minutes | Cook Time: 11 minutes | Serves: 6

240 ml apple juice	zest
240 ml dry white wine	3 large apples, peeled, cored, and
2 tablespoons honey	chopped
1 cinnamon stick	3 large pears, peeled, cored, and
¼ teaspoon ground nutmeg	chopped
1 tablespoon grated lemon zest	60 g dried cherries
1½ tablespoons grated orange	

1. Place all ingredients in the pot and stir well. Close the lid and move slider to PRESSURE. Make sure the pressure release valve is in the SEAL position. The temperature will default to HIGH, which is the correct setting. Set time to 1 minute. Select START/STOP to begin cooking. 2. When cooking is complete, turn the pressure relief valve

to the VENT position for quick pressure relief. Move slider to the right to unlock the lid, then carefully open it. 3. Use a slotted spoon to transfer fruit to a serving bowl. Remove and discard cinnamon stick. Move slider to AIR FRY/STOVETOP. Select SEAR/SAUTÉ and set to Hi5. Select START/STOP to begin cooking. Bring juice in the pot to a boil. Cook, stirring constantly, until reduced to a syrup that will coat the back of a spoon, about 10 minutes. 4. Stir syrup into fruit mixture. Allow to cool slightly, then cover with plastic wrap and refrigerate overnight.
Per Serving: Calories 228; Fat 4.41g; Sodium 298mg; Carbs 46.52g; Fibre 6.8g; Sugar 34.56g; Protein 4.94g

Pear-Applesauce

Prep time: 20 minutes | Cook time: 10 minutes | Serves: 10

900g variety of apples, peeled, cored, and chopped	120ml freshly squeezed orange juice
1 tablespoon ground cinnamon	75g light brown sugar
2 whole star anise	½ teaspoon salt
6 whole allspice	80ml water

1. Add apples, cinnamon, star anise, whole allspice, orange juice, sugar, salt, and water to the cooking pot. 2. Install the pressure lid and turn the pressure release valve to the SEAL position. 3. Select PRESSURE COOK, set the cooking temperature to HI and adjust the cooking time to 8 minutes. 4. When cooked, let the unit naturally release pressure. 5. Remove star anise and allspice. 6. Use a blender to blend the ingredients in pot, or use a stand blender to blend applesauce in batches until desired consistency is reached. Serve warm or cold.
Per Serving: Calories 70; Fat 0.73g; Sodium 123mg; Carbs 17.88g; Fibre 3.5g; Sugar 10.62g; Protein 0.73g

White Chocolate Cocoa with Raspberry

Prep time: 5 minutes | Cook time: 10 minutes | Serves: 4

1.2L whole milk	⅛ teaspoon salt
85g white chocolate chips	2 teaspoons vanilla extract
120ml Chambord (raspberry liqueur)	2 tablespoons granulated sugar

1. Add all ingredients to the cooking pot. 2. Install the pressure lid and turn the pressure release valve to the VENT position. 3. Select STEAM and set the cooking time to 8 minutes. 4. When cooked, let the unit naturally release pressure. 5. Whisk ingredients to ensure smoothness. 6. Ladle cocoa into four mugs and serve warm.
Per Serving: Calories 440; Fat 16.23g; Sodium 232mg; Carbs 63.7g; Fibre 1.1g; Sugar 62.29g; Protein 10.58g

Honey Blueberry Compote

Prep time: 10 minutes | Cook time: 5 minutes | Serves: 4

455g fresh blueberries	1 teaspoon vanilla extract
1 tablespoon granulated sugar	⅛ teaspoon salt
2 tablespoons honey	2 tablespoons water
2 tablespoons orange zest	1 teaspoon cornflour
Juice from 1 medium orange	

1. Add blueberries, sugar, honey, orange zest, orange juice, vanilla, salt, and water to the the cooking pot. 2. Install the pressure lid and turn the pressure release valve to the SEAL position. 3. Select PRESSURE COOK, set the cooking temperature to HI and adjust the cooking time to 4 minutes. 4. When cooked, let the unit naturally release pressure. 5. Stir in cornflour to thicken mixture, smooshing blueberries against the sides of the pot as you stir. 6. Transfer blueberry mixture to an airtight container and refrigerate until ready to eat. Serve warm or cold.
Per Serving: Calories 159; Fat 0.43g; Sodium 82mg; Carbs 39.55g; Fibre 1.9g; Sugar 36.37g; Protein 0.97g

Orange-Glazed Blueberry Cake

Prep time: 15 minutes | Cook time: 25 minutes | Serves: 6

For Cake
120g fresh blueberries
125g gluten-free flour
2 teaspoons gluten-free baking powder
½ teaspoon baking soda
50g granulated sugar
⅛ teaspoon salt

½ teaspoon vanilla extract
3 tablespoons unsalted butter, melted
2 large eggs
2 tablespoons whole milk
1 tablespoon orange zest
480ml water

For Orange Glaze
5 tablespoons granulated sugar
5 teaspoons fresh orange juice,

strained of pulp

1. Lightly grease a suitable spring-form pan with either oil or cooking spray. Pour blueberries into cake pan until the bottom of the pan is covered. Set aside. 2. In a large bowl, combine flour, baking powder, baking soda, sugar, and salt. 3. In a medium bowl, combine vanilla, butter, eggs, milk, and orange zest. 4. Pour wet ingredients from the medium bowl into the large bowl with dry ingredients. Gently combine ingredients. Do not over-mix. Spoon mixture into the greased cake pan. 5. Add the water to the cooking pot, place the reversible rack in the pot in the lower position and drop the lower rack through the reversible rack handles. 6. Arrange the pan onto the rack. 7. Install the pressure lid and turn the pressure release valve to the SEAL position. 8. Select PRESSURE COOK, set the cooking temperature to HI and adjust the cooking time to 25 minutes. 9. When cooked, let the unit naturally release pressure. 10. Remove the pan from pot and set aside to cool 5 minutes. 11. Remove the spring-form pan side and flip cake onto a serving plate and allow to completely cool for 30 minutes. 12. Whisk together glaze ingredients until the consistency of corn syrup. 13. If glaze is too thick, add more juice; if glaze is too runny, add more sugar. 14. Gently pour glaze evenly over cooled cake. Slice cake and serve.

Per Serving: Calories 223; Fat 6g; Sodium 171mg; Carbs 39.14g; Fibre 1.3g; Sugar 21.22g; Protein 3.88g

Yummy Cake with Peanut Butter Ganache

Prep time: 10 minutes | Cook time: 20 minutes | Serves: 6

2 large eggs, whisked
1 teaspoon vanilla extract
40g gluten-free flour
2 tablespoons unsweetened cocoa powder
70g granulated sugar
2 teaspoons gluten-free baking powder
1 teaspoon baking soda

⅛ teaspoon salt
4 tablespoons unsalted butter, melted
2 tablespoons whole milk
55g semisweet chocolate chips
240ml water
60g heavy cream
85g peanut butter chips

1. In a large bowl, combine eggs, vanilla, flour, cocoa powder, sugar, baking powder, baking soda, and salt. Stir in melted butter and milk and then fold in chocolate chips. Do not over-mix them. Pour batter into a suitable cake pan greased with either oil or cooking spray. 2. Add the water to the cooking pot, place the reversible rack in the pot in the lower position and drop the lower rack through the reversible rack handles. 3. Arrange the pan onto the rack. 4. Install the pressure lid and turn the pressure release valve to the SEAL position. 5. Select PRESSURE COOK, set the cooking temperature to HI and adjust the cooking time to 20 minutes. 6. When cooked, let the unit naturally release pressure. 7. Remove cake pan from pot and transfer to a rack to cool 10 minutes. Flip cake onto a serving platter. Let cool completely 30 minutes. 8. In a small saucepan, bring heavy cream to a light rolling boil over medium heat (do not overheat, as it will scorch). Remove from heat. 9. Add peanut butter chips to heated cream and stir until melted. Gently pour ganache over cake. 10. Let the dish set for 30 minutes. Serve.

Per Serving: Calories 245; Fat 14.76g; Sodium 325mg; Carbs 25.94g; Fibre 1.5g; Sugar 14.94g; Protein 4.78g

Strawberry Cupcakes

Prep time: 10 minutes | Cook time: 10 minutes | Serves: 6

For Strawberry Cupcakes
150g gluten-free baking flour
2 teaspoons gluten-free baking powder
½ teaspoon baking soda
⅛ teaspoon salt
½ teaspoon vanilla extract
1 teaspoon lime zest

3 tablespoons unsalted butter, melted
2 large eggs
50g granulated sugar
55g finely diced fresh strawberries, hulled
240ml water

For Vanilla Buttercream
130g icing sugar
75g unsalted butter, softened

½ teaspoon vanilla extract
2 teaspoons whole milk

1. In a large bowl, combine flour, baking powder, baking soda, and salt. 2. In a medium bowl, combine vanilla, lime zest, butter, eggs, and sugar. 3. Pour wet ingredients from the medium bowl into the large bowl with dry ingredients. Gently combine ingredients. Do not over-mix. 4. Fold in strawberries, and then spoon mixture into six silicone cupcake liners lightly greased with either oil or cooking spray. 5. Add the water to the cooking pot, place the reversible rack in the pot in the lower position and drop the lower rack through the reversible rack handles. 6. Arrange the cupcake liners onto the rack. 7. Install the pressure lid and turn the pressure release valve to the SEAL position. 8. Select PRESSURE COOK, set the cooking temperature to HI and adjust the cooking time to 9 minutes. 9. When cooked, let the unit naturally release pressure. 10. Remove cupcakes from pot and set aside to cool 20 minutes. 11. Once cupcakes have cooled, cream together icing sugar, softened butter, vanilla extract, and milk. Spread topping on cooled cupcakes and serve.

Per Serving: Calories 301; Fat 12.58g; Sodium 172mg; Carbs 43.01g; Fibre 0.9g; Sugar 21.56g; Protein 4.42g

Cheesecake with Peaches

Prep time: 25 minutes | Cook time: 30 minutes | Serves: 6

1 pkg. (200 g) reduced-fat cream cheese
100 g fat-free cream cheese
100 g sugar
120 g reduced-fat sour cream
2 tbsp. unsweetened apple juice

1 tbsp. flour
½ tsp. vanilla
3 large eggs, room temperature, lightly beaten
2 medium ripe peaches, peeled and thinly sliced

1. Add 240 ml water to the pot and place the bottom layer of the Deluxe Reversible Rack in the lower position in the pot. 2. Grease a 15 cm springform pan; place on a double thickness of heavy-duty foil. Wrap securely around pan. 3. In a bowl, beat cream cheeses and sugar until smooth. 4. Beat in flour, sour cream, apple juice, and vanilla. Add the eggs; beat on low speed just until blended. Pour into the prepared pan. 5. Cover pan with foil. Fold an 46x30 cm piece of foil lengthwise into thirds, making a sling. Use the sling to lower the pan on the rack in the pot of your pressure cooker. 6. Close the lid and move slider to PRESSURE. Ensuring the pressure release valve is in the SEAL position. The temperature will default to HIGH, which is the correct setting. Set time to 30 minutes. Select START/STOP to begin cooking. 7. When cooking is complete, naturally release the pressure for 10 minutes. Then release the pressure quickly by turning the pressure release valve to the VENT position. Move slider to AIR FRY/ STOVETOP to unlock the lid, then carefully open it. 8. Using foil sling, carefully remove the springform pan. Let it sit for 10 minutes. Remove foil from the pan. Cool the cheesecake on a wire rack for about 1 hour. 9. Loosen sides from pan with a knife. Refrigerate overnight, covering when cooled. To serve, remove rim from springform pan. Serve with peaches.

Per Serving: Calories 202; Fat 8.7g; Sodium 308mg; Carbs 22.7g; Fibre 0.8g; Sugar 16.38g; Protein 8.64g

Classic Cheesecake

Prep time: 15 minutes | Cook time: 35 minutes | Serves: 8

Nonstick cooking spray
16 crushed digestive biscuits
4 tablespoons unsalted butter, melted
2 tablespoons granulated sugar
400 g cream cheese, at room temperature
110 g brown sugar
60 g sour cream
1 tablespoon flour
½ teaspoon fine sea salt
2 teaspoons vanilla extract
2 large eggs, at room temperature
480 ml water, for steaming

1. Line the bottom of a 18 cm springform pan with a piece of parchment paper and grease with nonstick cooking spray. 2. Mix together the butter, graham cracker crumbs, and granulated sugar in a large bowl and mix until moist. Pour the mixture into the prepared pan and press firmly to the bottom and up the sides about 5 cm. 3. In another mixing bowl, use an electric mixer to beat the cream cheese and brown sugar until creamy. Add the sour cream and mix, scraping the sides of the bowl. Add the flour, salt, and vanilla and stir to combine. Add the eggs, one at a time, and stir just until incorporated; do not overbeat. 4. Pour the mixture into the prepared crust. Cover the pan with a paper towel and then aluminum foil. 5. Pour the water into the pot and place the bottom layer of the Deluxe Reversible Rack in the lower position in the pot. Place the pan on the rack. 6. Close the lid and move slider to PRESSURE. Ensuring the pressure release valve is in the SEAL position. The temperature will default to HIGH, which is the correct setting. Set time to 35 minutes. Select START/STOP to begin cooking. 7. When cooking is complete, naturally release the pressure for 20 minutes. Then release the pressure quickly by turning the pressure release valve to the VENT position. Move slider to AIR FRY/ STOVETOP to unlock the lid, then carefully open it. 8. Using the sling, lift the pan out of the pot. Allow the cheesecake to cool on a cooling rack to room temperature and then refrigerated, still covered with foil, for at least 4 hours before serving.
Per Serving: Calories 303; Fat 22.25g; Sodium 419mg; Carbs 20.84g; Fibre 0.1g; Sugar 18.04g; Protein 5.46g

Peach-Berry Cobbler

Prep time: 5 minutes | Cook time: 15 minutes | Serves: 4

2 cans peach pie filling
120 g fresh berries
3 tablespoons unsalted butter, melted
1 large egg
120 g Greek yogurt (for
homemade)
70 g granulated sugar
½ teaspoon vanilla extract
150 g plain flour
2 teaspoons baking powder
240 ml water, for steaming

1. Place the peach pie filling in the bottom of a 16 cm round cake pan. Add the berries and gently fold them in. 2. Combine the butter, sugar, egg, yogurt, and vanilla in a bowl, mix well. 3. In a small bowl, mix together the flour and baking powder, and add to the wet ingredients. Stir until combined. The batter should be fairly stiff. 4. Spoon the topping over the top of the fruit. It's okay if the topping is slightly uneven or doesn't completely cover the fruit. Cover the pan with aluminum foil to prevent water from getting into the cobbler. 5. Add water to the pot and place the bottom layer of the Deluxe Reversible Rack in the lower position in the pot. 6. Place the pan on the rack. Close the lid and move slider to PRESSURE. Ensuring the pressure release valve is in the SEAL position. The temperature will default to HIGH, which is the correct setting. Set time to 15 minutes. Select START/STOP to begin cooking. 7. When cooking is complete, naturally release the pressure for 10 minutes. Then release the pressure quickly by turning the pressure release valve to the VENT position. Move slider to AIR FRY/ STOVETOP to unlock the lid, then carefully open it. 8. Lift the cobbler out of the pot. Remove the foil and allow it to rest for 5 minutes.
Per Serving: Calories 669; Fat g10.76; Sodium 260mg; Carbs 140.56g; Fibre 5.1g; Sugar 62.28g; Protein 7.22g

Chapter 8 Beans and Grains Recipes

Cheesy Mushroom and Herb Risotto

Prep Time: 20 minutes | Cook Time: 11 minutes | Serves: 4

6 tablespoons salted butter, cut into 1-tablespoon pieces, divided
2 medium shallots, chopped
200 g mixed fresh mushrooms, tough stems removed, thinly sliced
2 tablespoons fresh sage, finely chopped
240 ml vegetable stock, low-sodium

185 g Arborio or carnaroli rice
35 g Parmesan cheese, finely grated, plus more to serve
4 tablespoons sliced fresh chives (1 cm lengths), divided
4 teaspoons white balsamic vinegar
A pinch of salt and ground black pepper

1. Add 2 tablespoons of the butter to the pot. Move slider to AIR FRY/STOVETOP. Select SEAR/SAUTÉ and set to 3. Select START/STOP to begin cooking. Once the butter has melted, add the shallots and mushrooms, stirring occasionally, cook until the mushrooms have released all of their moisture, about 5 minutes. 2. Add the rice and cook, stirring, until the grains are translucent at the edges, 1 to 2 minutes. Stir in the sage, stock and 360 ml water, then distribute the mixture in an even layer. Press START/STOP to turn off the SEAR/SAUTÉ function. 3. Close the lid and move the slider to PRESSURE. Make sure the pressure release valve is in the SEAL position. Set the heat to LOW and set time to 3 minutes. Select START/STOP to begin cooking. 4. When cooking is complete, turn the pressure release valve to the vent position for a quick pressure release. Move slider to the right to unlock the lid, then carefully open it. 5. Vigorously stir in the Parmesan and the remaining 4 tablespoons butter, adding the butter one piece at a time. Taste and season with salt and pepper, then stir in 3 tablespoons of the chives and the vinegar. 6. Sprinkle with the remaining 1 tablespoon chives. 7. Serve with additional Parmesan on the side.
Per Serving: Calories 436; Fat 21.49g; Sodium 331mg; Carbs 64.86g; Fibre 13.8g; Sugar 5.15g; Protein 13.67g

Italian Sausage and Rocket Risotto

Prep Time: 15 minutes | Cook Time: 10 minutes | Serves: 4

5 tablespoons salted butter, cut into 1-tablespoon pieces, divided
185 g Arborio or carnaroli rice
4 medium garlic cloves, finely chopped
200 g sweet or hot Italian sausage, casing removed, sausage broken into 1 cm pieces

35 g Parmesan cheese, finely grated, plus more to serve
Salt and ground black pepper
60 g lightly packed baby rocket, roughly chopped
4 teaspoons white balsamic vinegar

1. Add 1 tablespoon of butter to the pot. Move slider to AIR FRY/STOVETOP. Select SEAR/SAUTÉ and set to 3. Select START/STOP to begin cooking. Once the butter is melted, add the rice and garlic, then cook, stirring, until the grains are translucent at the edges, 1 to 2 minutes. 2. Stir in the sausage and 600 ml water, scraping up any browned bits stuck to the bottom of the pot, then distribute the mixture in an even layer. Press START/STOP to turn off the SEAR/SAUTÉ function. 3. Close the lid and move the slider to PRESSURE. Make sure the pressure release valve is in the SEAL position. Set the heat to LOW and set time to 3 minutes. Select START/STOP to begin cooking. 4. When cooking is complete, turn the pressure release valve to the vent position for a quick pressure release. Move slider to the right to unlock the lid, then carefully open it. 5. Stir in the Parmesan, 1 teaspoon pepper and the remaining 4 tablespoons butter, adding the butter one piece at a time. Add the rocket and stir until slightly wilted, about 30 seconds. 6. Taste and season with salt, then stir in the vinegar. Serve sprinkled with pepper and with additional Parmesan on the side.
Per Serving: Calories 325; Fat 23.58g; Sodium 602mg; Carbs 21.02g; Fibre 6.7g; Sugar 2.09g; Protein 17.16g

Garlic Black Beans Stew

Prep Time: 15 minutes | Cook Time: 35 minutes | Serves: 6

455 g dried black beans, rinsed and drained

200 g grape or cherry tomatoes
1 large white or yellow onion,

chopped
1 head garlic, outer papery skins removed, top third sliced off and discarded

1 tablespoon chili powder
3 bay leaves
Salt

1. Add the beans, tomatoes, garlic, onion, chili powder, bay, 1 teaspoon salt and 1.2 L water to the pot. Stir to combine, then distribute in an even layer. 2. Close the lid and move the slider to PRESSURE. Make sure the pressure release valve is in the SEAL position. The temperature will default to HIGH, which is the correct setting. Set time to 35 minutes. Select START/STOP to begin cooking. 3. When cooking is complete, naturally release the pressure for 20 minutes. Then quick release pressure by turning the pressure release valve to the VENT position. Move slider to AIR FRY/STOVETOP to unlock the lid, then carefully open it. 4. Remove and discard the bay. Using tongs, squeeze the garlic cloves from the head into the beans and stir to combine. Taste and season with salt.
Per Serving: Calories 239; Fat 1.21g; Sodium 237mg; Carbs 44.38g; Fibre 11.2g; Sugar 2.71g; Protein 14.54g

Spicy Creamy Black Beans

Prep Time: 15 minutes | Cook Time: 17 minutes | Serves: 4

1.3 kg Simple Black Beans, drained (cooking liquid reserved)
2 tablespoons coconut oil or lard
5 medium garlic cloves, finely chopped

4 teaspoons ground cumin
4 teaspoons ground coriander
1 tablespoon chili powder
Salt and ground black pepper

1. Using a potato masher to mash the beans until mostly smooth. Add 120 ml of the reserved cooking liquid and vigorously stir until the beans are as smooth as possible. 2. Add oil to the pot. Move slider to AIR FRY/STOVETOP. Select SEAR/SAUTÉ and set to 3. Select START/STOP to begin cooking. Heat the oil until shimmering. Add the cumin, garlic, coriander and chili powder, then cook, stirring occasionally, until fragrant, about 30 seconds. 3. Stir in the mashed beans and cook, stirring frequently, until beginning to brown, 8 to 10 minutes. Continue to cook and stir, adding additional reserved cooking liquid as needed, until the mixture is thick and creamy, about 5 minutes. 4. Taste and season with salt and pepper.
Per Serving: Calories 423; Fat 8.99g; Sodium 65mg; Carbs 65.41g; Fibre 23.6g; Sugar 0.81g; Protein 23.97g

Simple Garlic Chickpeas

Prep Time: 15 minutes | Cook Time: 25 minutes | Serves: 6

455 g dried chickpeas, rinsed and drained
Salt and ground black pepper
½ teaspoon baking soda

4 medium garlic cloves, smashed and peeled
3 bay leaves

1. Add chickpeas, 2 teaspoons salt, the baking soda and 1.4 L water to the pot, stir to mix well and then distribute in an even layer. 2. Close the lid and move the slider to PRESSURE. Make sure the pressure release valve is in the SEAL position. The temperature will default to HIGH, which is the correct setting. Set time to 5 minutes. Select START/STOP to begin cooking. 3. When cooking is complete, turn the pressure release valve to the vent position for a quick pressure release. Move slider to the right to unlock the lid, then carefully open it. 4. Using potholders, carefully remove the pot from the housing. Drain the chickpeas in a colander; return the pot to the housing. Rinse the chickpeas under cool water, then return them to the pot. Add the garlic, bay and 1.4 L water; stir to combine, then distribute in an even layer. 5. Close the lid and still cook on PRESSURE mode, making sure the pressure release valve is in the SEAL position. The temperature will default to HIGH, which is the correct setting. Set time to 20 minutes. Select START/STOP to begin cooking. 6. When pressure cooking is complete, naturally release the pressure for 20 minutes, then release the remaining steam by moving the pressure valve to Venting. Press START/STOP, then carefully open the pot. 7. Using potholders, carefully remove the pot from the housing and drain the chickpeas in a colander. Remove and discard the bay and garlic. Taste and season with salt and pepper.
Per Serving: Calories 261; Fat 4.13g; Sodium 122mg; Carbs 44.01g; Fibre 8.5g; Sugar 7.54g; Protein 13.99g

Easy Soaked Beans

Prep Time: 5 minutes | Cook Time: 5 minutes | Serves: 6

455 g dried beans   Water to cover beans

1. Rinse dried beans in a colander and pick out and dispose of any stones. 2. Place the rinsed beans in the pot. Pour into the water until water is 2 cm above top of beans. 3. Close lid and move slider to PRESSURE. Make sure the pressure release valve is in the SEAL position. The temperature will default to HIGH, which is the correct setting. Set time to 5 minutes. Select START/STOP to begin cooking. 4. When cooking is complete, turn the pressure release valve to the vent position for a quick pressure release. Move slider to the right to unlock the lid, then carefully open it and drain out any access water. 5. Store any unused beans in an air-tight container in the refrigerate up to seven days or in the freezer up to three months.

Per Serving: Calories 17; Fat 0.35g; Sodium 2mg; Carbs 3.27g; Fibre 1.4g; Sugar 0.59g; Protein 0.85g

Cheesy Black Beans and Green Chilies

Prep Time: 15 minutes | Cook Time: 30 minutes | Serves: 8

2 tablespoons olive oil	1 bay leaf
½ medium yellow onion, peeled and diced	1 teaspoon cumin
2 cloves garlic, minced	1 teaspoon dried oregano
1.4 L vegetable stock	¼ teaspoon salt
455 g dry black beans	⅛ teaspoon black pepper
1 (100 g) can mild diced green chilies	200 g shredded sharp Cheddar cheese

1. Add oil to the pot. Move slider to AIR FRY/STOVETOP. Select SEAR/SAUTÉ and set to 3. Select START/STOP to begin cooking. Once the oil is hot, add in onion and cook for 5 minutes, stirring occasionally. 2. Add in garlic and cook for 30 seconds. 3. Pour stock into the pot and deglaze bottom of pot. Press START/STOP to turn off the SEAR/SAUTÉ function. 4. Add in beans, diced green chilies, bay leaf, oregano, cumin, salt, and pepper. 5. Close lid and move slider to PRESSURE. Make sure the pressure release valve is in the SEAL position. The temperature will default to HIGH, which is the correct setting. Set time to 25 minutes. Select START/STOP to begin cooking. 6. When cooking is complete, turn the pressure release valve to the vent position for a quick pressure release. Move slider to the right to unlock the lid, then carefully open it. 7. Stir in cheese. Serve once the cheese is melted.

Per Serving: Calories 417; Fat 15.96g; Sodium 718mg; Carbs 48.16g; Fibre 11.3g; Sugar 4.15g; Protein 22.47g

Garlic Green Beans and Bacon

Prep Time: 10 minutes | Cook Time: 5 minutes | Serves: 6

240 ml water	1 tsp sea salt
680 g green beans, ends trimmed	115 g precooked crispy bacon or turkey bacon, crumbled
43 g grass-fed butter or ghee	
4 cloves garlic, minced	

1. Pour the water into the pot and place the r Cook & Crisp Basket in the pot. insert a steamer basket. Layer the green beans in the basket. 2. Close the lid and move the slider to PRESSURE. Make sure the pressure release valve is in the SEAL position. The temperature will default to HIGH, which is the correct setting. Set time to 2 minutes. Select START/STOP to begin cooking. 3. When cooking is complete, naturally release the pressure for 10 minutes. Then quick release pressure by turning the pressure release valve to the VENT position. Move slider to AIR FRY/ STOVETOP to unlock the lid, then carefully open it. 4. Carefully remove the green beans and basket, setting the green beans aside. Pour out and discard the water that remains in the pot. 5. Place your healthy fat of choice in the pot and move slider to AIR FRY/STOVETOP. Select SEAR/SAUTÉ and set to 3. Select START/STOP to begin cooking. Once the fat has melted, add the garlic and sauté for 2 minutes, stirring occasionally. 6. Add the green beans back to the pot and stir in the salt and crumbled bacon. Give everything a stir, then sauté for 1 minute to warm the bacon. Press START/STOP. Serve immediately.

Per Serving: Calories 137; Fat 11.87g; Sodium 669mg; Carbs 6.76g; Fibre 2.7g; Sugar 0.91g; Protein 3.48g

Green Beans with Bacon & Toasted Walnuts

Prep Time: 15 minutes | Cook Time: 7 minutes | Serves: 4

5 strips raw bacon, chopped	beans
15 g unsalted butter	Salt
60 ml low-sodium chicken stock	Freshly ground black pepper
340 g washed and trimmed green	55 g walnuts

1. Move slider to AIR FRY/STOVETOP. Select SEAR/SAUTÉ and set to 3. Select START/STOP to begin preheating. Allow unit to preheat for 5 minutes. After 5 minutes, add the chopped bacon. Cook for 5 to 6 minutes, or until crispy. 2. Remove the crisp bacon with a slotted spoon. Transfer to a paper towel–lined plate. Press START/STOP. 3. Add the butter and stock to the bacon fat. Use a wooden spoon to scrape up any browned bits from the bottom of the pot. 4. Add the green beans to the pot. Season with salt and pepper. Toss to evenly coat the beans. 5. Close the lid and move the slider to PRESSURE. Make sure the pressure release valve is in the SEAL position. The temperature will default to HIGH, which is the correct setting. Set time to 1 minute. Select START/STOP to begin cooking. 6. In the meantime, heat a small and dry frying pan over medium heat. Add the walnuts and toast them for 2 minutes. Remove from the heat and chop. 7. When cooking is complete, turn the pressure release valve to the vent position for a quick pressure release. Move slider to the right to unlock the lid, then carefully open it. 8. Toss the beans with tongs and transfer the beans and sauce to a plate. Top with the bacon and walnuts.

Per Serving: Calories 151; Fat 13.5g; Sodium 245mg; Carbs 6.3g; Fibre 2.8g; Sugar 1.05g; Protein 4.21g

Curried Beans & Broccoli Salad

Prep Time: 15 minutes | Cook Time: 25 minutes | Serves: 6

250 g dried navy beans, soaked for 8 hours	45 g tahini
480 ml water	60 ml freshly squeezed lemon juice
1 head broccoli	2 tablespoons pure maple syrup
1 large carrot	1 clove garlic, minced
5 green onions, tender white and green parts only	2 teaspoons curry powder
Small handful of fresh coriander	1 teaspoon minced fresh ginger (about 1 cm knob)
60 g dried cranberries	1 teaspoon fine sea salt
60 g sliced almonds (optional)	Freshly ground black pepper
Curried Tahini Dressing:	

1. Drain the soaked navy beans and add them to the pot with the water. Close the lid and move the slider to PRESSURE. Make sure the pressure release valve is in the SEAL position. The temperature will default to HIGH, which is the correct setting. Set time to 25 minutes. Select START/STOP to begin cooking. 2. Meanwhile, finely chop the broccoli and shred the carrot, adding them to a big mixing bowl. Chop the green onions and coriander, but leave them on the cutting board for now. 3. To make the dressing, in a separate bowl, mix together the tahini, lemon juice, garlic, maple syrup, ginger, curry powder, salt, and black pepper. Whisk well to combine, then add water, 1 tablespoon at a time, and whisk until the dressing is creamy and easy to pour. 4. When the cooking cycle on the beans is complete, naturally release the pressure for 10 minutes. Then quick release pressure by turning the pressure release valve to the VENT position. Move slider to AIR FRY/ STOVETOP to unlock the lid, then carefully open it. 5. Use a fork to mash a bean against the side of the pot to be sure it is tender. If the beans don't mash easily, close the lid and cook at high pressure for 5 minutes more. 6. Let the pressure naturally release for 10 minutes so no foam spurts from the vent, then test the beans for tenderness again. 7. When ready, drain the beans and add them to the bowl with the broccoli and carrots. Stir well and let the beans cool for 15 minutes; the heat from the beans will soften the broccoli slightly. 8. Once cool, stir in the green onions, cranberries, coriander, and almonds and pour the dressing over the top. Toss well to coat evenly. 9. Serve right away, or chill the salad in the fridge for 1 hour to let the flavours meld. Store leftovers in an airtight container in the fridge for 3 days.

Per Serving: Calories 288; Fat 6.6g; Sodium 450mg; Carbs 48.51g; Fibre 11.3g; Sugar 14.4g; Protein 13.65g

Tasty Sweet Potato Risotto

Prep Time: 15 minutes | Cook Time: 13 minutes | Serves: 4

4 tablespoons olive oil	4 cloves garlic, minced
4 tablespoons butter, divided	270 g arborio rice
1 medium shallot, peeled and diced	960 ml vegetable stock
	½ teaspoon salt
1 medium sweet potato, cut into small chunks	¼ teaspoon black pepper

1. Add oil and 2 tablespoons butter to the pot. Move slider to AIR FRY/STOVETOP. Select SEAR/SAUTÉ and set to 3. Select START/STOP to begin cooking. Once the butter is melted, add shallot and sweet potatoes. Cook, stirring occasionally, 5 minutes. 2. Add garlic and rice and cook for an additional 30 seconds. 3. Pour in stock and deglaze bottom of pot. Press START/STOP to turn off the SEAR/SAUTÉ function. 4. Close the lid and move the slider to PRESSURE. 5. Make sure the pressure release valve is in the SEAL position. The temperature will default to HIGH, which is the correct setting. Set time to 7 minutes. Select START/STOP to begin cooking. 6. When cooking is complete, turn the pressure release valve to the vent position for a quick pressure release. Move slider to the right to unlock the lid, then carefully open it. 7. Mix in remaining 2 tablespoons butter, salt, and pepper. 8. Serve hot.

Per Serving: Calories 485; Fat 36.36g; Sodium 962mg; Carbs 44.81g; Fibre 13.2g; Sugar 6.29g; Protein 11.08g

Lentils Burger Salad with Special Sauce

Prep Time: 15 minutes | Cook Time: 10 minutes | Serves: 6

Burger "Meat":	60 g raw cashews, soaked for 1 hour
1 tablespoon extra-virgin olive oil	120 ml water
1 yellow onion, chopped	1 tablespoon raw apple cider vinegar
1 teaspoon garlic powder	
1 teaspoon paprika	2 tablespoons pure maple syrup
⅛ teaspoon cayenne pepper	2 tablespoons tomato paste
½ teaspoon ground cumin	2 tablespoons yellow mustard
¼ teaspoon freshly ground black pepper	½ teaspoon onion powder
150 g green lentils	¾ teaspoon fine sea salt
300 ml water	Chopped lettuce, tomatoes, and green onions; pickle slices; and shredded Cheddar cheese, for serving
1 teaspoon fine sea salt	
60 g finely chopped raw walnuts	
Special Sauce:	

1. To make the burger "meat," add the olive oil to the pot. Move slider to AIR FRY/STOVETOP. Select SEAR/SAUTÉ and set to 3. Select START/STOP to begin cooking. Once the oil is hot, add the onion and sauté until softened, about 5 minutes. Press START/STOP. 2. Stir in the garlic powder, cumin, cayenne, paprika, and black pepper while the pot is hot. Add the green lentils and water, and stir until the lentils are covered in the liquid for even cooking. 3. Close the lid and move the slider to PRESSURE. Make sure the pressure release valve is in the SEAL position. The temperature will default to HIGH, which is the correct setting. Set time to 5 minutes. Select START/STOP to begin cooking. 4. Meanwhile, make the special sauce. Drain and rinse the cashews, then add them to a blender along with the water, tomato paste, vinegar, mustard, maple syrup, onion powder, and salt. 5. Blend until very smooth, set aside. 6. When the cooking cycle on the burger "meat" is complete, quick release pressure by turning the pressure release valve to the VENT position. Move slider to the right to unlock the lid, then carefully open it. Stir in the salt and chopped walnuts. 7. Fill a bowl with chopped lettuce, the burger "meat," tomatoes, green onions, pickles, and cheese. 8. Drizzle plenty of special sauce over the top before serving. Store leftovers in three separate airtight containers—for the dressing, the burger "meat," and the vegetables—in the fridge for 1 week.

Per Serving: Calories 246; Fat 18.62g; Sodium 829mg; Carbs 18.27g; Fibre 2.3g; Sugar 7.65g; Protein 5.66g

Vegetarian Red Kidney Beans & Brown Rice

Prep Time: 15 minutes | Cook Time: 30 minutes | Serves: 4

220 g dried red kidney beans,	soaked for 8 hours

600 ml water	2 tablespoons tomato paste
1 yellow onion, chopped	185 g long-grain brown rice, rinsed
4 celery ribs, chopped	
1 red pepper, seeded and chopped	1 tablespoon soy sauce or tamari
4 cloves garlic, minced	¾ teaspoon fine sea salt
1 teaspoon dried thyme	Chopped green onions, tender white and green parts only, for garnish
1 teaspoon dried oregano	
⅛ teaspoon cayenne pepper	
¼ teaspoon freshly ground black pepper	Chopped fresh coriander, for garnish

1. Pour the drained beans into the pot, add 360 ml of the water, and stir to make sure the beans are submerged for even cooking. Add the onion, celery, red pepper, garlic, oregano, thyme, cayenne, black pepper, and tomato paste on top. 2. Place the Deluxe Reversible Rack in the lower position in the pot and place a 18 cm oven-safe bowl on top. 3. Add the rice and remaining 240 ml water to the bowl. Close the lid and move the slider to PRESSURE. Make sure the pressure release valve is in the SEAL position. The temperature will default to HIGH, which is the correct setting. Set time to 30 minutes. Select START/STOP to begin cooking. 4. When cooking is complete, naturally release the pressure for 10 minutes. Then quick release pressure by turning the pressure release valve to the VENT position. Move slider to AIR FRY/ STOVETOP to unlock the lid, then carefully open it. 5. Use oven mitts to lift the rack and the bowl out of the pot. Use a spoon to press a bean against the side of the pot to make sure it's tender. 6. When the beans are tender, stir in the soy sauce and salt. 7. Taste and adjust the seasonings as needed, then serve the beans with a scoop of brown rice topped with the green onions and coriander. Store leftovers in an airtight container in the fridge for 1 week.

Per Serving: Calories 299; Fat 6.71g; Sodium 600mg; Carbs 53.2g; Fibre 5.2g; Sugar 9.24g; Protein 7.41g

Cheese Beans Burritos

Prep Time: 20 minutes | Cook Time: 50 minutes | Serves: 2

1 tablespoon olive oil	480 ml water
2 tablespoons chopped red onion	½ teaspoon ground cumin
½ jalapeño pepper, stemmed, seeded, and finely chopped	Salt
	Freshly ground black pepper
1 garlic clove, finely minced	50 g shredded Cheddar cheese
90 g canned pinto beans, rinsed and drained	4 (20 cm) flour tortillas

1. Preheat the oven to 175°C. Line a baking sheet with aluminum foil. 2. Move slider to AIR FRY/STOVETOP. Select SEAR/SAUTÉ and set to 3. Select START/STOP to begin preheating. Allow unit to preheat for 5 minutes. After 5 minutes, heat the olive oil. Add the onion, garlic and jalapeño and cook for 1 - 2 minutes, stirring often. 3. Add the beans, water, salt and pepper. Press START/STOP to turn off the SEAR/SAUTÉ function. 4. Close the lid and move slider to PRESSURE. Make sure the pressure release valve is in the SEAL position. The temperature will default to HIGH, which is the correct setting. Set time to 35 minutes. Select START/STOP to begin cooking. 5. When cooking is complete, naturally release the pressure for 10 minutes. Then turn the pressure relief valve to the VENT position for quick pressure relief. Move slider to AIR FRY/ STOVETOP to unlock the lid, then carefully open it. 6. Drain the beans, reserving 480 ml of the cooking liquid in a bowl. Using an immersion blender or potato masher, process or mash the beans to your desired consistency, adding some of the reserved cooking water if needed for a smoother purée. 7. Mix together the beans and Cheddar cheese in a medium bowl. 8. Lay out the tortillas on a work surface. Scoop about some of the bean mixture onto one tortilla just below centre. Fold the bottom edge of the tortilla up and over the filling. Fold the sides in, overlapping them to enclose the filling. 9. Place the Deluxe Reversible Rack in the lower position in the pot. 10. Roll up the tortilla from the bottom, then place seam-side down on the rack. Repeat with the remaining tortillas and filling. 11. Close the lid and Move slider to AIR FRY/STOVETOP. Select BAKE/ ROAST, setting temperature to 175°C, set the time to 12 minutes and press START/STOP to begin cooking. 12. Bake until heated through. Serve with white rice and fresh salsa.

Per Serving: Calories 627; Fat 22.58g; Sodium 1093mg; Carbs 80.73g; Fibre 10.2g; Sugar 4.83g; Protein 24.94g

Mushroom, Peas & Barley "Risotto"

Prep Time: 15 minutes | Cook Time: 25 minutes | Serves: 4

1 tablespoon extra-virgin olive oil
1 yellow onion, chopped
200 g cremini mushrooms, chopped
2 cloves garlic, minced
1 teaspoon dried thyme
170 g pearled barley
120 g dried black-eyed peas, unsoaked
480 ml water
1 teaspoon fine sea salt
1 tablespoon soy sauce or tamari
1 generous handful baby spinach
1 tablespoon freshly squeezed lemon juice
25 g grated Parmesan cheese, plus more for serving

1. Add oil to the pot. Move slider to AIR FRY/STOVETOP. Select SEAR/SAUTÉ and set to 3. Select START/STOP to begin cooking. 2. Once the oil is hot, add the onion and mushrooms and sauté until the onion is softened, about 5 minutes. Press START/STOP to end the cooking function and stir in the garlic while the pot is still hot. 3. Stir in the thyme, barley, peas, and water. 4. Close the lid and move the slider to PRESSURE. Make sure the pressure release valve is in the SEAL position. The temperature will default to HIGH, which is the correct setting. Set time to 20 minutes. Select START/STOP to begin cooking. 5. When cooking is complete, naturally release the pressure for 10 minutes. Then quick release pressure by turning the pressure release valve to the VENT position. Move slider to AIR FRY/STOVETOP to unlock the lid, then carefully open it. 6. Stir in the spinach, salt, soy sauce, lemon juice, and Parmesan until the spinach wilts and the cheese melts. 7. Taste and adjust the seasoning as needed, and serve immediately with additional Parmesan on the side. 8. Store leftovers in an airtight container in the fridge for 5 days.
Per Serving: Calories 447; Fat 7.8g; Sodium 869mg; Carbs 89.09g; Fibre 16.7g; Sugar 3.87g; Protein 15.23g

Taco Beans Salad

Prep Time: 15 minutes | Cook Time: 45 minutes | Serves: 6

120 g dried black beans
120 g dried red beans
1 tablespoon avocado oil
1 small onion, peeled and diced
480 ml vegetable stock
½ teaspoon garlic powder
½ teaspoon chili powder
½ teaspoon ground cumin
½ teaspoon sea salt
10 g chopped fresh coriander
75 g mixed greens
1 medium avocado, pitted and sliced
2 large tomatoes, diced
135 g corn kernels
120 g sour cream
24 tortilla chips

1. Rinse and drain beans. 2. Move slider to AIR FRY/STOVETOP. Select SEAR/SAUTÉ and set to 3. Select START/STOP to begin cooking. Heat the oil in the pot. Add onion and sauté 3–5 minutes until onions are translucent. Deglaze the pot by adding stock and scraping the bottom and sides of the pot. Press START/STOP to turn off the SEAR/SAUTÉ function. 3. Stir in the beans, garlic powder, cumin, chili powder, salt, and coriander. 4. Close the lid and move the slider to PRESSURE. Make sure the pressure release valve is in the SEAL position. The temperature will default to HIGH, which is the correct setting. Set time to 30 minutes. Select START/STOP to begin cooking. 5. When cooking is complete, naturally release the pressure for 10 minutes. Then quick release pressure by turning the pressure release valve to the VENT position. Move slider to AIR FRY/ STOVETOP to unlock the lid, then carefully open it. 6. Select SEAR/SAUTÉ and set the heat to Lo1. Simmer the bean mixture unlidded for 10 minutes to thicken. 7. Distribute mixed greens evenly among six bowls. Add a spoonful of beans to each bowl. 8. Garnish with equal amounts of avocado, tomatoes, corn, and sour cream. Top each with 4 tortilla chips and serve.
Per Serving: Calories 332; Fat 13.22g; Sodium 582mg; Carbs 44.93g; Fibre 11.6g; Sugar 5.19g; Protein 12.62g

Wild Rice with Hazelnuts & Apricots

Prep Time: 15 minutes | Cook Time: 5 minutes | Serves: 8

380 g wild rice, rinsed
720 ml vegetable stock
600 ml water
2 teaspoons sea salt
1 tablespoon butter
60 g chopped hazelnuts
60 g chopped dried apricots

1. Place all ingredients into the pot, stir well. 2. Close the lid and move the slider to PRESSURE. Make sure the pressure release valve is in the SEAL position. The temperature will default to HIGH, which is the correct setting. Set time to 30 minutes. Select START/STOP to begin cooking. 3. When cooking is complete, naturally release the pressure for 5 minutes. Then quick release pressure by turning the pressure release valve to the VENT position. Move slider to AIR FRY/ STOVETOP to unlock the lid, then carefully open it. 4. Transfer to a dish and serve warm.
Per Serving: Calories 261; Fat 7.8g; Sodium 810mg; Carbs 41.94g; Fibre 4.9g; Sugar 7.02g; Protein 9.04g

Chickpea Yogurt Pita Salad with Mint

Prep Time: 10 minutes | Cook Time: 4 minutes | Serves: 6

340 g Simple Chickpeas
1½ teaspoons ground cumin, divided
Salt and ground black pepper
240 g plain whole-milk yogurt
55 g tahini
2 medium garlic cloves, finely chopped
1 teaspoon lemon zest, plus 1 tablespoon lemon juice, grated
30 g pine nuts
3 tablespoons salted butter, cut into 3 pieces
120 g pita chips
45 g lightly packed fresh mint, torn if large

1. In a medium bowl, mix the chickpeas with 1 teaspoon of cumin and 1 teaspoon salt. In a small bowl, mix together the yogurt, tahini, lemon zest and juice, garlic, ½ teaspoon salt and ¼ teaspoon pepper. 2. Move slider to AIR FRY/STOVETOP. Select SEAR/SAUTÉ and set to 3. Select START/STOP to begin cooking. 3. Toast the pine nuts in the pot, stirring often, until golden brown and fragrant, 3 to 4 minutes. Add the butter, the remaining ½ teaspoon cumin and ¼ teaspoon each salt and pepper, stir until the butter is melted. Press START/STOP to turn off the SEAR/SAUTÉ function. Set aside. 4. Place the pita chips in a shallow serving bowl, then scatter on the chickpeas. Spoon on the yogurt mixture, then top with mint and the pine-nut butter mixture.
Per Serving: Calories 478; Fat 19.43g; Sodium 167mg; Carbs 60.62g; Fibre 10.9g; Sugar 11.54g; Protein 20.02g

Spicy Curried Chickpeas and Cucumbers Salad

Prep Time: 15 minutes | Cook Time: 0 minute | Serves: 6

1 kg boiled chickpeas
1 small red onion, finely chopped
2 teaspoons curry powder
Salt and ground black pepper
60 g tamarind chutney
1½ tablespoons hot sauce (such as Tabasco), plus more as needed
3 tablespoons lime juice, plus lime wedges, to serve
2 tablespoons packed brown sugar
100 g fried wonton strips
1 English cucumber, quartered lengthwise and cut crosswise into 1 cm pieces
30 g lightly packed fresh coriander leaves

1. In a big bowl, toss the chickpeas with the onion, 2 teaspoons salt, curry powder and 1 teaspoon pepper; set aside. 2. In a small bowl, mix together the chutney, lime juice, hot sauce and sugar, whisk until the sugar dissolves. Taste and season with more hot sauce, if desired. 3. Pour the chutney mixture over the chickpeas and stir. Toss in the wonton strips, cucumber and half the coriander. Taste and season with salt and pepper. Sprinkle with the remaining coriander. Serve with the lime wedges.
Per Serving: Calories 327; Fat 4.56g; Sodium 135mg; Carbs 56.98g; Fibre 13.9g; Sugar 14.84g; Protein 15.85g

Cider-Braised Lentils with Leeks & Apple

Prep Time: 15 minutes | Cook Time: 4-5 hours | Serves: 6

3 medium leeks, white and light green parts thinly sliced, rinsed and dried
4 tablespoons salted butter
2 medium garlic cloves, finely chopped
1½ teaspoons fresh thyme leaves, minced
1 medium Granny Smith apple, peeled, cored and finely chopped
Salt and ground black pepper
400 g lentils du Puy, rinsed and drained
720 ml apple cider
1 bunch chives, thinly sliced
1 to 2 tablespoons balsamic vinegar (optional)

1. Move slider to AIR FRY/STOVETOP. Select SEAR/SAUTÉ and set to 3. Select START/STOP to begin preheating. Allow unit to preheat for 5 minutes. After 5 minutes, add the butter and melt. Add the leeks and cook, stirring occasionally, until lightly browned, 5 to 7 minutes. Stir in the garlic, apple, thyme, 2 teaspoons salt and ¼ teaspoon pepper. Cook, stirring, until fragrant, about 30 seconds. 2. Add the lentils, cider and 480 ml water; stir to combine well, then distribute in an even layer. Press START/STOP to turn off the SEAR/SAUTÉ function. 3. Close the lid and move slider to PRESSURE. Make sure the pressure release valve is in the SEAL position. The temperature will default to HIGH, which is the correct setting. Set time to 8 minutes. Select START/STOP to begin cooking. 4. When cooking is complete, press START/STOP and naturally release the pressure for 10 minutes. Then turn the pressure relief valve to the VENT position for quick pressure relief. Move slider to AIR FRY/STOVETOP to unlock the lid, then carefully open it. 5. Move slider to AIR FRY/STOVETOP. Select SEAR/SAUTÉ and set to Hi5. Select START/STOP to begin cooking. Bring the mixture to a boil. 6. Close the lid in place and select Slow Cook and set the temperature to Low. Set the cooking time for 4 to 5 hours; the lentils are done when they are fully tender but still hold their shape. Press START/STOP, then carefully open the pot. 7. Stir in the chives and balsamic vinegar (if using), then taste and season with salt and pepper. Serve warm.

Per Serving: Calories 158; Fat 5.57g; Sodium 56mg; Carbs 26.28g; Fibre 3.5g; Sugar 10.87g; Protein 4.11g

Turmeric Yellow Split Pea & Carrot Soup

Prep Time: 15 minutes | Cook Time: 6½-7½ hours | Serves: 6

2 tablespoons coconut oil, preferably unrefined
1 large yellow onion, finely chopped
6 medium garlic cloves, finely chopped
1 teaspoon dried thyme
1 teaspoon ground allspice
1 habanero or Scotch bonnet chili, stemmed
1.5 L low-sodium chicken stock
270 g yellow split peas, rinsed and drained
3 medium carrots, peeled, halved lengthwise and thinly sliced
Salt and ground black pepper
1 tablespoon ground turmeric
10 g finely chopped fresh coriander
Lime wedges, to serve

1. Move slider to AIR FRY/STOVETOP. Select SEAR/SAUTÉ and set to Hi5. Select START/STOP to begin cooking. Add the oil and heat until shimmering. Add the onion and cook, stirring frequently, until softened and golden brown at the edges, 5 to 7 minutes. 2. Stir in the garlic, thyme and allspice, then cook until fragrant, about 30 seconds. Add the stock, chili, and split peas; stir to combine well, then distribute in an even layer. Press START/STOP to turn off the SEAR/SAUTÉ function. 3. Close the lid and move slider to PRESSURE. Make sure the pressure release valve is in the SEAL position. The temperature will default to HIGH, which is the correct setting. Set time to 18 minutes. Select START/STOP to begin cooking. 4. When cooking is complete, turn the pressure relief valve to the VENT position for quick pressure relief. Move slider to the right to unlock the lid, then carefully open it. 5. With the pot still on SEAR/SAUTÉ function and set to Hi5, bring the mixture to a boil. 6. Close the lid in place and select Slow Cook and set the temperature to Low. Set the cooking time for 6 to 7 hours; the soup is done when the split peas have completely broken down. Press START/STOP, then carefully open the pot. 7. Stir the split pea mixture, scraping the bottom of the pot, then stir in the carrots. 8. Select SEAR/SAUTÉ and set to Hi5, stirring occasionally, until the carrots are tender, about 5 minutes.

Press START/STOP to turn off the SEAR/SAUTÉ function. 9. Let rest for 10 minutes, then whisk in the turmeric and coriander. Remove and discard the chili. 10. Taste and season with salt and pepper.

Per Serving: Calories 140; Fat 7.59g; Sodium 159mg; Carbs 14.09g; Fibre 2.3g; Sugar 4.69g; Protein 5.61g

Lentil Salad with Greens

Prep Time: 15 minutes | Cook Time: 5 minutes | Serves: 6

260 g green lentils
480 ml water
60 ml raw apple cider vinegar
2 tablespoons extra-virgin olive oil
1½ teaspoons fine sea salt
Freshly ground black pepper
1 tablespoon spicy brown mustard
1 tablespoon pure maple syrup
1 clove garlic, minced
2 small minced shallots
1 English cucumber
1 red pepper
20 g lightly packed chopped fresh flat-leaf parsley
90 g raisins
90 g sliced almonds
Leafy greens, like arugula, for serving

1. Place the lentils and water in the pot and close the lid. 2. Move slider to PRESSURE. Make sure the pressure release valve is in the SEAL position. The temperature will default to HIGH, which is the correct setting. Set time to 4 minutes. Select START/STOP to begin cooking. 3. When cooking is complete, naturally release the pressure for 10 minutes. Then turn the pressure relief valve to the VENT position for quick pressure relief. Move slider to AIR FRY/ STOVETOP to unlock the lid, then carefully open it. 4. While the lentils are cooking, mix together the vinegar, salt, olive oil, several grinds of pepper, the mustard, garlic, maple syrup, and shallots to make a dressing. 5. Dice the cucumber and add it to the bowl of dressing to marinate. Seed and dice the red pepper, then add it and parsley to the bowl of dressing to marinate. 6. Pour the cooked lentils into a fine-mesh sieve and rinse with cold water to quickly cool them off. Add the cooked lentils to the bowl with the dressing and vegetables and toss well to coat. Stir in the raisins and almonds, then chill in the fridge for 1 hour. 7. Once the salad is chilled, taste and adjust the seasoning as needed. Serve the lentil salad along with the leafy greens. 8. Store leftovers in an airtight container in the fridge for 5 days.

Per Serving: Calories 70; Fat 2.47g; Sodium 666mg; Carbs 10.85g; Fibre 1.3g; Sugar 4.26g; Protein 3.06g

Chapter 9 Soup, Stock and Stock Recipes

Basic Cream Soup

Prep Time: 15 minutes | Cook Time: 11 minutes | Serves: 8

4 tablespoons unsalted butter	30 g plain flour
2 stalks celery, diced	½ teaspoon salt
½ medium yellow onion, peeled and diced	960 ml chicken stock
	120 g heavy whipping cream

1. Move slider to AIR FRY/STOVETOP. Select SEAR/SAUTÉ and set to Lo1. Select START/STOP to begin cooking. Melt butter in the pot. Add celery and onion. Sauté until soft, about 8 minutes. Add the flour and salt and cook for one minute. Press the START/STOP button. 2. Whisk in stock slowly. Close the lid and move the slider to PRESSURE. Make sure the pressure release valve is in the SEAL position. The temperature will default to HIGH, which is the correct setting. Set time to 1 minute. Select START/STOP to begin cooking. 3. When the timer beeps, quick-release the pressure. Open lid, press the START/STOP button, then select the SEAR/SAUTÉ button and set to 3. Cook, whisking frequently, until the desired thickness is achieved. Stir in cream. Use immediately.
Per Serving: Calories 86; Fat 6.95g; Sodium 616mg; Carbs 4.51g; Fibre 0.3g; Sugar 1.1g; Protein 1.69g

Classic Beef Stock

Prep Time: 15 minutes | Cook Time: 65 minutes | Serves: 8

1 tablespoon olive oil	4 cloves garlic, peeled and crushed
455 g chuck or round beef, cut into 8 cm pieces	1 tablespoon tomato paste
1 teaspoon sea salt	2 sprigs fresh thyme or ½ teaspoon dried thyme
2 stalks celery, cut into 6cm pieces	2 sprigs fresh oregano or ½ teaspoon dried oregano
1 medium white onion, peeled and quartered	1 teaspoon (about 10) whole black peppercorns
1 medium carrot, peeled and cut into 6 cm pieces	2 L water

1. Move slider to AIR FRY/STOVETOP. Select SEAR/SAUTÉ and set to 3. Select START/STOP to begin cooking. Heat oil in the pot. Add in beef and season with salt and brown on all sides, about 5 minutes per side. Press the START/STOP button. 2. Add celery, onion, carrot, tomato paste, garlic, peppercorns, thyme, oregano, and water to pot and stir well. 3. Close the lid and move the slider to PRESSURE. Make sure the pressure release valve is in the SEAL position. The temperature will default to HIGH, which is the correct setting. Set time to 60 minutes. Select START/STOP to begin cooking. 4. When cooking is complete, naturally release the pressure for 30 minutes. Then quick release pressure by turning the pressure release valve to the VENT position. Move slider to AIR FRY/ STOVETOP to unlock the lid, then carefully open it. 5. Carefully lift out beef and reserve for another use. Strain stock into a jar and use immediately, refrigerate the leftover for up to seven days or freeze for up to three months.
Per Serving: Calories 109; Fat 5.31g; Sodium 351mg; Carbs 3.38g; Fibre 0.8g; Sugar 1.31g; Protein 12.22g

Turkey Celery Stock

Prep Time: 15 minutes | Cook Time: 40 minutes | Serves: 8

1 carcass from a 5.5 kg turkey, broken into pieces	1 medium carrot, chopped
3 stalks celery, chopped	2 cloves garlic, peeled and crushed
20 g celery leaves	2 bay leaves
1 medium yellow onion, peeled and quartered	10 whole black peppercorns
	1 sprig fresh sage

1. Place all ingredients in the pot, then fill pot with water to the Max Fill line. 2. Close the lid and move the slider to PRESSURE. Make sure the pressure release valve is in the SEAL position. The temperature will default to HIGH, which is the correct setting. Set time to 40 minutes. Select START/STOP to begin cooking. 3. When cooking is complete, naturally release the pressure for 30 minutes. Then quick release pressure by turning the pressure release valve to the VENT position. Move slider to AIR FRY/ STOVETOP to unlock the lid, then carefully open it. 4. Strain stock into a jar and use

immediately, refrigerate for up to seven days, or freeze for up to three months.
Per Serving: Calories 288; Fat 25.34g; Sodium 41mg; Carbs 3.36g; Fibre 1g; Sugar 1.13g; Protein 11.25g

Thyme Beef Stock

Prep Time: 15 minutes | Cook Time: 2½ hours | Serves: 8

2.3 kg beef bones	120 ml water
2 tablespoons olive oil, divided	2 cloves garlic, peeled and crushed
2 stalks celery, chopped	
1 medium white onion, peeled and quartered	2 sprigs fresh thyme or ½ teaspoon dried thyme
1 medium carrot, peeled and cut into 6 cm pieces	1 sprig fresh flat-leaf parsley
	1 tablespoon tomato paste

1. Move slider to AIR FRY/STOVETOP. Select BAKE/ROAST, setting temperature to 200°C, and setting time to 5 minutes. Select START/STOP to begin preheating. 2. While unit is preheating, toss beef bones in 1 tablespoon oil and arrange on a large rimmed baking sheet that fits the pot. In a big bowl, toss celery, carrot and onion with remaining 1 tablespoon oil and set aside. 3. Place the Deluxe Reversible Rack in the lower position in the pot. Then place the baking sheet with beef bones on the rack. 4. Roast bones for 30 minutes. Turn bones over, and add vegetable mixture to the baking sheet and roast for 30 minutes more until bones are browned and vegetables are soft. Watch bones carefully to avoid scorching. Remove the baking sheet and rack from the pot. 5. Transfer bones and vegetables to the pot. Pour water onto baking sheet and scrape up browned bits. Pour into the pot. 6. Add garlic, parsley, thyme, and tomato paste to the pot, then cover with water to the Max Fill line. Close the lid and move the slider to PRESSURE. Make sure the pressure release valve is in the SEAL position. Set the temperature to LOW and set time to 2 hours. Select START/STOP to begin cooking. 7. When the timer beeps, let pressure release naturally, about 30 minutes. Open the lid. Strain stock into a jar and use immediately, refrigerate for up to seven days, or freeze for up to three months.
Per Serving: Calories 644; Fat 32.85g; Sodium 201mg; Carbs 2.93g; Fibre 0.7g; Sugar 1.26g; Protein 79.4g

Chinese Style Bamboo Shoots Soup

Prep Time: 15 minutes | Cook Time: 15 minutes | Serves: 6

1.7 L vegetable stock	455 g baby bella mushrooms, sliced (or shiitake mushrooms, tough stems removed)
60 ml reduced-sodium soy sauce	
3 tablespoons rice vinegar	1 can bamboo shoots, drained
1 tablespoon rapeseed or vegetable oil	1 bunch spring onions, thinly sliced
1 tablespoon red wine vinegar	250 g baby spinach
2 teaspoons chili-garlic sauce or sriracha	30 g cornflour
2 teaspoons ground ginger	200 – 350 g firm or extra-firm tofu, cut into small cubes (optional)
2 teaspoons seasoned salt	
1½ teaspoons sugar	2 large eggs, whisked (optional)
1 teaspoon white pepper	
1 teaspoon sesame oil (any kind)	

1. Place all the ingredients in the pot except for the spinach, cornflour, tofu, and eggs. Stir well and top with the spinach. 2. S Close the lid and move the slider to PRESSURE. Make sure the pressure release valve is in the SEAL position. The temperature will default to HIGH, which is the correct setting. Set time to 5 minutes. Select START/ STOP to begin cooking. 3. In the meantime, mix the cornflour with 60 ml water to form a slurry. Set aside. 4. When cooking is complete, quick release pressure. Press START/STOP. Move slider to AIR FRY/STOVETOP. Select SEAR/SAUTÉ and set to Hi5. Select START/STOP to begin cooking. 5. Once the liquid begins to bubble, immediately add the cornflour slurry, stir well, and simmer about 2 minutes. 6. Stir in the tofu followed by the eggs (if using). Stir well for about a minute until little egg ribbons form before serving topped with some crispy Chinese noodles, if desired.
Per Serving: Calories 176; Fat 7.36g; Sodium 1226mg; Carbs 21.93g; Fibre 3.6g; Sugar 5.05g; Protein 8.78g

Curried Red Lentil Soup

Prep Time: 10 minutes | Cook Time: 20 minutes | Serves: 6

2 tablespoons salted butter	2 teaspoons grated fresh ginger
1 medium white onion, peeled and chopped	3 tablespoons tomato paste
1 tablespoon red curry paste	180 g red lentils
½ teaspoon garam masala	960 ml chicken stock or vegetable stock
½ teaspoon turmeric	120 ml full-fat canned coconut milk, shaken well
½ teaspoon brown sugar	
2 cloves garlic, minced	

1. Move slider to AIR FRY/STOVETOP. Select SEAR/SAUTÉ and set to 3. Select START/STOP to begin cooking. Melt butter in the pot. Add the onion and cook until tender, about 3 minutes. 2. Add curry paste, garam masala, garlic, brown sugar, turmeric, and ginger and cook until fragrant, about 30 seconds. Stir in tomato paste and cook for 30 seconds. Press the START/STOP button. 3. Add lentils and stock, close lid and move slider to PRESSURE. Make sure the pressure release valve is in the SEAL position. The temperature will default to HIGH, which is the correct setting. Set time to 15 minutes. Select START/STOP to begin cooking. 4. When the timer beeps, let pressure release naturally, about 15 minutes. Open the lid and stir in coconut milk. Serve warm.

Per Serving: Calories 299; Fat 12.84g; Sodium 362mg; Carbs 36.21g; Fibre 6.3g; Sugar 6.64g; Protein 12.72g

Savoury Beef and Lentil Soup

Prep Time: 15 minutes | Cook Time: 40 minutes | Serves: 6

2 tablespoons olive oil	½ teaspoon salt
455 g beef stew meat	375 g red lentils
2 stalks celery, chopped	1 large sweet potato, peeled and diced
1 medium onion, chopped	480 ml chicken stock
1 medium carrot, chopped	
2 cloves garlic, minced	

1. Move slider to AIR FRY/STOVETOP. Select SEAR/SAUTÉ and set to 3. Select START/STOP to begin cooking. Heat oil in the pot. Add beef and cook, stirring frequently, until well browned, about 10 minutes. 2. Add onion, celery, and carrot and cook until just tender, about 3 minutes. Add the garlic and salt and cook until fragrant, about 30 seconds. Press the START/STOP button. 3. Add lentils, sweet potato, and stock. Close the lid and move the slider to PRESSURE. Make sure the pressure release valve is in the SEAL position. The temperature will default to HIGH, which is the correct setting. Set time to 25 minutes. Select START/STOP to begin cooking. 4. When the timer beeps, let pressure release naturally, about 15 minutes. Open the lid and stir. Serve warm.

Per Serving: Calories 432; Fat 9.97g; Sodium 397mg; Carbs 52.76g; Fibre 8.6g; Sugar 4.55g; Protein 34.88g

Tomato and Beans Soup

Prep Time: 15 minutes | Cook Time: 37 minutes | Serves: 4

1 tablespoon vegetable oil	½ teaspoon black pepper
1 medium white onion, peeled and chopped	220 g cannellini beans, soaked overnight and drained
2 cloves garlic, minced	960 ml vegetable stock
1 pound tomatoes, chopped	1 teaspoon salt
½ teaspoon dried sage	

1. Move slider to AIR FRY/STOVETOP. Select SEAR/SAUTÉ and set to 3. Select START/STOP to begin cooking. Heat oil in the pot. Add onion and cook until tender, about 5 minutes. Add garlic and cook until fragrant, about 1 minute. Add tomatoes and cook for one minute. 2. Press the START/STOP button and add sage, beans, pepper, and stock. 3. Close the lid and move slider to PRESSURE. Make sure the pressure release valve is in the SEAL position. The temperature will default to HIGH, which is the correct setting. Set time to 30 minutes. Select START/STOP to begin cooking. 4. When the timer beeps, let pressure release naturally. Open the lid, stir well, and season with salt. Serve hot.

Per Serving: Calories 162; Fat 5.9g; Sodium 1156mg; Carbs 24.03g; Fibre 5.5g; Sugar 7.95g; Protein 6.13g

Green Split Pea & Ham Soup

Prep Time: 15 minutes | Cook Time: 35 minutes | Serves: 4

1 tablespoon bacon grease	1.2 L chicken stock
1 large sweet onion, peeled and diced	1 teaspoon dried oregano
2 celery stalks, sliced	1 pound smoked ham hock
2 large carrots, peeled and diced	½ teaspoon sea salt
210 g dried green split peas, rinsed	½ teaspoon ground black pepper
	4 tablespoons sour cream

1. Move slider to AIR FRY/STOVETOP. Select SEAR/SAUTÉ and set to 3. Select START/STOP to begin cooking. Heat the bacon grease in the pot. Add the onion, celery, and carrots. Sauté for 3-5 minutes until the onions are translucent. Add peas, chicken stock, ham hock, oregano, salt, and pepper. 2. Close the lid and move the slider to PRESSURE. Make sure the pressure release valve is in the SEAL position. The temperature will default to HIGH, which is the correct setting. Set time to 30 minutes. Select START/STOP to begin cooking. 3. When cooking is complete, turn the pressure release valve to the vent position for a quick pressure release. Move slider to the right to unlock the lid, then carefully open it. 4. Ladle into four bowls and garnish each with 1 tablespoon sour cream. Serve warm.

Per Serving: Calories 289; Fat 6.92g; Sodium 1419mg; Carbs 29.53g; Fibre 8.2g; Sugar 9.75g; Protein 29.1g

Creamy Tomato Basil Soup

Prep Time: 15 minutes | Cook Time: 15 minutes | Serves: 4

1 tablespoon olive oil	10 g julienned fresh basil
1 small onion, peeled and diced	1 teaspoon sea salt
1 celery stalk, sliced	720 ml chicken stock
8 medium heirloom tomatoes, seeded and quartered	240 g heavy cream
	1 teaspoon ground black pepper

1. Move slider to AIR FRY/STOVETOP. Select SEAR/SAUTÉ and set to 3. Select START/STOP to begin cooking. Heat oil in the pot. Add the onion and celery and sauté for 3-5 minutes until the onions are translucent. Add the tomatoes. Continue to sauté for 3 minutes until tomatoes are tender and start to break down. Add basil, salt, and stock. 2. Close the lid and move the slider to PRESSURE. Make sure the pressure release valve is in the SEAL position. The temperature will default to HIGH, which is the correct setting. Set time to 7 minutes. Select START/STOP to begin cooking. 3. When cooking is complete, turn the pressure release valve to the vent position for a quick pressure release. Move slider to the right to unlock the lid, then carefully open it. 4. Add heavy cream and pepper to the pot, purée the soup with an immersion blender. Ladle into bowls and serve warm.

Per Serving: Calories 199; Fat 15.42g; Sodium 1302mg; Carbs 13.49g; Fibre 3.5g; Sugar 8.92g; Protein 4.32g

Flank Steak and Pickle Soup

Prep Time: 15 minutes | Cook Time: 22 minutes | Serves: 6

675 g beef flank steak	2 tablespoons jarred prepared white horseradish
1.2 L beef or chicken stock	1 teaspoon dried thyme
240 ml unsweetened apple cider	¼ teaspoon celery seeds
3 large dill pickles, quartered lengthwise and sliced into 1 cm pieces	¼ teaspoon ground cloves
	¼ teaspoon ground black pepper

1. Run your hand along the flank steak to determine the grain of the meat. Slice the meat into 1 cm-thick strips against the grain, then cut these strips widthwise into 2.5 cm pieces. Put them and all the remaining ingredients in the pot. 2. Close the lid and move the slider to PRESSURE. Make sure the pressure release valve is in the SEAL position. The temperature will default to HIGH, which is the correct setting. Set time to 22 minutes. Select START/STOP to begin cooking. 3. When cooking is complete, naturally release the pressure for 10 minutes. Then quick release pressure by turning the pressure release valve to the VENT position. Move slider to AIR FRY/ STOVETOP to unlock the lid, then carefully open it. 4. Stir the soup well before serving.

Per Serving: Calories 182; Fat 6.22g; Sodium 880mg; Carbs 4.37g; Fibre 0.7g; Sugar 3.32g; Protein 25.82g

Thai Curried Coconut Carrot Soup

Prep Time: 15 minutes | Cook Time: 26 minutes | Serves: 6

1 tablespoon coconut oil	240 ml canned coconut milk
1 small onion, peeled and diced	1 tablespoon fresh lime juice
1 pound carrots, peeled and diced	¼ teaspoon red pepper flakes
2 cloves garlic, minced	1 teaspoon sea salt
1 tablespoon Thai red curry paste	½ teaspoon ground black pepper
960 ml vegetable stock	10 g julienned fresh basil, plus 3
1 teaspoon honey	tablespoons for garnish

1. Move slider to AIR FRY/STOVETOP. Select SEAR/SAUTÉ and set to 3. Select START/STOP to begin cooking. Heat the coconut oil in the pot. Add the onion and carrots. Sauté for 3-5 minutes until onions are translucent. Add the garlic and curry paste. Continue to sauté for 1 minute. Add remaining ingredients, except 3 tablespoons basil. 2. Close the lid and move the slider to PRESSURE. Make sure the pressure release valve is in the SEAL position. The temperature will default to HIGH, which is the correct setting. Set time to 20 minutes. Select START/STOP to begin cooking. 3. When cooking is complete, naturally release the pressure for 10 minutes. Then quick release pressure by turning the pressure release valve to the VENT position. Move slider to AIR FRY/ STOVETOP to unlock the lid, then carefully open it. 4. In the pot, purée soup with an immersion blender, or use a stand blender and purée in batches. 5. Ladle into bowls, garnish each bowl with ½ tablespoon basil, and serve warm.
Per Serving: Calories 151; Fat 5.31g; Sodium 836mg; Carbs 22.65g; Fibre 4.9g; Sugar 9.8g; Protein 5.3g

Cream Mushroom Soup

Prep Time: 15 minutes | Cook Time: 20 minutes | Serves: 6

4 tablespoons salted butter	or chicken stock
900 g baby bella mushrooms, sliced	2 teaspoons dried thyme, plus more for garnish
1 tablespoon cooking sherry	3 cloves garlic, minced or pressed
1 yellow onion, diced	1 tablespoon seasoned salt
30 g plain flour	240 ml heavy cream
1.4 L mushroom stock (e.g. Mushroom Better Than Bouillon)	A few drops truffle oil, to taste (optional)

1. Move slider to AIR FRY/STOVETOP. Select SEAR/SAUTÉ and set to Hi5. Select START/STOP to begin cooking. Melt the butter in the pot. 2. Add the mushrooms, stir well to coat with the butter, and cook, stirring occasionally, for 10 minutes, pausing to add the cooking sherry after 5 minutes. 3. Using a slotted spoon, remove about half of the cooked mushrooms and set aside. 4. Add the onion to the pot with the remaining mushrooms and cook for another 3 minutes, until the onion has softened, and then add the flour and quickly stir to coat everything. 5. Add the stock, thyme, and garlic to the pot, stir to mix well. 6. Close the lid and move the slider to PRESSURE. Make sure the pressure release valve is in the SEAL position. The temperature will default to HIGH, which is the correct setting. Set time to 5 minutes. Select START/STOP to begin cooking. Quick release the pressure when done. 7. With an immersion blender or working in batches with a countertop blender, blend the soup for about 1 minute, until it's a smooth puree. 8. Stir in the seasoned salt, the reserved mushrooms and the heavy cream. 9. Serve topped with any reserved mushrooms, a sprinkle of thyme, and a few drops of truffle oil (if using).
Per Serving: Calories 564; Fat 7.49g; Sodium 1268mg; Carbs 126.83g; Fibre 18.8g; Sugar 7.68g; Protein 18.97g

Savoury Ham and Potato Soup

Prep Time: 15 minutes | Cook Time: 15 minutes | Serves: 6

2 L chicken stock	1 small yellow onion, chopped
675 g russet potatoes, peeled and diced	2 tablespoons butter, cut into small bits
675 g deli ham, any coating or fat removed, the meat diced	1 teaspoon dried sage
2 medium celery stalks, thinly sliced	½ teaspoon ground black pepper
	240 ml whole or low-fat milk
	30 g plain flour

1. Add the stock, potatoes, ham, onion, celery, sage, butter, and pepper to the pot. 2. Close the lid and move the slider to PRESSURE. Make sure the pressure release valve is in the SEAL position. The temperature will default to HIGH, which is the correct setting. Set time to 8 minutes. 3. When cooking is complete, turn the pressure release valve to the vent position for a quick pressure release. Move slider to the right to unlock the lid, then carefully open it. Stir well. 4. Move slider to AIR FRY/STOVETOP. Select SEAR/SAUTÉ and set to 3. Select START/STOP to begin cooking. 5. Bring the soup to a simmer, stirring occasionally, about 5 minutes. Whisk the milk and flour in a medium bowl until smooth. Whisk this slurry into the bubbling soup. Continue cooking, whisking constantly, until thickened, 1 to 2 minutes. Turn off the SEAR/SAUTÉ function. 6. Whisk a few more times to stop the bubbling, then serve hot.
Per Serving: Calories 379; Fat 13.78g; Sodium 1722mg; Carbs 31.1g; Fibre 2g; Sugar 3.03g; Protein 33.82g

Prawns & Noodle Soup

Prep Time: 15 minutes | Cook Time: 11 minutes | Serves: 4

1.5 L vegetable or chicken stock	preferably reduced-sodium
100 g brown or white rice stick noodles, or rice noodles for pad Thai	1 tablespoon minced peeled fresh ginger
80 g shiitake mushroom caps, thinly sliced	455 g medium prawns, peeled and deveined
2 tablespoons soy sauce,	200 g small bok choy, washed well for grit and roughly chopped

1. Combine the stock, mushrooms, noodles, soy sauce, and ginger in the pot. 2. Close the lid and move the slider to PRESSURE. Make sure the pressure release valve is in the SEAL position. The temperature will default to HIGH, which is the correct setting. Set time to 4 minutes. Select START/STOP to begin cooking. 3. When cooking is complete, turn the pressure release valve to the vent position for a quick pressure release. Move slider to the right to unlock the lid, then carefully open it. 4. Move slider to AIR FRY/STOVETOP. Select SEAR/SAUTÉ and set to Lo1. Select START/STOP to begin cooking. 5. Bring the soup to a simmer, about 5 minutes. Stir the prawns and bok choy into the soup. Cook, stirring occasionally, until the prawns are pink and firm, about 2 minutes. Turn off the SEAR/SAUTÉ function and serve warm.
Per Serving: Calories 288; Fat 12.62g; Sodium 2122mg; Carbs 7.64g; Fibre 0.3g; Sugar 4.66g; Protein 35.01g

Beef Reuben Soup

Prep Time: 20 minutes | Cook Time: 20 minutes | Serves: 6

1 tablespoon unsalted butter	720 ml beef stock
1 medium yellow onion, peeled and chopped	1 medium russet potato, peeled and chopped
3 cloves garlic, peeled and minced	455 g cooked corned beef, chopped
¼ teaspoon ground fennel	140 g drained sauerkraut
¼ teaspoon salt	60 g heavy cream
¼ teaspoon ground black pepper	75 g grated Swiss cheese
2 tablespoons plain flour	2 spring onions, chopped

1. Add the butter to the pot. Select SEAR/SAUTÉ. Select Lo3, and then press START/STOP to begin cooking. 2. When the butter melted, add onion and cook them for 5 minutes until tender; add garlic, fennel, salt, and pepper, and cook them for 30 seconds until fragrant; add flour and cook for 1 minute, making sure flour coats the onions; stir in the stock, making sure to scrape any bits off the bottom of pot; mix in the potato, corned beef, and sauerkraut. 3. Stop the process. 4. Close the lid, turn the pressure release valve to SEAL position, and then move the slider to PRESSURE. Select HI and set the cooking time to 20 minutes. Press START/STOP to begin cooking. When finished, release the pressure quickly. 5. Open the lid and stir soup well. Add cream and cheese and stir until cheese is completely melted. 6. Serve the dish hot with spring onions for garnish.
Per Serving: Calories 313; Fat: 14.54g; Sodium: 780mg; Carbs: 17.98g; Fibre: 2.1g; Sugar: 2.17g; Protein: 28.38g

Italian Sausage & White Bean Soup

Prep Time: 15 minutes | Cook Time: 15 minutes | Serves: 6

2 tablespoons olive oil	2 teaspoons dried oregano
455 g sweet Italian sausage links, cut into 2.5 cm pieces	Up to ½ teaspoon saffron threads (optional)
4 medium carrots, peeled and chopped	½ teaspoon table salt
1 medium yellow onion, chopped (	1.5 L chicken stock
2 medium garlic cloves, peeled and minced (2 teaspoons)	2 large round red tomatoes, stemmed and chopped
2 teaspoons finely grated orange zest	One can white beans, drained and rinsed
	Up to 2 dried chiles de arbol (optional)

1. Move slider to AIR FRY/STOVETOP. Select SEAR/SAUTÉ and set to 3. Select START/STOP to begin cooking. Heat oil in the pot. Add the sausage pieces. Cook, stirring once in a while, until lightly browned, about 5 minutes. 2. Add the carrots and onion; continue cooking, stirring often, until the onion begins to soften, about 3 minutes. 3. Stir in the garlic, zest, saffron (if using), oregano, and salt until aromatic, just a few seconds. 4. Pour in the stock and scrape up the most of the browned bits on the pot's bottom. Turn off the SEAR/ SAUTÉ function and stir in the tomatoes, white beans, and dried chiles (if using). 5. Close the lid and move the slider to PRESSURE. Make sure the pressure release valve is in the SEAL position. The temperature will default to HIGH, which is the correct setting. Set time to 6 minutes. Select START/STOP to begin cooking. 6. When cooking is complete, turn the pressure release valve to the vent position for a quick pressure release. Move slider to the right to unlock the lid, then carefully open it. If you've included the dried chiles, find and discard them. Stir well before serving.
Per Serving: Calories 303; Fat 11.87g; Sodium 1533mg; Carbs 29.18g; Fibre 6.8g; Sugar 5.72g; Protein 21.82g

Spiced Beef & Bok Choy Soup

Prep Time: 15 minutes | Cook Time: 20 minutes | Serves: 6

455 g boneless beef chuck, cut into 2.5 cm pieces	2 tablespoons minced peeled fresh ginger
1.5 L beef or chicken stock	1 teaspoon five-spice powder
60 ml soy sauce	1 large head of bok choy (about 455 g) cored and thinly sliced
1 medium red onion, chopped	
2 medium carrots, thinly sliced	

1. Add the beef, onion, carrots, stock, soy sauce, ginger, and five-spice powder to the pot. Lock the lid onto the pot. 2. Close the lid and move the slider to PRESSURE. Make sure the pressure release valve is in the SEAL position. The temperature will default to HIGH, which is the correct setting. Set time to 20 minutes. Select START/STOP to begin cooking. 3. When cooking is complete, naturally release the pressure for 30 minutes. Then quick release pressure by turning the pressure release valve to the VENT position. Move slider to AIR FRY/ STOVETOP to unlock the lid, then carefully open it. 4. Stir in the bok choy. Set the lid askew over the top of the pot and set aside for 5 minutes to partially wilt the vegetable. Stir well before serving.
Per Serving: Calories 165; Fat 6.89g; Sodium 1125mg; Carbs 7.5g; Fibre 1.4g; Sugar 4.57g; Protein 19.24g

Delicious Chicken Noodle Soup

Prep Time: 15 minutes | Cook Time: 15 minutes | Serves: 8

1 whole chicken chopped into quarters (leg, breast, thigh, and wing)	seasoning
	3 bay leaves
1.9 L water	Salt and black pepper
1 Spanish (or yellow) onion, peeled and cut into large chunks	200 – 300 g egg noodles
	240 g carrots, peeled and sliced into 1 cm disks
3 cloves garlic, minced or pressed	
1 heaping tablespoon Chicken Better Than Bouillon or 4 chicken bouillon cubes	240 g celery, sliced into 1 cm pieces with leafy green tops reserved
1 teaspoon Italian seasoning	15 g fresh dill leaves
1 teaspoon lemon pepper	3 tablespoons fresh parsley, chopped (or 1 tablespoon dried

parsley)
2 tablespoons cooking sherry

1½ teaspoons seasoned salt (more to taste)

1. Place the chicken in the pot and pour in water to cover the chicken. Add the onion, garlic, bouillon, lemon pepper seasoning, Italian seasoning, bay leaves, salt and pepper. Stir to mix well. 2. Close the lid and move the slider to PRESSURE. Make sure the pressure release valve is in the SEAL position. The temperature will default to HIGH, which is the correct setting. Set time to 10 minutes. Select START/ STOP to begin cooking. 3. In the meantime, cook the egg noodles according to package directions and set aside. 4. When the cooking time of the chicken is up, quick release the pressure. Remove the chicken with tongs and set aside to cool. Remove and discard the bay leaves and onion (if you wish) using a slotted spoon. 5. Add all of the remaining ingredients to the pot except for the chicken and egg noodles, and stir. Close the lid and move the valve to the sealing position. Cook on High Pressure for 5 minutes. Quick release when done. 6. While the pot is cooking the soup, pick the slightly cooled chicken meat from the bones, discarding the bones, skin, and cartilage. Shred the meat and set aside. 7. Stir in the shredded chicken and serve in bowls topped with egg noodles.
Per Serving: Calories 180; Fat 3.86g; Sodium 671mg; Carbs 9.21g; Fibre 1.2g; Sugar 1.24g; Protein 25.93g

Cheese Macaroni Soup

Prep Time: 15 minutes | Cook Time: 10 minutes | Serves: 8

3 tablespoons unsalted butter	1 teaspoon dried mustard
2 medium carrots, peeled and finely chopped	720 ml chicken stock
	200 g elbow macaroni
2 stalks celery, diced	240 g heavy cream
1 medium onion, peeled and diced	200 g shredded sharp Cheddar cheese
1 clove garlic, minced	100 g shredded American cheese

1. Add the butter to the pot. Select SEAR/SAUTÉ. Select Lo3, and then press START/STOP to begin cooking. 2. When the butter melted, add carrots, celery, and onion, and cook them for 5 minutes until softened; add garlic and cook them for 30 seconds until fragrant, then add mustard and stir them well. 3. Stop the process and pour in the stock. 4. Close the lid, turn the pressure release valve to SEAL position, and then move the slider to PRESSURE. Select HI and set the cooking time to 5 minutes. Press START/STOP to begin cooking. When finished, release the pressure naturally. 5. Open lid and stir soup well. Stir in cream, and then stir in cheese 100 g at a time, stirring each addition until completely melted before adding another. 6. Serve hot.
Per Serving: Calories 540; Fat: 30.26g; Sodium: 990mg; Carbs: 29g; Fibre: 1.7g; Sugar: 4.81g; Protein: 36.61g

Spicy Chicken

Prep Time: 15 minutes | Cook Time: 40 minutes | Serves: 8

1 tablespoon olive oil	rinsed
455 g chicken mince	1 teaspoon Worcestershire sauce
1 medium yellow onion, peeled and diced	1 can diced tomatoes, including liquid
3 cloves garlic, minced	1 can diced green chilies, including liquid
3 canned chipotle chilies in adobo sauce	1 teaspoon sea salt
1 can dark red kidney beans, drained and rinsed	2 teaspoons hot sauce
	1 teaspoon smoked paprika
1 can black beans, drained and	1 teaspoon chili powder

1. Add the oil to the pot. Select SEAR/SAUTÉ. Select Lo3, and then press START/STOP to begin cooking. 2. When the oil is hot, add the chicken mince and onion, and sauté them for 5 minutes until chicken is no longer pink. 3. Stir in the remaining ingredients and stop the process. 4. Close the lid, turn the pressure release valve to SEAL position, and then move the slider to PRESSURE. Select HI and set the cooking time to 35 minutes. Press START/STOP to begin cooking. When finished, release the pressure naturally. 5. Ladle the dish into individual bowls and serve warm.
Per Serving: Calories 272; Fat: 12.3g; Sodium: 1472mg; Carbs: 27.06g; Fibre: 11g; Sugar: 9.43g; Protein: 17.87g

Enchilada Chicken Soup

Prep Time: 25 minutes | Cook Time: 30 minutes | Serves: 6

1 tablespoon vegetable oil	¼ teaspoon ground coriander
1 medium yellow onion, peeled and chopped	¼ teaspoon salt
10 g chopped fresh coriander	¼ teaspoon ground black pepper
3 cloves garlic, peeled and minced	720 ml chicken stock
1 small jalapeño pepper, seeded and minced	2 (150 g) boneless, skinless chicken breasts
1 (250 g) can diced green tomatoes with green chilies, drained	60 g water
	3 tablespoons masa
	100 g grated sharp Cheddar cheese
½ teaspoon ground cumin	120 g sour cream
	75 g tortilla chips

1. Add the oil to the pot. Select SEAR/SAUTÉ. Select Lo3, and then press START/STOP to begin cooking. 2. When the oil is hot, add onion and cook them for 5 minutes until tender; add coriander, garlic, jalapeño, tomatoes, cumin, coriander, salt, and pepper, and cook them for 1 minute until fragrant. 3. Stop the process, and stir in the stock and chicken. 4. Close the lid, turn the pressure release valve to SEAL position, and then move the slider to PRESSURE. Select HI and set the cooking time to 20 minutes. Press START/STOP to begin cooking. When finished, release the pressure naturally. 5. Open lid and transfer chicken to a cutting board. Shred meat with two forks and set aside. 6. In a small bowl, combine water and masa, then whisk into soup. 7. Select the SEAR/SAUTÉ mode and cook them for 8 minutes until the soup has thickened, stirring constantly. 8. Once soup stops bubbling, stir in chicken, cheese, and sour cream and stir until the cheese is completely melted. 9. Serve the soup hot with tortilla chips for garnish.
Per Serving: Calories 451; Fat: 22.96g; Sodium: 1212mg; Carbs: 23.53g; Fibre: 2g; Sugar: 7.21g; Protein: 36.67g

Chili without Bean

Prep Time: 10 minutes | Cook Time: 40 minutes | Serves: 4

1 tablespoon olive oil	3 cloves garlic, minced
225 g pork mince	2 tablespoons chili powder
225 g beef mince	1 teaspoon sea salt
1 medium onion, peeled and diced	2 teaspoons ground black pepper
1 small green pepper, seeded and diced	1 small jalapeño, seeded and diced
1 large carrot, peeled and diced	1 can puréed tomatoes (including juice)

1. Add the oil to the pot. Select SEAR/SAUTÉ. Select Lo3, and then press START/STOP to begin cooking. 2. When the oil is hot, add the pork mince, beef mince, and onion, and sauté them for 5 minutes until the pork is no longer pink. 3. Stop the process and stir in the remaining ingredients. 4. Close the lid, turn the pressure release valve to SEAL position, and then move the slider to PRESSURE. Select HI and set the cooking time to 35 minutes. Press START/STOP to begin cooking. When finished, release the pressure naturally. 5. Serve warm.
Per Serving: Calories 422; Fat: 25.59g; Sodium: 1033mg; Carbs: 17.37g; Fibre: 7.1g; Sugar: 8.84g; Protein: 32.29g

Vegetables & Chicken Breasts

Prep Time: 25 minutes | Cook Time: 15 minutes | Serves: 4

1 tablespoon olive oil	Salt and freshly ground black pepper
1 medium yellow onion, chopped	
2 medium carrots, chopped	720 ml store-bought chicken stock
2 celery ribs, sliced	240 ml Bisquick
455 g boneless, skinless chicken breasts	80 ml milk

1. Season the chicken breasts all over with salt and pepper. 2. Add the oil to the pot. Select SEAR/SAUTÉ. Select Lo3, and then press START/STOP to begin cooking. 3. When the oil is hot, add onion, carrot, and celery, and cook them for 4 minutes until tender. 4. Add the chicken and stock to the pot, and stop the process. 5. Close the lid, turn the pressure release valve to SEAL position, and then move the slider

to PRESSURE. Select HI and set the cooking time to 5 minutes. Press START/STOP to begin cooking. When finished, release the pressure quickly. 6. Transfer the chicken to a clean cutting board and chop into bite-size pieces. Return the chicken pieces to the pot. 7. In a medium bowl, mix the Bisquick with the milk until the mixture comes together into a sticky batter. 8. Drop the batter by tablespoons into the pot. Cover with a regular pan lid that fits snugly on top. 9. Select SEAR/SAUTÉ mode, and cook the dumplings at Lo3 for 5 minutes until they are fluffy and cooked through. 10. Serve the dish immediately.
Per Serving: Calories 280; Fat: 11.19g; Sodium: 1037mg; Carbs: 31.81g; Fibre: 3.2g; Sugar: 10.92g; Protein: 13.06g

Beef mince Stew

Prep Time: 25 minutes | Cook Time: 25 minutes | Serves: 6

1 tablespoon solid or liquid fat of your choice	Up to 1½ tablespoons dried herbs and/or spices
675 g lean beef mince	1 tablespoon soy sauce
240 ml stock of your choice	1 teaspoon ground black pepper
2 tablespoons tomato paste	Up to 1 teaspoon red pepper flakes (optional)
800 g chopped quick-cooking vegetables	100 – 200 g shredded semi-firm cheese
2 tablespoons vinegar	

1. Add the oil to the pot. Select SEAR/SAUTÉ. Select Lo3, and then press START/STOP to begin cooking. 2. When the oil is hot, add the beef mince and cook them for 2 to 3 minutes until the meat loses its raw, pink color, breaking up any clumps; pour in the stock and add the tomato paste, and then stir them until the paste has dissolved. 3. Stop the process, and stir in the quick-cooking vegetables, vinegar, dried herb and/or spice blend, soy sauce, black pepper, and red pepper flakes (optional). 4. Close the lid, turn the pressure release valve to SEAL position, and then move the slider to PRESSURE. Select HI and set the cooking time to 5 minutes. Press START/STOP to begin cooking. When finished, release the pressure quickly. 5. Unlatch the lid and open the cooker. Stir in the cheese, and then set the lid askew over the pot for 5 minutes to melt the cheese and blend the flavors. 6. Stir the dish again before serving.
Per Serving: Calories 462; Fat: 21.63g; Sodium: 769mg; Carbs: 24.12g; Fibre: 7.4g; Sugar: 7.85g; Protein: 40.45g

Lamb Stew in Beef Stock

Prep Time: 15 minutes | Cook Time: 40 minutes | Serves: 6

2 tablespoons olive oil	45 g diced pitted dates
900 g cubed boneless lamb	45 g diced dried apricots
1 medium onion, peeled and diced	2 teaspoons ground cumin
4 garlic cloves, minced	¼ teaspoon ground cinnamon
60 ml freshly squeezed orange juice	¼ teaspoon cayenne pepper
	2 teaspoons minced fresh ginger
480 ml beef stock	1 teaspoon sea salt
150 g crushed tomatoes	½ teaspoon ground black pepper
	20 g chopped fresh coriander

1. Add the oil to the pot. Select SEAR/SAUTÉ. Select Lo3, and then press START/STOP to begin cooking. 2. When the oil is hot, add the lamb cubes and onion, and cook them for 3 to 5 minutes until the onions are translucent; add the garlic and sauté them for 1 minute. 3. Add orange juice and beef stock to the pot and deglaze by scraping any of the bits from the side of the pot. Stir in the remaining ingredients (except coriander). 4. Close the lid, turn the pressure release valve to SEAL position, and then move the slider to PRESSURE. Select HI and set the cooking time to 35 minutes. Press START/STOP to begin cooking. When finished, release the pressure naturally. 5. Ladle the dish into individual bowls, garnish with coriander, and serve warm.
Per Serving: Calories 343; Fat: 16.66g; Sodium: 719mg; Carbs: 15.16g; Fibre: 2.3g; Sugar: 10.16g; Protein: 33.12g

Loaded Bacon Potato Soup

Prep Time: 10 minutes | Cook Time: 30 minutes | Serves: 4

2 slices bacon, diced
4 tablespoons butter
1 medium sweet onion, peeled and chopped
1 large carrot, peeled and diced
2 cloves garlic, chopped

600 g peeled and diced potatoes
960 ml chicken stock
1 teaspoon sea salt
1 teaspoon ground black pepper
Pinch of ground nutmeg
240 ml whole milk

1. Select SEAR/SAUTÉ. Select Lo3, and then press START/STOP to begin cooking. 2. Add the bacon to the pot and stir-fry the bacon until almost crisp; add the butter, onion, and carrot, and sauté them for 3 to 5 minutes until the onions are translucent; add garlic and sauté for an additional minute; add potatoes and continue to sauté for 2 to 3 minutes until potatoes are browned. 3. Stir in the stock, salt, pepper, and nutmeg, and stop the process. 4. Close the lid, turn the pressure release valve to SEAL position, and then move the slider to PRESSURE. Select HI and set the cooking time to 20 minutes. Press START/STOP to begin cooking. When finished, release the pressure naturally. 5. Add the milk to the pot, and then purée the soup with an immersion blender in it. 6. Ladle the soup into bowls and serve warm.
Per Serving: Calories 742; Fat: 35.38g; Sodium: 1777mg; Carbs: 44.97g; Fibre: 4.8g; Sugar: 14.14g; Protein: 59.46g

Minestrone Soup

Prep Time: 10 minutes | Cook Time: 30 minutes | Serves: 4

320 g dried butter beans
230 g orzo
2 large carrots, peeled and diced
1 bunch Swiss chard, ribs removed and roughly chopped
1 medium courgette, diced
2 stalks celery, diced
1 medium onion, peeled and diced
1 teaspoon minced garlic

1 tablespoon Italian seasoning
1 teaspoon salt
½ teaspoon ground black pepper
2 bay leaves
1 can diced tomatoes, including juice
960 ml vegetable stock
240 ml tomato juice
4 sprigs fresh parsley for garnish

1. Rinse beans and add to the pot with remaining ingredients except parsley. 2. Close the lid, turn the pressure release valve to SEAL position, and then move the slider to PRESSURE. Select HI and set the cooking time to 30 minutes. Press START/STOP to begin cooking. When finished, release the pressure naturally. 3. Ladle the soup into bowls, garnish each bowl with a sprig of parsley, and serve warm.
Per Serving: Calories 581; Fat: 5.65g; Sodium: 2327mg; Carbs: 106.93g; Fibre: 27.9g; Sugar: 14.21g; Protein: 30.21g

Conclusion

The Ninja Foodi is a culinary companion that revolutionizes how we cook; it is more than just a kitchen tool. Its versatility and multifunctionality enable home cooks to discover new culinary frontiers. We've dived deeply into the principles of the Ninja Foodi throughout this cookbook, giving you priceless insights into its capabilities, advantages, and usage. We've given you the knowledge to get the most out of this wonderful equipment, from comprehending its incredible possibilities to mastering its functioning. We've also provided crucial advice on using attachments wisely and keeping your Ninja Foodi in top shape. Our step-by-step instructions and frequently asked questions have been created to help your culinary adventure, whether you are an experienced cook or a newbie in the kitchen. This will ensure that you produce great results with each meal. The Ninja Foodi is a game-changer that enables you to experiment with a variety of culinary techniques, from pressure cooking to air frying and beyond. It saves time without sacrificing quality.

Appendix 1 Measurement Conversion Chart

VOLUME EQUIVALENTS (LIQUID)

US STANDARD	US STANDARD (OUNCES)	METRIC (APPROXIMATE)
2 tablespoons	1 fl.oz	30 mL
¼ cup	2 fl.oz	60 mL
½ cup	4 fl.oz	120 mL
1 cup	8 fl.oz	240 mL
1½ cup	12 fl.oz	355 mL
2 cups or 1 pint	16 fl.oz	475 mL
4 cups or 1 quart	32 fl.oz	1 L
1 gallon	128 fl.oz	4 L

TEMPERATURES EQUIVALENTS

FAHRENHEIT (F)	CELSIUS© (APPROXIMATE)
225 °F	107 °C
250 °F	120 °C
275 °F	135 °C
300 °F	150 °C
325 °F	160 °C
350 °F	180 °C
375 °F	190 °C
400 °F	205 °C
425 °F	220 °C
450 °F	235 °C
475 °F	245 °C
500 °F	260 °C

VOLUME EQUIVALENTS (DRY)

US STANDARD	METRIC (APPROXIMATE)
⅛ teaspoon	0.5 mL
¼ teaspoon	1 mL
½ teaspoon	2 mL
¾ teaspoon	4 mL
1 teaspoon	5 mL
1 tablespoon	15 mL
¼ cup	59 mL
½ cup	118 mL
¾ cup	177 mL
1 cup	235 mL
2 cups	475 mL
3 cups	700 mL
4 cups	1 L

WEIGHT EQUIVALENTS

US STANDARD	METRIC (APPROXINATE)
1 ounce	28 g
2 ounces	57 g
5 ounces	142 g
10 ounces	284 g
15 ounces	425 g
16 ounces (1 pound)	455 g
1.5pounds	680 g
2pounds	907 g

Appendix 2 Recipes Index

Printed in Great Britain
by Amazon